STONE SOUP

とってもかんたんマイレシピ

Edited by
Setsuko Watanabe

講談社インターナショナル

Tokyo • New York • London

STONE SOUP: Tottemo Kantan Mai Reshipi

Published by Kodansha International, Ltd.
17-14 Otowa 1-chome, Bunkyo-ku, Tokyo 112-8652, Japan

ISBN 4-7700-2061-9

99 00   01 02 5 4 3

Jacket design by Point Line

PREFACE

STONE SOUP started out as a completely homemade project. My students in English classes at Bunkyo Women's College worked together to present their favorite recipes in both Japanese and English. The resulting STONE SOUP was chock-a-block with tips they'd gotten from their grandmothers, recipes their mothers had always especially liked, and simple time-tested meals and snacks that the students themselves regularly prepared when good friends came over.

In preparing to publish the book, we have added some more traditional family fare, rewritten extensively to make the book as helpful as possible, and simplified all the steps in the cooking process. We've retained the original principles, though: focusing on easy-to-find, affordable ingredients, uncomplicated recipes, and nutritious and delicious results.

There were two reasons for building the class around this kind of large-scale project. First, I chose cooking because it is a logical, practical area that demands that students express themselves clearly and without any fuss. Secondly, I wanted them to immerse themselves in Japanese- and English-language cooking culture—in other words, I wanted them to experience culture shock. When they actually started, I think the cultural gap was very intense for them, more so than they'd expected. Not only did they have to name ingredients in two languages, but explain all kinds of complicated techniques that are taken for granted in Japan. They were surprised to find, for instance, that while Japanese has a wealth of terms to describe fish, a recipe in English may just call for "flatfish" or "whitefish." On the other hand, they were similarly amazed by the number of English words for different cuts of meat and by the detailed illustrations English-language cookbooks often provide. Finally, units of weight, measure and temperature are all calibrated differently in different countries. This project provided students with all kinds of opportunities to explore their own culture and learn about others.

Our priority in putting together STONE SOUP, then, was not just to compile delicious and easy recipes, but to make the recipes truly bilingual, in order to create a bridge between cultures. But just as people's names are untranslatable, there are some terms that simply can't be rendered neatly in another language. This is especially true with cooking, which is so closely linked to culture.

In such cases we've incorporated the Japanese term into the English—thus, *daikon* radish and *naganegi* leek—to make it easier for non-Japanese readers to shop for these ingredients, and also to help students of Japanese. All the recipes in the book and the handy Japanese-English/English-Japanese glossaries at the back provide a fun and practical learning opportunity for students of English and Japanese.

As the phrase "stone soup" (page 7) would suggest, there are many people who contributed various ingredients this book. First of all I would like to thank President Akiko Shimada of Bunkyo Women's College, who approved and encouraged this project from the start. I would also like to thank Professor Hiroshi Fukuda for patiently advising students on the use of the word processor. Thanks also to Professors Shūichi Takeda and Yōichi Tōma for their cooperation. Thanks also to Dale Bay, who not only suggested the title, but provided his version of the centuries-old story, "Stone Soup" and to Masami Ōno of the *Asahi Shimbun*, who provided invaluable support throughout. Finally, I would like to thank all the students who contributed their favorite recipes, which became the most important element in this book.

In the course of preparing the book for publication, many others made invaluable contributions. Professor Sachiko Kobayashi of Wayō Women's College checked all the recipes from a nutritional standpoint and offered a generous comment for the book's jacket. Nutritionist Yūko Murakami checked the calories in all the recipes and gave professional advice. I would like to thank Mamiko Murakami, Janice Nimura and Misha Taniuchi for their editorial advice. I am also grateful to Wakana Hanaoka, who reworked students' original drawings into simple and charming illustrations.

Finally, a million thanks to Shigeyoshi Suzuki and Elizabeth Floyd of Kodansha International. No matter how many excellent ingredients I might have received from hundreds of people, without these two editors the soup could not have been cooked. Shigeyoshi Suzuki first saw the potential for a beautiful book in our simple project. Elizabeth Ogata then came along to correct our English like magic. I am lucky to have these two wonderful editors.

Setsuko Watanabe
March, 1996

はじめに

　この本は、文京女子短期大学英文科の学生が授業の一環として制作したSTONE SOUPという本にもとづいてつくられました。学生たちが自分の気に入ったレシピを持ち寄って一冊にしたもので、おばあちゃん秘伝の料理、おかあさんの十八番、パーティーに欠かせない定番料理などがにぎやかに詰まっています。

　この度、講談社インターナショナルから出版することになり、日本人はもちろんのこと、海外で、あるいは日本にいる外国人の方々に本格的に役立ててもらえるようレシピでは伝統的な家庭料理を加えたり、調理法をさらにわかりやすく書き直したりといった配慮をいたしました。手に入れやすい材料で、簡単につくれて経済的、しかもヘルシーでおいしいというポイントはそのまま生かしています。

　ところで学生にこのような授業を課したのは2つの理由からです。ひとつは調理の仕方という合理的で具体的なものに挑戦して、自分の納得したこと、伝えたいことを論理的に正確に表現する訓練をさせたかったこと。もうひとつは、日本語と英語で食文化に体当たりしてもらい、直に文化の相違を体験してもらいたかったこと。実際に作業がはじまると、予想をはるかに上回ってこの異文化体験は強烈だったと思います。食材の適切な訳語を見つけるのも大変、野菜の切り方を説明するのにも四苦八苦。魚をよく食べる日本では、出世魚にあるように細やかに呼び方を変えたりするのに、英語では「平たい魚」、「白い魚」といった程度にしか分類しない。しかし肉では反対に、牛肉の部位の図や細分化された呼び名を見ているとめまいがするほど詳しい。このほか度量や単位なども一筋縄では訳せず、学生たちはまさに文化と言葉の関係の深さを痛感したと思います。

　STONE SOUPで重要視したのはレシピの内容もさることながら、今述べたように言葉の問題、日本語と英語の間を橋渡しすることでした。しかし、人の名前がそうであるように、いくら訳そうとしてももとから無い以上訳せないというものが、食文化を語るときにはたくさん存在します。そうした場合、本書を使用する方々の便を考慮して日本語を残し *daikon* radish のように表現するか、Japanese leeks *(naganegi)* と表記し、外国人読者が買い物をするときなど実際に役立ち、しかも勉強にもなるように配慮しました。英語表現では、今回ネイティヴの編集者が腕によりをかけて文章に磨きをかけてくれましたので、巻末の料理用語集などとあわせて本書が生きた英語を学ぶ絶好の材料になると確信しています。

　この本は、STONE SOUPの寓話（7頁参照）どおりたくさんの人々の協力でできあがりました。学生のこのプロジェクトに理解を示され、終始はげましをくださった文京女子短期大学学長島田煇子先生をはじめ、コンピュータ操作の上で、全面的に学生の指導にあたってくださった情報処理の福田博先生、また當真洋一先生、武田修一先生および教務課の皆さまにも学生の作業にいろいろな便宜をはかっていただきました。STONE SOUPという気の利いたタイトルはデイル・ベイさんがつけてくれたものです。朝日新聞社の大野正美さんには、この仕事の意義をみとめていただき、作業を進める上で大変勇気づけられました。授業の一環とはいいながら、学生たちの努力、本書への協力は大変うれしいものでした。みなさんの名前は巻末にあげさせてもらいました。

　今回講談社インターナショナルからの出版にあたって、さらに多くの方々の援助を得て内容が充実いたしました。和洋女子大学の小林幸子先生にはご専門の立場からレシピを1点1点検討していただいた上、推薦のお言葉まで頂戴しました。管理栄養士の村上祐子さんにはカロリー計算を詳細に校閲していただき、村上真美子さん、ジャニス・二村さん、ミッシャ・谷内さんには編集上いくつもの貴重なアドバイスをいただきました。学生のイラストをシンプルでチャーミングな画に仕上げてくださったのは花岡わかなさんです。

　最後に、学生の手作りの小冊子に目をとめてくださり、このような美しい書物としての出版を企画実行してくださった鈴木重好さん、英文の立場から編集に情熱を傾けてくださったエリザベス・フロイドさんに心から感謝いたします。多くの人々に材料を提供していただいたSTONE SOUPですが、お二人の名シェフなくしては、広く味わっていただけるものにはならなかったと思います。

1996年3月
渡辺節子

"STONE SOUP"

Long ago, a ragged traveler arrived in a small village and asked for something to eat. "We have nothing for you," said the villagers, eyeing him suspiciously. They shut their doors in his face. "Well then," said the traveler, "could you spare me a pot? The stones here are just perfect for stone soup." "Stone soup!" the villagers exclaimed. "Who ever heard of stone soup?"

A crowd gathered as the traveler built a fire under a large pot of water and carefully added a handful of stones. After a while he tasted a steaming spoonful, and sighed. "Not bad," he said, "but it's a pity I don't have a carrot." A bunch of carrots was quickly produced. "Mmm, much better," said the traveler, "but an onion would really bring out the flavor of the stones." A bag of onions was eagerly passed forward. Everyone wanted to have a hand in this mysterious soup, and soon the pot was brimming with celery, potatoes, mushrooms, peas, barley, and meat. A delicious fragrance rose from the bubbling soup. The traveler tried it one last time, and pronounced it ready. There was enough for everyone in the village. And everyone was amazed that such a delicious soup could be made from stones.

ストーンスープの話

むかし、貧しい身なりの旅人が、小さな村にやってきて、食べ物を乞いながら歩きました。「おまえにやる分は、ない」と村人たちは、疑わしげな目つきで睨み、旅人の顔前で、ぴしゃっとドアを閉めてしまいました。「それでは、鍋を貸してくれませんか。ストーンスープ（石のスープ）を作りますから、この村には、ちょうどおいしそうな石もあるし。」村人たちは、たまげました。「ストーンスープだって！」「見たことも聞いたこともない！」
旅人は、火をおこし、大鍋に湯をたぎらせた中に一握りの石ころをそっと入れました。見物人で周りはいっぱいです。しばらくすると、旅人は、湯気のたったスープを一匙味見して、「悪くない」とつぶやきました。「にんじんがあればな…」と彼が言うと、どこからか、一束のにんじんが、手際よく手渡されました。「うん…うまい。玉ねぎがあれば、石の風味がもっとよくでるんだがな。」と旅人が言うと、玉ねぎ一袋が、まちきれないように、さっとでてきました。だれもが、この摩訶不思議なスープに一口乗りたいと思っていました。まもなく、セロリ、じゃがいも、きのこ、まめ、麦や肉で、大鍋は溢れそうになりました。ぐらぐら煮立ったスープからおいしそうな匂いが漂ってきます。旅人がもう一度味見をして、できたと宣言しました。スープはたっぷりできていて、村中の人がお腹一杯飲めました。こんなにおいしいスープが石からできたなんてと、村人は口々に言い合ったことでした。

How to Use This Book

• Japanese and English Expressions

The Japanese and English expressions in this book mean the same thing but have been written with a view to producing the most natural Japanese and English, and so are somewhat independent.

• Weights and Measures

In Japan, the U.S. and England, not only are the standard units for expressing weights and measures different, but even the method of measuring various ingredients for use in cooking differs. For the sake of convenience, this book uses the measuring cup and spoons considered standard in Japan. For the reader's convenience, the standards in the three countries are as follows:

Japan	1 cup = 200 cc	1 Tbsp. = 15 cc	1 tsp. = 5 cc
U.S.	1 U.S. cup = 240 cc	1 Tbsp. = 15 cc	1 tsp. = 5 cc
England	1 cup = 280 cc	1 Tbsp. = 19 cc	1 tsp. = 6 cc

(English "cup" here refers to the English breakfast-cup.)

1 pound (1 lb.) = 16 ounces (16 oz.) = 450 g   1 oz. = 30 g

1 inch = $2\frac{1}{2}$ cm   2 inches = 5 cm

300°F = 150°C   325°F = 160°C   350°F = 180°C   400°F = 200°C

• Calculation of Energy

Energy was calculated using the Standard Tables of Food Composition in Japan, Fourth Revised Edition (Resources Council, Science and Technology Agency, Japan).

Energy available from deep-fried foods was calculated by factoring in the amount of oil absorbed by ingredients.

In all recipes, "kcal" represents the energy in one serving.

(The term "kcal" used here is identical in meaning to the "calorie" used in the U.S.)

この本の使い方

◆和文・英文について

本書の和文と英文は同じ意味を表していますが、日本語は日本語として、英語は英語として自然な表現になるようにそれぞれが独立して書かれています。

◆度量や単位の換算について

日米英では、料理に用いられる度量や単位が異なるばかりか、食材の種類で計量の方法が異なります。本書では、便宜上和文・英文とも日本での計量単位を用いました。各国で使用されている計量カップ等の容量はおよそ次のとおりです。

日本: カップ1 = 200 cc、大さじ1 = 15 cc、小さじ1 = 5 cc
米国: 1 cup = 240 cc、1 Tbsp. = 15 cc、1 tsp. = 5 cc
英国: 1 cup = 280 cc、1 Tbsp. = 19 cc、1 tsp. = 6 cc
（英国の cup は English breakfast-cup と呼ばれるカップです）

1 pound (1 lb.) = 16 ounces (16 oz.) = 450 g   1 oz. = 30 g
1 inch = $2\frac{1}{2}$ cm   2 inches = 5 cm
300°F = 150°C 325°F = 160°C 350°F = 180°C 400°F = 200°C

◆エネルギー（kcal）算出について

算出は「四訂日本食品標準成分表」（科学技術庁資源調査会編）によりました。
揚げ物については、材料重量に対する吸油率を加えて算出しました。
それぞれのレシピに表示した kcal は一人分の量です。
アメリカで用いられている cal は、日本のkcalと同じ単位です。

CONTENTS

SALADS AND SALAD DRESSINGS
サラダとサラダドレッシング

SOUPS
スープ

VEGETABLES
野菜

EGGS
たまご

TOFU
豆腐

PASTA & NOODLES
パスタ・ヌードル

FRIED FOODS
揚げ物

RICE
ご飯

MEAT
肉

FISH
魚

SEAFOOD
海産物

DESSERTS
デザート

APPENDICES
付録

Snacks and Light Foods

おつまみ・軽食

FRIED POTATO KABOBS
じゃがまるくん

Serves 4　4人分　25 min.　25分　　　　　　　　　238 kcal

---

6 potatoes (*jagaimo*)　じゃがいも　6個（900g）

1 Tbsp. cornstarch　コーンスターチ　大さじ1

1 Tbsp. flour　小麦粉　大さじ1

1 egg　卵　1個

pinch salt　塩　少量

oil for deep frying　揚げ油

Worcestershire sauce　ウスターソース

---

1. Peel and quarter the potatoes.

   じゃがいもの皮をむき、4等分する。

2. Rub the potatoes with salt, and rinse.

   じゃがいもに塩をまぶしてから水で洗う。

3. Steam the potatoes for 10 minutes.

   じゃがいもを10分ほど蒸す。

4. Combine the cornstarch, flour, egg and salt and mix, to make the batter. Roll potatoes in batter one by one.

   コーンスターチ、小麦粉、卵、塩をまぜ合わせて衣をつくり、じゃがいもをくぐらせてつける。

5. Deep fry ④ in oil heated to 350°F (170°–180°C).

   ④ のじゃがいもを170〜180℃の油で揚げる。

   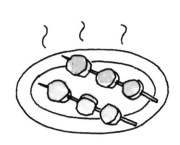

6. Skewer the potatoes, 3 to each skewer. Sprinkle with Worcestershire sauce.

   ⑤ でできたものを、3つずつ串に刺す。好みでソースをつけて食べる。

Note: Fried Potato Kabobs taste best when they're hot.

熱いうちに食べるととてもおいしい。

GREEN SOYBEANS BOILED ON THE STALK (*EDAMAME*)

枝豆

15 min. 15分   348 kcal

1 bunch green soybeans on the stalk (*edamame*) (about ½ lb.) 枝豆 250g

a generous amount of salt ひとつかみの塩

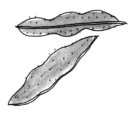

1. Rinse the soybean stalks and rub the pods well with salt to help keep them bright green.

   枝豆を水で洗い、色を鮮やかに仕上げるためひとつかみの塩でよくもむ。

2. Bring a large pot of water to a boil.

   鍋にたっぷりの水を入れ沸騰させる。

bean

3. Add the soybean stalks and continue to cook. (If you prefer, take pods from the stems and add just the pods). When water boils again, lower the heat to medium and cook another 5–10 minutes (depending on how soft you like your beans).

   沸騰したところで枝豆を入れ、再び沸騰させて中火で5〜10分間ぐらいゆでる（豆のかたさをみながら時間は調整する）。

4. When beans are done, quickly turn off the heat and set them in a colander. Cool beans right away by passing them briefly under running water or fanning them.

   豆がやわらかくなったら火を止めて、ざるにあげたら、さっと冷水をかけるか、うちわなどであおいで冷ます。

5. Sprinkle beans with a little more salt. Serve as they are, on the stalk!

   冷めた枝豆に、少量の塩をふりかけてできあがり。

salt

Note: These are finger food, set out in baskets or bowls.
ざるやボールにとり、おつまみとして楽しむことができる。

♥ **By the way:** *Edamame* are soybeans picked when the plants are still young. Soybeans, of course, are full of protein, so much so that in Japan they're called "meat from the garden."
大豆を若いうちに収穫した枝豆は、タンパク質を多く含み、"畑の肉"ともよばれる。

SAUTÉED GARLIC STEMS

にんにくの茎いため

Serves 4　4人分　10 min.　10分　　　　　　　103 kcal

---

2 bunches garlic stems　にんにくの茎　**2わ**

½ Tbsp. butter　バター　大さじ½

4 strips bacon　ベーコン　**4枚**

1 tsp. soy sauce　醤油　小さじ**1**

1. Cut garlic stems into 2–in. (5–cm.) lengths. Boil about 30 seconds in lightly salted water, till the color brightens.

   にんにくの茎を5cmに切り、ひとつまみの塩を入れた熱湯で、さっと30秒くらい色が鮮やかになる程度ゆでる。

2. Melt butter in a frying pan. Cut bacon strips into half-inch (1–cm.) lengths and sauté them with the garlic stems.

   フライパンにバターを溶かし、① と1cm幅ぐらいに切ったベーコンをいためる。

3. Sauté 1 or 2 minutes, till stems are done but not soft. Add soy sauce, stir up just a bit and remove from heat.

   にんにくの茎の歯ごたえが残る程度まで1〜2分いためたら、醤油を加えてさっとまぜ、火を止める。

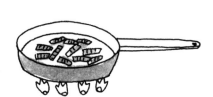

soy sauce

MINI HOT DOGS
ミニ アメリカン ドッグ

Serves 4　4人分　30 min.　30分　　　　　　　　　　192 kcal

12 miniature hot dogs　ウィンナーソーセージ　12本

1 cup pancake mix　ホットケーキミックス　カップ1（100g）

4 Tbsp. water　水　大さじ4

ketchup　ケチャップ

mustard　マスタード

1. Skewer each hot dog on a wooden toothpick.
   楊枝にウィンナーソーセージを刺す。

2. To make batter, combine pancake mix and water in a small bowl and mix well.
   ホットケーキミックスを水で固めに溶き、衣をつくる。

3. Dip hot dogs in the batter one at a time.
   ② にウィンナーソーセージをくぐらせて衣をつける。

4. Deep fry hot dogs till coating turns golden brown.
   衣がきつね色になるまで揚げる。

5. Serve with ketchup and mustard to taste.
   揚がったミニアメリカンドッグにケチャップやマスタードをつけて食べる。

Note: This dish is especially popular with young people, as a snack or as something to serve when friends come over.
子供のおやつ、パーティー、ティータイムに最適。

KOREAN-STYLE GRIDDLECAKE
韓国風お好み焼き

Serves 4　4人分　20 min.　20分　　　　　　　　611 kcal./1

6 dried *shiitake* mushrooms　干ししいたけ　6枚

1 bunch Japanese scallions (*nira*)　にら　1わ

2 7–in. carrots　にんじん　2本

7 oz. beef round　牛もも肉　200g

2 fillets of white fish　白身の魚　2切れ

8 egg yolks　卵黄　8個

1½ cups flour　小麦粉　カップ1½（150g）

4 Tbsp. dried bonito shavings (*kezuribushi*)　削り節　大さじ4

pinch salt　塩　少量

10 scallops　帆立貝柱（生でもボイルしたものでもよい）　10個

Ⓐ

> Dipping Sauce　たれ
>
> 3 Tbsp. soy sauce　醤油　大さじ3
>
> 2 Tbsp. sugar　砂糖　大さじ2
>
> small amount of *tōbanjan* (red, spicy Chinese miso)　トウ バンジャン　少量
>
> 2 Tbsp. dried bonito shavings (*kezuribushi*)　削り節　大さじ2

1. Cut hard edges from the *shiitake* mushrooms, slice mushrooms thin. Cut Japanese scallions into pieces 1 in. (3 cm.) long and julienne carrots the same length. Cut the beef and fish fillets into bite-sized pieces.

   しいたけは石づきをとり薄切り。にらは3cmくらいに切り、にんじんは3cmほどのせん切りにする。牛肉、白身の魚は、一口大に切る。

2. Place egg yolks in a bowl and add the flour, bonito and salt to make the batter.

   卵黄に、小麦粉、削り節、塩をまぜて衣をつくる。

3. Soak the scallops and all ingredients from ① in batter ② for 1 minute.

   ②の生地に、①と帆立貝柱を1分ほどまぜ込んでおく。

4. Spread ③ out thin on a griddle and cook well on both sides, watching to be sure it doesn't burn.

③ をホットプレート上に適当な大きさに薄く伸ばし、こがさないように両面焼く。

5. Make the dipping sauce by combining and mixing Ⓐ. If you like, add some chopped Japanese leek (*naganegi*). If you prefer, substitute ready-made barbecue sauce.

④ を Ⓐ のソースにつけて食べる。長ねぎの刻んだものを入れると、よりおいしい。焼肉のタレを代用してもよい。

Note: To reconstitute dried *shiitake* mushrooms, rinse well and soak in 2 cups cold water for 2 hours. (If you're in a hurry, use lukewarm water, but add a pinch of sugar.)

干ししいたけをもどすには、さっと水洗いした後、水（カップ2）に2時間くらい浸す。短時間でもどすには、ぬるま湯に砂糖を少々加えるとよい。

CHEESE AND *MOCHI* SPRING ROLLS

餅とチーズの春巻き

Serves 4　4人分　20 min.　20分　　　　　　　　　331 kcal

---

6 wrapping sheets for *harumaki* spring rolls　春巻きの皮　6枚

3 glutinous rice cakes (*mochi*)　餅　3切れ

5 slices (3⅓ oz.) pizza cheese　スライスチーズ（溶けるタイプ）5枚（100g）

pinch flour　小麦粉　少量

dash water　水　少量

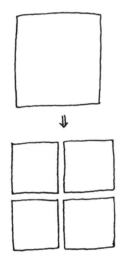

1. Cut the spring roll sheets into fourths.

   春巻きの皮を4等分に切る。

2. Cut each *mochi* cake crosswise into 8 sticks. Cut pizza cheese into rectangular blocks the same size as the *mochi*.

   餅を棒状に8等分する。溶けるチーズを餅と同じ大きさに切る。

3. Wrap *mochi* and cheese in the spring roll sheets. Paste the edges shut with a little flour mixed with water.

   餅とチーズを春巻きの皮で包む。皮の端に小麦粉少々を水で溶いたものをつけてとめる。

4. Deep fry in oil heated to 350°F (180°C), till golden brown.

   春巻きがきつね色になるまで180℃の油で揚げる。

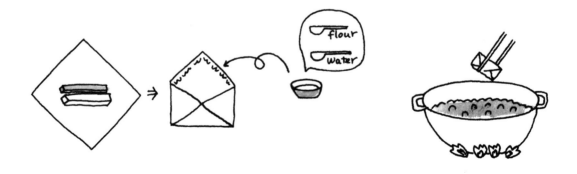

MINI PIZZA
ミニピザ

Serves 4　4人分　15 min.　15分　　　　　　　　　　153 kcal

8 wrapping sheets for *gyōza* **dumplings**　ギョウザの皮　**8** 枚

1 Tbsp. pizza sauce　市販のピザソース　大さじ**1**

1 onion (*tamanegi***)**　玉ねぎ　**1**個

2 green peppers　ピーマン　**2**個

½ salami sausage　サラミソーセージ　½本

1¼ cup pizza cheese　チーズ（溶けるタイプ）　**100g**

1. Spread pizza sauce onto the *gyōza* sheets.

   ギョウザの皮にピザソースをぬる。

2. Scatter sliced green peppers, sausage and onion over the pizza sauce.

   ① の上にスライスした玉ねぎ、ピーマン、ソーセージをのせる。

3. Sprinkle with cheese.

   ② の上にチーズをのせる。

4. Bake 3 minutes in an oven heated to 350°F (170–180°C).

   ③ を170～180℃のオーブンで約3分ほど焼く。

❤ **By the way:** Use your imagination in coming up with variations. For instance, half an English muffin can be used as the base, instead of a *gyōza* sheet. Other delicious toppings include: black olives, canned corn, steamed or boiled chicken (shredded), sliced mushrooms (sautéed in butter), dried oregano and basil, garlic powder.

バリエーションはあなた次第。たとえば、ギョウザの皮の代わりにマフィンを半分に割りピザ台にするとか、トッピングとして黒オリーブ、スイートコーン（缶詰）、蒸したりゆでたりして細く裂いた鶏肉、きのこの細切りバターいためをのせるとか、スパイスとしてオレガノやバジリコを使ってもおいしくなる。

ODEN

おでん

Serves 4 4人分   120 min. 120分   450 kcal

---

1 cup dried bonito shavings (*kezuribushi*) 削り節 カップ1 (10g)

8 cups water 水 カップ8

2 cups *dashi* だし カップ2

8 *musubi-konbu* (knotted pieces of kelp) 結びこんぶ 8個

2 tsp. salt 塩 小さじ2

4 Tbsp. soy sauce 醤油 大さじ4

2 Tbsp. *mirin* (sweet saké) みりん 大さじ2

2 *chikuwa* (hollow, tube-shaped fish cakes) ちくわ 2本

2 *chikuwabu* (*fu* wheat gluten formed into the shape of *chikuwa*) ちくわぶ 2本

1 8–in. length *daikon* radish 大根 ½本

1 cake *konnyaku* ("devil's tongue jelly") こんにゃく 1丁 (250g)

4 potatoes (*jagaimo*) じゃがいも 4個

2 *satsuma-age* (fried fish cakes) さつまあげ 2枚

2 *abura-age* (deep-fried tofu pouches) 油揚げ 2枚

4 glutinous rice cakes (*mochi*) もち 4切れ

1 28–in. length gourd ribbon (*kanpyō*) かんぴょう 70cm

---

1. To make the broth, simmer water and bonito for about an hour. Pass through a colander lined with paper towels, discard solids.

   鍋に水と削り節を入れて、1時間ほどぐつぐつ煮てスープをとる。スープはペーパータオルをひいたざるで静かにこす。

2. Cut *daikon* radish into slices about ¾–in. (2–cm.) thick. With a knife, score a cross about half an inch (1 cm.) deep in the center of each.

   大根を2cm厚さの輪切りにし、深さ1cmくらいの十文字の切れ目を入れる。

3. Cut the cake of *konnyaku* once down the middle in each direction. Sprinkle with salt and boil 5 or 6 minutes.

こんにゃくは十字に4つに切り、塩をまぶして、熱湯で5〜6分ゆでておく。

4. Cut *satsuma-age* and *chikuwa* in half. Cut *abura-age* into two square pouches and blanch it for 1 or 2 minutes to make it less oily.

さつまあげ、ちくわは半分に切る。油揚げは半分に切り、油ぬきのためさっと湯どおしする。

5. Cut gourd ribbon into 8–in. (20–cm.) lengths. Soak in cold water just briefly. Drain and rub well with salt, soak in lukewarm water. When ribbon swells, rinse off any excess salt and boil till tender.

かんぴょうは20cmくらいの長さに切り、水にさっと浸けて、塩でよくもんだあと洗い落として、ぬるま湯か水に浸け、かんぴょうがふやけたところで、やわらかくなるまでゆでる。

6. Insert the *mochi* rice cake into the *abura-age* pocket. Tie the pocket shut using ⑤ like string.

油揚げの切り口を開き中にもちを入れ、⑤ のかんぴょうで結ぶ。

7. Cut *chikuwabu* in half and blanch.

ちくわぶを半分に切り、さっとゆがく。

8. Combine knotted pieces of kelp, peeled potatoes and ②, ③, ④, ⑤, ⑥ and ⑦ in a good-sized, deep pot. Pour broth from ① over so that it just about covers the other ingredients. Add some water if necessary.

深鍋に、結びこんぶ、皮をむいたじゃがいも、②③④⑥⑦ の材料を入れ、① のスープを注ぐ。足りない場合は水を材料がかぶるくらい足す。

9. Bring ⑧ to a boil. Turn down the heat to low and add a dash each of *mirin* and soy sauce to deepen the flavor. Simmer till *daikon* radish and potatoes soften.

⑧ を火にかけ、ひと煮立ちしたら火を弱め、みりん、醤油で少し濃いめの味をつけ、大根、じゃがいもがやわらかくなるまでゆっくり煮る。

FRIED POTATO BARS
じゃがいも餅

Serves 4　4人分　45 min.　45分　　　　　　　　　　184 kcal

---

5 potatoes (*jagaimo*)　じゃがいも　5個（750g）

½ cup starch (*katakuriko*)　片栗粉　カップ½（50g）

1 Tbsp. butter　バター　大さじ1

1. Cut the potatoes into eighths. Boil and then mash them.
   じゃがいもを8等分にし、ゆでてからつぶす。

2. Gradually add the starch to the potatoes, while mixing.
   片栗粉を少しずつ加えながらまぜる。

3. Form the mixture into a square about 4 in. (10 cm.) wide.
   それを四角い形（10cm×10cm）に整える。

4. Cover with plastic wrap and refrigerate overnight.
   ラップで包んで、1日冷蔵庫で寝かせる。

5. Cut into bite-sized squares. Heat butter in a frying pan and sauté the squares.
   ④を2cmぐらいの厚さに切り、フライパンにバターを熱し、焼く。

Note: Potatoes are good for you. They're full of vitamin C, potassium and iron.
じゃがいもはビタミンC、カリウム、鉄分を含んでいて体にとてもよい。

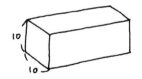

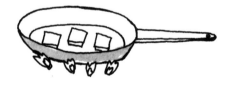

POTATO PANCAKES
じゃがいものパンケーキ

Serves 4　4人分　40 min.　40分　　　　　　　　　106 kcal

3 potatoes (*jagaimo*)　じゃがいも　3個

1 onion (*tamanegi*)　玉ねぎ　1個

1 Tbsp. grated cheese　粉チーズ　大さじ1

1 Tbsp. butter　バター　大さじ1

½ Tbsp. salt　塩　大さじ½

pinch pepper　こしょう　少量

dash vegetable oil　サラダ油　少量

1. Steam the potatoes till soft. Peel and mash them. Slice onion thinly and sauté it in butter. Mix onion through potatoes.

   じゃがいもを蒸して皮をむき、つぶしておく。玉ねぎは薄切りにしてバターでいため、じゃがいもによくまぜる。

2. Sprinkle ① with grated cheese and season with salt and pepper. Mix well and form into flattened patties.

   ① に粉チーズをまぜて、塩、こしょうをする。それを平たいだ円形にまとめる。

3. Cook in a lightly oiled frying pan, turning once, until both sides are nicely browned.

   フライパンに油を少量ひき② を両面に焦げめがつくまで焼く。

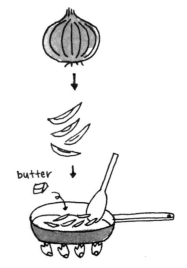

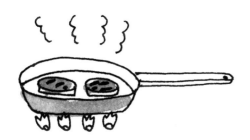

FRIED LOTUS ROOT WITH *SHISO* AND CHEESE

れんこんのしそチーズはさみ揚げ

Serves 4　4人分　30 min.　30分　　　　　　**153 kcal**

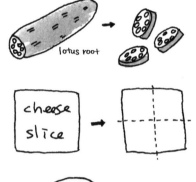

1½ sections lotus root (12 oz.)　れんこん　1½節（350g）

2 slices cheese　スライスチーズ　2枚

8 perilla (*shiso*) leaves　青じそ（大葉）　8枚

1 egg　卵　1個

1 Tbsp. flour (*komugiko*)　小麦粉　大さじ1

1 Tbsp. water　水　大さじ1

oil for deep frying　揚げ油

⅓ lemon　レモン　⅓個

salt and pepper　塩、こしょう

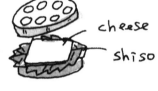

1. Cut lotus root into half-inch (1–cm.) slices.
   れんこんは皮をむき1cmの厚さの輪切りにする。

2. Cut each slice of cheese into fourths.
   チーズをそれぞれ4等分する。

3. Place 1 square of cheese and 1 *shiso* leaf between every 2 lotus root slices.
   輪切りにしたれんこん2枚でチーズひと切れとしそ1枚をはさむ。

4. Mix the flour, egg and water to make the batter.
   小麦粉、卵、水をまぜ、衣をつくる。

5. Dip ③ into ④.
   ③ を ④ にくぐらせる。

6. Deep fry ⑤, till golden, in oil heated to 350°F (180°C).
   ⑤ を180℃の油できつね色になるまで揚げる。

7. Season with salt and pepper and garnish with lemon slices.
   ⑥ を皿に盛り、塩、こしょうをふり、スライスしたレモンを添える。

POTATOES WRAPPED IN *SHISO*

じゃがいもとしそのはさみ揚げ

Serves 4 4人分 20 min. 20分   202.8 kcal

3 small potatoes (*jagaimo*) じゃがいも 小3個（300g）

20 perilla (*shiso*) leaves 青じそ（大葉） **20枚**

pinch salt 塩 少量

pinch starch (*katakuriko*) 片栗粉 少量

dipping sauce for tempura (*tentsuyu*) 天つゆ

soy sauce 醤油

---

1. Peel and grate the potatoes. Place them in a mixing bowl and add a little salt.

   じゃがいもをむき、すりおろす。ボールにじゃがいもを入れ塩を少々加える。

2. Sprinkle the glossy side of the *shiso* leaves with starch.

   しそのつやのある面に片栗粉をまぶす。

3. Place 1 portion of potato on the starch side of each leaf, and fold over.

   しその片栗粉をつけた面に① のじゃがいもをのせ、2つ折りにする。

4. Deep fry for 2 or 3 minutes in oil heated to 350°F (170°– 180°C).

   170〜180℃の油で2〜3分揚げる。

Note: To serve, sprinkle with *tentsuyu* (page 127) or soy sauce.

天つゆ（127頁参照）や醤油で食べるとおいしい。

PEANUT MISO

ピーナッツ味噌

Serves 4 4人分 20 min. 20分   **262 kcal**

²⁄₃ cup whole, raw peanuts 生ピーナツ　カップ²⁄₃ （70g）

4 Tbsp. miso 味噌　大さじ4

²⁄₃ cup sugar 砂糖　72g

dash *mirin* (sweet saké) みりん　少量

2¹⁄₃ Tbsp. vegetable oil サラダ油　大さじ2¹⁄₃

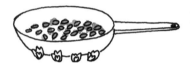

1. Mix the miso and sugar well in a small bowl. Add *mirin* and stir through. Set aside.

   味噌と砂糖はあらかじめよくまぜておくとよい。みりん（少量）を加えるとよくまざる。まざったらとっておく。

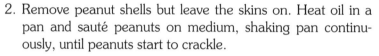
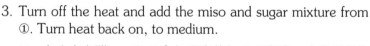

2. Remove peanut shells but leave the skins on. Heat oil in a pan and sauté peanuts on medium, shaking pan continuously, until peanuts start to crackle.

   薄皮つきの生ピーナツをサラダ油を熱して、フライパンで、パリパリと音がするまで絶えずゆり動かしながら中火でいる。

3. Turn off the heat and add the miso and sugar mixture from ①. Turn heat back on, to medium.

   いったん火を消し、① の合わせ味噌を ② に加え、中火でからめる。

4. Continue heating, stirring continuously to be sure peanut miso doesn't burn. When the mixture glazes, take it out of the pan right away.

   ピーナツと味噌がこげないように注意しながら、照りが出たところで火からおろす。

♥ **By the way:** Peanut miso goes very nicely with beer.

ピーナツ味噌はビールにあう。

Salads and Salad Dressings

サラダとサラダドレッシング

SWEET POTATO APPLE SALAD
りんごとさつまいものサラダ

Serves 4　4人分　30 min.　30分　　　　　　　　154 kcal

2 sweet potatoes (*satsumaimo*)　さつまいも　2本

½ apple　りんご　½個

1 lemon　レモン　1個

1 tsp. sugar　砂糖　小さじ1

pinch cinnamon　シナモン　少量

1. Peel the sweet potatoes. Boil them till they soften. Mash them.
   さつまいもの皮をむいて、やわらかくなるまでゆでてつぶす。

2. Peel the apple. Slice it thinly and lay it into an ovenproof bowl.
   りんごの皮をむいて、薄切りにして耐熱皿に入れる。

3. Sprinkle a little sugar over the apple. Slice ⅔ of the lemon thinly and lay it over the apple.
   ② に砂糖を少々入れ、⅔のレモンを輪切りにしてのせる。

4. Cover ③ with plastic wrap and warm 2 or 3 minutes in a microwave. (Or cover with foil instead, and warm 8 to 10 minutes in an oven preheated to 350°F/180°C).
   ③ にラップをして、電子レンジで2、3分温める。あるいは、あらかじめ180℃くらいに温めておいたオーブンで温める。（オーブンの場合はアルミホイルで器に蓋をする。）

5. Remove lemon slices. Mix ④ together with the sweet potatoes from ① and sprinkle with cinnamon and the juice from the remaining ⅓ lemon.
   ④ のレモンを取り除き、① のさつまいもとまぜ、シナモンと残り⅓のレモンをしぼってかける。

BEAN SPROUT AND CHINESE PICKLE SALAD

もやしとザーサイのあっさりサラダ

Serves 4 4人分 10 min. 10分   78 kcal

1 package bean sprouts　もやし　1袋

½ 6–in. carrot　にんじん　½本（80g）

⅓ 16–in. Japanese leek (*naganegi*)　長ねぎ　⅓本（30g）

generous Tbsp. (bottled) Chinese pickles (*zāsai*)　ザーサイ
（びん詰）　20g

white sesame seeds　白ごま　少量

4 Tbsp. *Wafū* (Japanese-style) Dressing　和風ドレッシング
大さじ4

1. Julienne the carrot and *naganegi* leek. Cut the Chinese pickles up small.

   にんじんと長ねぎはせん切りに、ザーサイは細かく刻む。

2. Plunge the bean sprouts briefly into boiling water. Remove and set in a colander to drain. Boil carrots for 5 or 6 minutes. Soak *naganegi* leek in water.

   もやしは熱湯にさっとくぐらせ、ざるにとり水気を切り、にんじんは5〜6分ゆでる。長ねぎは水にさらす。

3. Spread bean sprouts on a plate, and arrange carrots, *naganegi* leek and Chinese pickles on top. Sprinkle with white sesame seeds.

   皿にもやしをのせ、その上ににんじん、長ねぎ、ザーサイをのせ、白ごまをふりかける。

4. Sprinkle with *Wafū* (Japanese-style) Dressing (page 55).

   和風ドレッシング（55頁参照）をかける。

❤ **By the way:** Bean sprouts combat skin problems, stress, anemia and constipation.

もやしは肌荒れ、ストレス、貧血、便秘などの予防によい。

CHINESE SALAD

もやし・きゅうり・ハムのサラダ

Serves 4 4人分   30 min. 30分   199 kcal

1 package bean sprouts　もやし　**1袋**

2 8–in. cucumbers　きゅうり　**2本**

10 slices boneless ham　ボンレスハム　**10枚（200g）**

⅔ cup *Chūka* **(Chinese-style) Dressing**　中華ドレッシング　カップ⅔

---

1. Boil bean sprouts about 1 minute. Transfer to a colander to drain.

   沸騰したお湯で、もやしを1分ほどさっとゆで、ざるに上げておく。

2. Julienne the cucumbers and ham.

   きゅうりとハムをせん切りにする。

3. Transfer sprouts to a serving dish. Arrange ② attractively on top.

   もやしを皿に盛り、その上に ② を彩りよくのせる。

4. Just before serving, sprinkle *Chūka* (Chinese-style) Dressing (page 56) over the salad and mix lightly.

   食べる直前に中華ドレッシング（56頁参照）で和える。

BEAN SPROUTS WITH MUSTARD DRESSING

もやしのからし和え

Serves 4　4人分　15 min.　15分　　　　　　　　　　68 kcal

1 package bean sprouts　もやし　1袋

8 *kani-fūmi kamaboko* (crab-flavored cakes of pressed fish)
かに風味かまぼこ　8本

1 8–in. cucumber　きゅうり　1本

2 Tbsp. soy sauce　醤油　大さじ2

4 Tbsp. vinegar　酢　大さじ4

1 Tbsp. Japanese-style prepared mustard (*neri-garashi*)
練りがらし　大さじ1

1 tsp. salt　塩　小さじ1

kani kamaboko

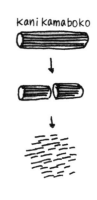

1. Rinse bean sprouts and boil in lightly salted water about 1 minute. Set in a colander to drain and cool.

   もやしを洗い、沸騰したお湯に塩を入れ1分ほどゆでたらざるにとり、冷ます。

2. Cut fish cakes in half and peel them into thin strips.

   かに風味かまぼこを2等分し、細く裂く。

3. Slice cucumber very thin.

   きゅうりを1mmの厚さの輪切りにする。

4. Mix soy sauce, vinegar and prepared mustard in a small bowl.

   醤油、酢、練りがらしをボールでまぜる。

5. Add bean sprouts, fish cakes and cucumber to ④ and toss.

   もやし、かに風味かまぼこ、きゅうりを④ に入れ、和える。

37

COD ROE POTATO SALAD
タラモ サラダ

Serves 4　4人分　15 min.　15分　　　　　　　　216 kcal

6 potatoes (*jagaimo*) じゃがいも　6個

1 pair cod roe sacs (*tarako*) たらこ　1腹

pinch each, salt and pepper 塩、こしょう　少量

¼ cup mayonnaise マヨネーズ　カップ¼

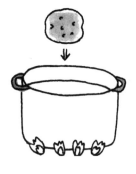

1. Boil the potatoes in their skins. Peel and mash them.

   じゃがいもは皮つきのままゆでて皮をむき、よく潰す。

2. Season potatoes with salt and pepper.

   ① に塩、こしょうし、まぜる。

3. Slit the cod roe sacs open with a fork. Scrape out the roe and combine it with ②, mix.

   たらこを潰し、② に入れる。

4. Add mayonnaise to ③, mix again.

   ③ にマヨネーズを入れ、まぜる。

❤ **By the way:** Cod roe is high in protein and vitamins A, B₁, B₂ and E. It is even said to prevent signs of ageing.

たらこには、タンパク質、ビタミンA、B₁、B₂、Eなどが含まれていて、老化防止に効果的とされている。

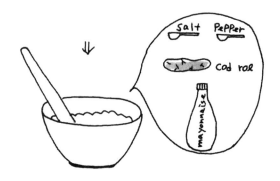

PLUM AND POTATO SALAD
梅干しポテトサラダ

Serves 4　4人分　25 min.　25分　　　　　146 kcal

4 pickled plums (*umeboshi*)　梅干し　4個

4 potatoes (*jagaimo*)　じゃがいも　4個

5 perilla (*shiso*) leaves　青じそ（大葉）　5枚

3 Tbsp. mayonnaise　マヨネーズ　大さじ3

pinch each, salt and pepper　塩、こしょう　少量

¼ bunch leafy salad greens　サラダ菜　8枚

1. Boil the potatoes in their skins. Peel and mash them.

   じゃがいもは皮つきのままゆで、皮をむき、潰す。

2. Remove the stones from the pickled plums and crush the fruit into a paste.

   梅干しの種を取り除き、フォークなどで果肉を潰す。

3. Julienne the *shiso* leaves.

   しその葉をせん切りにする。

4. Combine the mashed potatoes, pickled plum paste and strips of *shiso* together in a bowl and mix.

   潰したじゃがいもと、梅干し、せん切りにしたしそを、ボールに入れてまぜる。

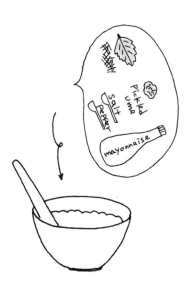

5. Season with salt and pepper. Add mayonnaise and mix.

   ④ に塩、こしょうし、マヨネーズを加える。

6. Arrange on a bed of salad greens.

   皿の上にサラダ菜をのせ、⑤ を盛りつける。

♥ **By the way:** Pickled plums are good for the digestion. They also stimulate appetite and combat fatigue.

梅干しは消化を助け、また食欲増進、疲労回復にも役立つ。

DAIKON RADISH–SHRIMP SALAD
大根のマヨネーズ和え

Serves 4 4人分 15 min. 15分   194 kcal

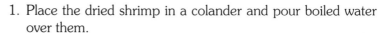

1 10–in. length *daikon* radish 大根 250g

$\frac{1}{3}$ cup dried shrimp (*hoshi-sakuraebi*) 干しさくらエビ カップ$\frac{1}{3}$（30g）

3 Tbsp. mayonnaise マヨネーズ 大さじ3

3 Tbsp. vegetable oil サラダ油 大さじ3

pinch each, salt and pepper 塩、こしょう 少量

1. Place the dried shrimp in a colander and pour boiled water over them.

   干しエビはざるに入れ、熱湯をかける。

2. Peel and julienne the *daikon* radish.

   大根の皮をむいて、せん切りにする。

3. Mix ① and ②. Sprinkle with salt and pepper.

   ①と②をまぜる。これに塩とこしょうを加える。

4. Mix mayonnaise and vegetable oil together in a small bowl and pour over ③. Mix lightly.

   マヨネーズとサラダ油を小さなボールに入れてよくまぜ合わせ、③に加えて和える。

Note: Increase or decrease the amount of oil at Step ④, as you like.
If you are using Chinese-style dried shrimp, which are harder, soak them 15 minutes in a large bowl of warm water. Canned scallops (*hotategai-bashira*) can also be substituted for shrimp.

Step ④ のサラダ油は好みで加減する。
さくらエビの代わりに中華材料の干しエビを使う場合は、たっぷりした量のぬるま湯に15分くらい浸けてもどす。缶詰（水煮）のホタテ貝柱を使ってもおいしい。

DAIKON RADISH AND CARROTS

大根とにんじんサラダとしそドレッシング

Serves 4　4人分　10 min.　10分　　　　　　　　132 kcal

1 12–in. length *daikon* radish　大根　¼本（300g）

½ 6–in. carrot　にんじん　小½本（50g）

dash vegetable oil　サラダ油　少量

4 Tbsp. *Shiso* Dressing　しそドレッシング　大さじ4

1. Make *Shiso* Dressing (page 52).

   しそドレッシングをつくる（52頁参照）。

2. Peel the *daikon* radish and carrots. Cut both into thin quarter-slices.

   大根とにんじんは皮をむき、薄めのいちょう切りにする。

3. Place ② in cold water for 1 or 2 minutes to make them crisper. Drain well.

   それらを冷水に1〜2分浸しシャキッとさせる。ざるにとり、よく水気を切る。

4. Sprinkle with a little vegetable oil.

   サラダ油を少量かける。

5. Spoon the dressing over just before serving.

   皿に盛り、ドレッシングをかけてできあがり。

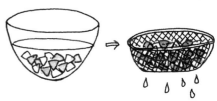

vegetable oil

❤ **By the way:** Carrots are said to fight anemia, low blood pressure, fatigue and poor eyesight.

にんじんは貧血、低血圧の改善、疲労回復、視力回復などに効果的。

dressing

CHERRY TOMATOES
JAPANESE-STYLE

プチトマトの和風サラダ

Serves 4　4人分　20 min.　20分　　　　　　　　63 kcal

16 cherry tomatoes　プチトマト　16個（240g）

4 Tbsp. Cucumber-*Daikon* Dressing　きゅうりと大根のドレッシング　大さじ4

1. Make Cucumber-*Daikon* Dressing (page 53).

   きゅうりと大根のドレッシングを作る（53頁参照）。

2. Rinse cherry tomatoes and remove the stems.

   プチトマトを水洗いし、ヘタを取り除く。

3. Quarter each tomato lengthwise.

   プチトマトを縦に四等分に切る。

4. Just before serving, sprinkle tomatoes with dressing. Toss gently and set out in small bowls.

   ③をドレッシングで和え、小さめのボールにきれいに盛りつける。

TOMATO SALAD

トマト サラダ

Serves 4　4人分　30 min.　30分　　　　　　　　47 kcal

2 or 3 whole fresh tomatoes　トマト　2〜3個

¼ onion (*tamanegi*)　玉ねぎ　¼個

1 stalk parsley　パセリ　1茎（5g）

Ⓐ

Dressing　ドレッシング

1 Tbsp. vegetable oil　サラダ油　大さじ1

2 Tbsp. vinegar　酢　大さじ2

⅔ tsp. salt　塩　小さじ⅔

pinch pepper　こしょう　少量

1. Score a cross on one end of each tomato and plunge them into boiling water for 1 minute. Drain and peel.

   トマトは十文字の切り込みを入れ沸騰した湯に1分ほど浸けてから皮をむく。

2. Slice and refrigerate tomatoes.

   トマトを薄く切って冷蔵庫に入れる。

3. Combine Ⓐ in a small bowl and mix.

   Ⓐ をボールに入れてまぜる。

4. Add minced onion to ③.

   ③ にみじん切りにした玉ねぎを加える。

5. Rinse the parsley, blot it dry with a paper towel and mince.

   パセリを水洗いし水気をペーパータオルで取り、みじん切りにする。

6. Arrange chilled tomatoes on a plate. Sprinkle dressing over and garnish with ⑤.

   皿に冷やしたトマトを盛り、ドレッシングをかけ ⑤ を散らす。

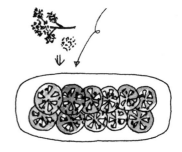

♥ **By the way:** Tomatoes are low in calories but rich in vitamins (like A and C). They also help reduce cholesterol and break down fats in the body.

トマトは低カロリーでビタミンAやCをたっぷり含み、コレステロールを低下させたり、脂肪の分解をたすけたり、とてもヘルシー。

43

SALAD BAR
サラダ バー

Serves 4　4人分　30 min.　30分　　　　　　　　　　**188 kcal**

2 blocks firm tofu (*momen-dōfu*)　もめん豆腐　2丁

½ head lettuce　レタス　½個

1 8–in. cucumber　きゅうり　1本（100g）

½ onion (*tamanegi*)　玉ねぎ　½個

½ 7–in. carrot　にんじん　½本（70g）

1¾ oz. fresh-packed seaweed (*nama-wakame*)　生ワカメ（50g）

8 cherry tomatoes　プチトマト　8個

Ⓐ

Dressing　ドレッシング

1 Tbsp. vegetable oil and 1 tsp. sesame oil　サラダ油　大さじ1
ごま油　小さじ1

5 Tbsp. vinegar　酢　大さじ5

pinch each, salt and pepper　塩、こしょう　少量

1. Rinse lettuce leaves and arrange them on a large dish. Set drained tofu blocks (page 101) on top.

   レタスを洗い、皿に敷き、その上に水切りをした豆腐（101頁参照）をのせる。

2. Cut the onions up finely. Julienne the cucumber and carrot. Cut the seaweed into bite-sized pieces.

   玉ねぎは薄切りに、きゅうり、にんじんはせん切りにする。わかめは食べやすい大きさに切る。

3. Scatter ② over and around the tofu blocks and set cherry tomatoes around the base.

   切った野菜と、わかめを ② の豆腐の上にのせ、プチトマトをまわりに飾る。

4. To make the dressing, combine Ⓐ and mix. Sprinkle over the salad and serve.

   Ⓐ の材料をよくまぜてドレッシングをつくり、サラダにかける。

❤ **By the way:** This dish is nutritious and low-calorie. And it's fine to use whatever vegetables you happen to have around the kitchen.
台所にあるあり合わせの野菜でつくれ、栄養のバランスがよく、低カロリー。

BEAN AND SEAFOOD SALAD

豆・たこ・イカのサラダ

Serves 4 4人分 30 min. 30分   213 kcal

10 oz. broad beans (*soramame*) そら豆 280g

3½ oz. peas (*endōmame*) えんどう豆 100g

3½ oz. boiled octopus (leg) meat (*yudedako no ashi*) ゆでだこの足 100g

meat of ½ squid いか ½尾 （50g）

2–3 leaves leafy salad greens (*sarada-na*) サラダ菜 葉 2〜3枚 （20g）

1 Tbsp. each, minced green, red and yellow peppers ピーマン、赤ピーマン、黄ピーマンのみじん切り 各大さじ1 （5g）

1 Tbsp. minced onion (*tamanegi*) 玉ねぎのすりおろし 大さじ1

2 Tbsp. *mirin* (sweet saké) みりん 大さじ2

2 Tbsp. olive oil オリーブ油 大さじ2

1 Tbsp. vinegar 酢 大さじ1

1 tsp. each, salt and pepper 塩、こしょう 小さじ各1

---

1. Place beans and peas in a pot of lightly salted water. Bring to a boil, then lower heat to medium and cook 10 or 15 minutes, till soft.

   塩水でえんどう豆とそら豆をゆでる。沸騰したら中火で10〜15分やわらかくなるまでゆで、水気を切る。

2. Boil octopus and squid meat about 5 minutes, till heated through. Cut both into bite-sized pieces.

   いかをさっとゆで、たこの足といっしょに食べやすい大きさに切る。

3. Cut the salad greens up roughly. Cut all the peppers into ¼-in. (7–8 mm.) squares.

   サラダ菜はざく切りにし、ピーマンはすべて7〜8mm角に切る。

4. Mix *mirin*, olive oil, vinegar and salt and pepper. Add the minced onion.

   みりん、オリーブ油、酢、塩、こしょうを合わせ、そこに玉ねぎのすりおろしを加えよくまぜる。

5. Combine all ingredients from ①, ② and ③. Sprinkle with ④ and toss lightly.

   ④ のソースですべての材料を和え、皿に盛る。

SALMON BONE SALAD

サケの骨のサラダ

Serves 4　4人分　15 min.　15分　　　　　　　　　　　156 kcal

---

1 head lettuce　レタス　1個

1 can salmon bones　サケの中骨缶　1缶（300g）

1 Tbsp. lemon juice　レモン汁　大さじ1

5 slices boneless ham　ボンレスハム　5枚　100g

3 Tbsp. mayonnaise　マヨネーズ　大さじ3

3 Tbsp. *Wafū* (Japanese-style) Dressing　和風ドレッシング 大さじ3

---

1. Separate and rinse the lettuce leaves. Spread them on a large plate.

   レタスの葉を一枚一枚よく洗い、水を切ってから大皿にたくさん敷く。

2. Scatter salmon bones over ①. Sprinkle a little lemon juice over.

   敷いたレタスの上にサケの骨を散らす。レモン汁をかけて、さわやかな味にする。

3. Scatter julienned ham over ②.

   その上に細切りにしたハムを散らす。

4. Make *Wafū* (Japanese-style) Dressing (page 55). Combine mayonnaise and *Wafū* Dressing in a small dish and mix. Sprinkle over the salad.

   小皿に、マヨネーズと和風ドレッシング（55頁参照）をまぜ、サラダにかける。

GREEN SALAD WITH SEAFOOD

シーフードサラダ

Serves 4　4人分　30 min.　30分　　　　　　　　　　**244 kcal**

5 medium shrimp　エビ　5尾（100g）

3½ oz. squid meat　イカ（胴）　1杯（100g）

6 large lettuce leaves　レタス　6枚（120g）

1 5–in. length fresh seaweed (*nama-wakame*)　生ワカメ　10g

1 small (3–oz.) can tuna　ツナ　小1缶（90g）

1 small (3–oz.) can scallops　ホタテ貝柱　1缶（90g）

4 Tbsp. *Wafū* (Japanese-style) Dressing　和風ドレッシング
大さじ4

1. Remove shells, heads and tails from the shrimp, devein.
   Boil shrimp and squid together, till heated through.

   エビは殻と頭を取り、背わたを抜く。エビ、イカを火が通るま
   でゆでる。

2. Rinse and drain lettuce.

   レタスを洗って水を切る。

3. Cut squid, seaweed and lettuce into bite-sized pieces.

   イカとワカメとレタスを一口大に切る。

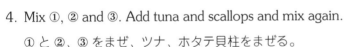

4. Mix ①, ② and ③. Add tuna and scallops and mix again.

   ① と ②、③ をまぜ、ツナ、ホタテ貝柱をまぜる。

5. Sprinkle *Wafū* (Japanese-style) Dressing (page 55) over the
   salad. Toss lightly.

   これらを和風ドレッシング（55頁参照）で和える。

❤ **By the way:** You can substitute crab for squid, if you prefer.

イカの代わりに、カニでつくるのもよい。

TUNA GLASS NOODLE SALAD

春雨とツナのサラダ

Serves 4　4人分　30 min.　30分　　　　　　　　　295 kcal

1 package (3⅓ oz.) *harusame* (thin glass noodles made of starch)　春雨　1パック（100g）

2 8–in. cucumbers　きゅうり　2本（200g）

1 large (6–oz.) can tuna　ツナ　大1缶（185g）

pinch each, salt and pepper　塩、こしょう　少量

⅔ cup *Chūka* (Chinese-style) Dressing　中華ドレッシング　カップ⅔

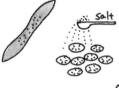

1. Cut *harusame* glass noodles into 2–in. (5–cm.) lengths. Bring pot of water to a boil. Turn off heat and add glass noodles. Let them soak 3 or 4 minutes, until transparent. Transfer to a colander, rinse with cold water and drain.

   春雨を食べやすい長さ（5cmくらい）に切っておく。沸騰湯に春雨を入れて火を止め、ふたをし、透きとおるまで蒸らし、ざるにとって冷水で洗い、水気を切る。

2. Slice cucumbers thin and sprinkle with salt.

   きゅうりを薄く輪切りにし、塩をふる。

3. Blot cucumber slices dry and place them in a bowl with the glass noodles.

   きゅうりの水気をしぼり、春雨と一緒にボールに入れる。

4. Drain the tuna and add it to ③.

   ツナを汁を除いて ③ に入れる。

5. Sprinkle salad with *Chūka* (Chinese-style) Dressing (page 56) and pepper.

   ④ に中華ドレッシング（56頁参照）をかけ、こしょうをふる。

LIGHT SALAD WITH *UNAGI* EEL
あっさりうなぎサラダ

Serves 4　4人分　20 min.　20分　　　　　　　　　　**87 kcal**

3 8–in. cucumbers　きゅうり　3本（300g）

1 broiled eel, with sauce (*unagi no kabayaki*)　うなぎの蒲焼き
1枚（80g）

3 Tbsp. vinegar　酢　大さじ3

1 Tbsp. sugar　砂糖　大さじ1

1 tsp. light soy sauce (*usukuchi shōyu*)　うす口醤油　小さじ1

1½ Tbsp. *dashi*　だし　大さじ1½

1. Slice cucumbers thin.

   きゅうりを薄い輪切りにする。

2. Dip cucumbers into lightly salted water for 2 or 3 minutes,
   then squeeze hard to remove any excess water.

   きゅうりを薄い塩水に2〜3分さらし、手で水気をぎゅっとしぼる。

3. Heat eel on a grilling tray (*yakiami*) or in a broiler.

   焼き網でうなぎをあぶる。

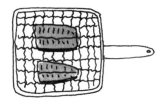

4. Cut eel into pieces about ½ in. (1 cm.) wide.

   うなぎを1cm幅に切る。

5. Combine vinegar, sugar, light soy sauce and *dashi* (page
   222) in a small bowl and mix. Pour over the sliced cucumbers, toss lightly.

   ボールに酢、砂糖、うす口醤油、だし（222頁参照）を入れて
   まぜ、きゅうりを和える。

6. Just before serving, add eel to ⑤.

   食べる直前にうなぎを加える。

CHICKEN KIMCHI SALAD
ささみときゅうりのピリ辛サラダ

Serves 4　4人分　10 min.　10分　　　　　　　　　58 kcal

6 chicken *sasami* (inner breast fillets), or 3 chicken breasts cut in half lengthwise 鶏ささみ　小6本（150g）

2 tsp. saké 酒　小さじ2

1 8–in. cucumber きゅうり　1本

1 Tbsp. kimchi base (*kimuchi no moto*) キムチの素　大さじ1

1 Tbsp. French dressing フレンチドレッシング　大さじ1

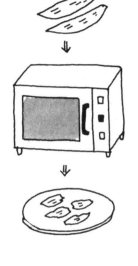

1. Cook the chicken fillets for 2 minutes in a microwave. When they cool, tear each into 4 or 5 pieces.

   ささみを皿にのせ、酒（小さじ2）をふりラップをかけ電子レンジで2分加熱する。冷めたら、1本を5〜6切れに裂く。

2. Julienne the cucumber.

   きゅうりをせん切りにする。

3. Mix the chicken and cucumber. Add the kimchi base and Vinaigrette Dressing (page 54). (Adjust the flavor by adding more or less kimchi base.)

   ささみときゅうりに、キムチの素とフレンチドレッシング（54頁参照）を加えてまぜる。キムチの素は、好みで加減するとよい。

♥ **By the way:** Kimchi is actually said to help burn off fat stored in the body. The *tōgarashi* red pepper which is one of kimchi's main ingredients stimulates the production of gastric juices, improving digestion.

キムチには体内の脂肪を燃焼させる作用があると言われている。またキムチに使われる唐がらしは、胃液の分泌を促し消化を助ける。

SPECIAL VEGETABLE DRESSING
野菜ドレッシング

400 cc (2 cups)　30 min.　30分　　　　　　　　　1430 kcal (2cups)

1 small onion (*tamanegi*)　玉ねぎ　小**1個**

¼ knob ginger root　しょうが　¼かけ（**10g**）

½ clove garlic　にんにく　½かけ（**10g**）

¼ tomato　トマト　¼個

¼ green pepper　ピーマン　¼個（**15g**）

¼ rib celery　パセリ　¼本

2⅓ Tbsp. salt　塩　大さじ2⅓

¾ tsp. Japanese-style prepared mustard (*neri-garashi*)　練りがらし　小さじ¾

¼ tsp. pepper　こしょう　小さじ¼

⅓ cup ketchup　ケチャップ　カップ⅓（**80g**）

¼ cup tomato juice　トマトジュース　カップ¼

¾ cup vegetable oil　サラダ油　カップ¾（**700g**）

¼ cup vinegar　酢　カップ¼

1. Peel the onion, ginger root, garlic and tomato.
   玉ねぎ、しょうが、にんにく、トマトの皮をむく。

2. Cut the green pepper in half lengthwise, take out the seeds.
   ピーマンは縦2つにし、種をとる。

3. Chop the onion, celery, tomatoes and green peppers.
   玉ねぎ、セロリ、トマト、ピーマンをざくざくと切る。

4. Place all ingredients in a food blender and mix.
   その他全ての材料といっしょにミキサーにかける。

❤ **By the way:** Try this dressing on Green Salad with Seafood (page 47).
シーフードサラダ（47頁参照）にピッタリ。

YOGURT LEMON DRESSING
ヨーグルトとレモンのドレッシング

Serves 4　4人分　5 min.　5分　　　　　　　　　　169 kcal

1 cup plain yogurt　ヨーグルト　カップ1

1 Tbsp. lemon juice　レモン汁　大さじ1

$\frac{1}{3}$ cup vegetable oil　サラダ油　カップ$\frac{1}{3}$

$\frac{1}{2}$ tsp. salt　塩　小さじ$\frac{1}{2}$

pinch pepper　こしょう　少量

1. Combine all ingredients in a small bowl and mix.
   材料をボールに入れよくまぜ合わせる。

SHISO DRESSING
しそドレッシング

Serves 4　4人分　5 min.　5分　　　　　　　　　　211 kcal

7 Tbsp. vegetable oil　サラダ油　大さじ7

2 Tbsp. rice vinegar　米酢　大さじ2

(scant $\frac{1}{2}$ tsp. salt)　塩　小さじ$\frac{1}{2}$弱

5 perilla (*shiso*) leaves　青じそ（大葉）　5枚

1. Combine all ingredients except the *shiso* leaves and mix well.
   しそ以外のすべての材料をよくまぜ合わせる。

2. Rinse the *shiso* leaves. Pat dry and mince finely.
   しそを洗い、よく水を切ったら細くきざむ。

3. Add the minced *shiso* just before serving.
   ドレッシングを使う直前にきざんだしそを加える。

CUCUMBER-*DAIKON* DRESSING
きゅうりと大根のドレッシング

Serves 4　4人分　10 min.　10分　　　　　　　　　10 kcal

2 8–in. cucumbers　きゅうり　2本（200g）

1½–in. length *daikon* radish　大根　4cm（100g）

2–3 Tbsp. lemon juice　レモン汁　大さじ2〜3

pinch salt　塩　少量

1. Cut off the ends of the cucumbers and peel the *daikon* radish. Grate both.

   両端を切り落としたきゅうりと皮をむいた大根をすりおろす。

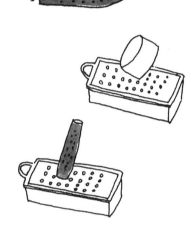

2. Transfer mixture to a colander and let drain 1 to 2 minutes.

   ① を目の細かいざるに入れ1〜2分そのままにし、水気を少なくする。

3. Transfer to a bowl, mix thoroughly. Add lemon juice and salt, mix again.

   それをボールに移し、レモン汁と塩を加えてまぜ合わせる。

Note: When this dressing is exposed to the air, it gets watery and loses its vitamin C, so it's best to make it just before serving.

このドレッシングは食べる直前につくるとよい。あまり長く放っておくと、水っぽくなったりビタミンCがとんだりしてしまう。

1-2 minutes

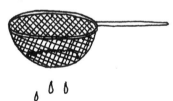

VINAIGRETTE DRESSING
フレンチドレッシング

Serves 4 4人分 5 min. 5分   315 kcal

¾ cup olive oil オリーブ油 カップ¾

¼ cup vinegar or lemon juice 酢またはレモン汁 カップ¼

¼–½ tsp. prepared mustard マスタード 小さじ¼〜½

½ tsp. salt 塩 小さじ½

pinch pepper こしょう 少量

1. Place all ingredients except the olive oil in a bowl. Blend well with a wire whisk.

   ボールにオリーブ油以外の材料を入れ、泡立て器でよくかきまぜる。

2. Add olive oil gradually, stirring between additions.

   かきまぜながら、少しずつオリーブ油を加える。

3. Refrigerate in a glass jar or other container till needed. Shake well again just before using.

   よくまざったら、瓶などに入れて冷蔵庫へ。使うときはよくまぜ合わせる。

♥ **By the way:** Optional additions: fresh herbs, garlic.
にんにくなどを加えてもドレッシングがおいしくなる。いろいろなスパイスを使って好みの味を作ってみよう。

WAFŪ (JAPANESE-STYLE) DRESSING
和風ドレッシング

Serves 4 4人分 10 min. 10分   120 kcal

¼ 16–in. Japanese leek (*naganegi*) 長ねぎ ¼本 （10cm）

4 Tbsp. vegetable oil サラダ油 大さじ4

2 Tbsp. rice vinegar 米酢 大さじ2

1 Tbsp. soy sauce 醤油 大さじ1

pinch brown sugar 黒砂糖 少量

1. Mince the *naganegi* leek. Place all ingredients in a small bowl and mix well.

   長ねぎをみじん切りにし、他の材料といっしょにボールに入れ、よくまぜ合わせる。

2. Refrigerate in a glass jar or other container till needed. Shake well again just before using.

   保存は、瓶などに入れて冷蔵庫へ。使うときにはよくまぜ合わせる。

naganegi leek

rice vinegar

vegetable oil

soy sauce

pinch brown sugar

shake well!

CHŪKA (CHINESE-STYLE) DRESSING

中華風ドレッシング

Serves 4　4人分　15 min.　15分　　　　　　　　　140 kcal

---

4 Tbsp. vegetable oil and 1 scant tsp. sesame oil　サラダ油 大さじ4とごま油　小さじ1弱

2 Tbsp. rice vinegar　米酢　大さじ2

2 tsp. light soy sauce (*usukuchi shōyu*)　うす口醤油　小さじ2

1 tsp. *mirin*　みりん　小さじ1

½ Tbsp. roasted and ground white sesame seeds　すり白ごま 大さじ½

¼ tsp. salt　塩　小さじ¼

---

1. Combine all the ingredients in a small bowl and mix well with a wire whisk.

   ボールにすべての材料を入れ、泡立て器でよくまぜ合わせる。

2. Refrigerate in a glass jar or other container till needed. Shake well again just before using.

   保存は、瓶などに入れて冷蔵庫へ。使うときにはよくまぜ合わせる。

♥ **By the way:** You can make this more "Chinese-style" by adding pressed or minced garlic and/or grated ginger.

おろしにんにくやおろししょうがを加えるとより中華風。

shake well !

Soups

スープ

SCALLION EGG SOUP
にらたまスープ

Serves 4　4人分　20 min.　20分　　　　　　　　　　　　23 kcal

½ bunch (5–10 stalks) Japanese scallions (*nira*)　にら　½わ

2 eggs　卵　2個

3 cups water　水　カップ3

½ chicken or vegetable bouillon cube　固形スープ　½個

dash saké　酒　少量

dash soy sauce　醤油　少量

pinch salt　塩　少量

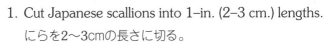

1. Cut Japanese scallions into 1–in. (2–3 cm.) lengths.

   にらを2〜3cmの長さに切る。

2. Combine water, bouillon, scallions, saké, soy sauce and salt in a soup pot and bring to a simmer.

   鍋に水、固形スープ、にら、調味料を入れ煮る。

3. Beat the eggs and add them to ②. As soon as they boil up, turn off the heat.

   そこに卵を溶いて入れ、卵が浮いてきたら、火を止める。

Note: You may want to mellow the scallions' flavor by blanching them first.

にらの香りをやわらかくするには、前もってさっとゆでておくとよい。

COUNTRY SOUP
田舎スープ

Serves 4　4人分　30 min.　30分　　　　　　　　　　378 kcal

$\frac{1}{3}$ lb. pork (shoulder butt), sliced thin　豚肩ロース薄切り肉 150g

$3\frac{2}{3}$ Tbsp. butter　バター　大さじ$3\frac{2}{3}$

4 cups water　水　カップ4

2 bouillon cubes　固形スープ　2個

salt and pepper　塩、こしょう

Ⓐ

2 celery ribs　セロリ　2本

1 7–in. carrot　にんじん　1本

5 potatoes (*jagaimo*)　じゃがいも　5個

3 Japanese turnips (*kabu*)　かぶ　3個

$\frac{1}{2}$ head cabbage　キャベツ　$\frac{1}{2}$個

1 onion (*tamanegi*)　玉ねぎ　1個

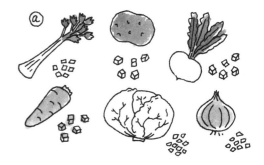

1. Dice the celery, carrot, potatoes and turnip. Cut cabbage and onion into half-inch (1–cm.) squares.

   セロリ、にんじん、じゃがいも、かぶはさいの目に、キャベツと玉ねぎは1cm角くらいに切る。

2. Cut pork into bite-sized pieces. Melt the butter in a stew pot, add pork and sauté it until meat turns whitish throughout.

   豚肉は一口大に切る。鍋にバターを溶かし、豚肉を色が変わるまでいためる。

3. Add Ⓐ to the pot and sauté with the pork 1 or 2 minutes.

   Ⓐを鍋に入れ、豚肉と一緒に1〜2分いためる。

4. Add the water to ③. When water is hot, add the bouillon cubes. Let simmer, skimming the fat now and then. Season with salt and pepper.

   ③に水を入れ、温まったら固形スープを加えて、アクを除きながら煮込み、塩とこしょうで味を調える。

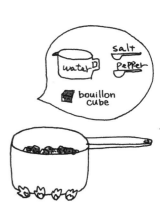

5. Cook until all vegetables, including the carrot, are heated through.

   にんじんがやわらかくなったらできあがり。

GROUND CHICKEN SOUP WITH WAX GOURD

とうがんの鶏そぼろスープ

Serves 4　4人分　40 min.　40分　　　　　　　　　245 kcal

1½ cups (10 oz.) ground chicken　鶏ひき肉　300g

1 *tōgan* wax gourd (4 cups)　冬瓜　900g

¾ cup green soybeans (*edamame*)　枝豆　100g

3 cups *dashi* broth　だし汁　カップ3

½ Tbsp. salt　塩　大さじ½

1 Tbsp. soy sauce　醤油　大さじ1

2 Tbsp. *mirin* (sweet saké)　みりん　大さじ2

1 Tbsp. starch (*katakuriko*)　片栗粉　大さじ1

1. Peel the gourd, cutting away some of the harder pulp just beneath the peel as well. Remove seeds and cut pulp into 2–in. (4–5 cm.) chunks. Sprinkle pulp with salt to soften, set aside.

   とうがんは種を取って皮を厚めにむき、4〜5cm大に切る。それに塩少々を振りかけて、しんなりとさせておく。

2. Boil green soybeans in salted water about 5 minutes, till fairly soft. Drain and cool. Hull beans and discard the pods.

   枝豆は約5分、多少やわらかくなるまで塩ゆでにし、ざるに上げ、冷めたら実を取り出しておく。

3. Heat the *dashi* broth (page 222) and the wax gourd. Add the ground chicken and stir. When mixture returns to a boil, turn heat down to low. Skim the fat.

   鍋にだし（222頁参照）ととうがんを入れ火にかける。鶏ひき肉を加えてかきまぜ、沸騰したら火を弱め、アクをすくい取る。

4. When the wax gourd's color grows lighter, season the soup with salt, soy sauce and *mirin*. Heat uncovered on low for 20 to 30 minutes.

   とうがんが透き通ってきたら、塩、醤油、みりんで味をつけ、弱火で20〜30分煮る。

5. Dissolve starch in cold water (1 part starch to 2 parts water). Add this mixture to ④, to thicken it.

   水で溶いた片栗粉（水の量は片栗粉の約2倍）でとろみをつける。

6. Add the soybeans from ② to ⑤.

   ②の枝豆を入れる。

WHOLE ONION SOUP
まるごと玉ねぎスープ

Serves 4　4人分　45 min.　45分　　　　　　　　　84 kcal

4 onions (*tamanegi*)　玉ねぎ　4個

4 (chicken- or beef-flavored) bouillon cubes　固形スープ　4個

4 cups water　水　カップ4

pinch each, salt and pepper　塩、こしょう　少量

parsley　パセリ　少量

1. Peel the onions and cut off the tops. Score a cross into the bottom of each, to let heat pass through more quickly.

   玉ねぎの皮をむき、上部を切り落とす。短時間で火が通るように、下部に十字に切り目を入れておく。

2. Place water, onions and bouillon cubes in a soup pot. Simmer 30 or 40 minutes, till onions can easily be cut with chopsticks. Season to taste with salt and pepper.

   鍋に水、玉ねぎ、固形スープを入れ、30〜40分弱火で煮る（箸でちぎれるくらい）。塩とこしょうで味を調える。

3. Mince the parsley. Pour soup into individual serving bowls and sprinkle with parsley.

   1人分ずつスープ皿に分け、みじん切りにしたパセリを散らす。

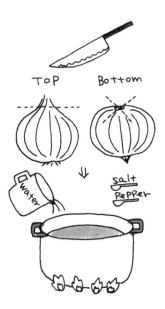

CHICKEN TOMATO SOUP
鶏肉とトマトのスープ

Serves 4　4人分　30 min.　30分　　　　　　　　　　**237 kcal**

2 chicken legs　骨付き鶏もも　**2本**

2 chicken-flavored bouillon cubes　固形スープ　**2個**

½ clove garlic　にんにく　**½かけ**

6 whole tomatoes　トマト　**6個**

2 cups water　水　カップ**2**

pinch each, salt and pepper　塩、こしょう　少量

1. Cut each leg into several large pieces, and rinse. Mince the garlic clove, or crush it under the blade of a heavy knife.

   鶏肉を3つに切って洗う。にんにくは大きめの包丁でたたいてつぶす。

2. Place bouillon cubes and water in a pot. Add the meat from ① and the crushed garlic, simmer about 20 minutes.

   鍋に固形スープ、水を入れ、① の鶏肉、つぶしたにんにくを加え弱火で20分煮る。

3. Remove chicken from the pot. Pass soup through a colander lined with paper towels.

   鶏肉を鍋から出して、ペーパータオルを敷いたざるでスープをこす。

4. Discard the chicken bones and return broth and chicken to the pot. Add roughly chopped tomatoes and season with salt and pepper. Simmer about 10 more minutes.

   こしたスープと鶏肉を鍋に戻し、ざく切りにしたトマトを加え塩、こしょうで味を調えて10分ほど煮る。

Note: If you like a clearer soup, peel the tomatoes at Step ④.
トマトの皮はむいておくと、口当たりがよい。

❤ **By the way:** This soup is great with French bread.
フランスパンとよく合います。

SQUASH SOUP

パンプキンポタージュ

Serves 4 4人分 50 min. 50分   175 kcal

---

1 Japanese squash (*kabocha*), or acorn squash かぼちゃ 小**1**個

½ onion (*tamanegi*) 玉ねぎ **½**個

5 cups water 水 カップ**5**

3 bouillon cubes 固形スープ **3**個

2 Tbsp. butter バター 大さじ**2**

2 Tbsp. flour (*komugiko*) 小麦粉 大さじ**2**

a small amount of parsley パセリ 少量

a few croutons クルトン 少量

salt and pepper 塩、こしょう

---

1. Peel squash, remove seeds. Slice pulp and onion thin.

   かぼちゃは皮をむき、種とわたを取って小切りに、玉ねぎは薄切りにする。

2. Combine water and bouillon cubes in a soup pot and bring to a boil. Set aside 1 cup of the soup. In the remaining 4 cups, simmer the squash and onion till soft. Just before mixture returns to a boil, lower heat. Simmer until squash is soft. Blend or pass through a sieve (reserve the solids).

   鍋に水と固形スープを入れ煮立てる。1カップ分のスープは別にとっておく。残りのスープでかぼちゃと玉ねぎをやわらかくなるまで煮て、煮えたら裏ごしするかミキサーにかけ、煮汁はとっておく。

3. Combine butter and flour in a large, sturdy soup pot. Heat slowly, stirring continuously. Don't let mixture burn. Add the rest of the liquid from ② a little at a time. When mixture is smooth, add the strained squash and onion. Season with salt and pepper.

   厚手の鍋にバターと小麦粉を入れ、こがさないようにへらでまぜながらいため、さらさらにする。残したスープを少しずつ加え、なめらかになったら、裏ごししたかぼちゃと玉ねぎを入れてさっとまぜ、塩とこしょうで味を調える。

4. Mince the parsley. Pour soup into small serving dishes and sprinkle with parsley and croutons.

   器にとり分け、クルトンとパセリのみじん切りを浮かせる。

EGG SOUP

かきたま汁

Serves 4　4人分　20 min.　20分　　　　　　　　　67 kcal

3 cups *dashi* broth　だし　カップ3

3 eggs　卵　3個

a few trefoil leaves (*mitsuba*)　みつば　少量

a small amount of Japanese leek (*naganegi*)　長ねぎ　少量

1 Tbsp. soy sauce　醤油　大さじ1

½ tsp. salt　塩　小さじ½

1. In a soup pot, bring *dashi* broth (page 222) to a simmer. Season with soy sauce and salt.

   鍋にだし（222頁参照）を入れ、煮立ったら醤油と塩を加えつゆを作る。

2. Beat eggs.

   卵を溶いておく。

3. Add the eggs gently to ① with a soup ladle and then swirl them through.

   煮立ったつゆに、おたまでまぜながら ② を静かに流す。

4. When eggs are half-cooked, sprinkle soup with trefoil leaves and minced *naganegi* leek. Remove from heat and serve.

   卵が半熟状になったら、みつばと刻みねぎを散らし火を止める。

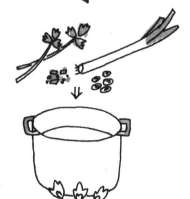

BACON AND CHINESE CABBAGE SOUP

白菜とベーコンのスープ

Serves 4 4人分 35 min. 35分   **371 kcal**

8 leaves Chinese cabbage (*hakusai*) 白菜 葉8枚

1 16–in. Japanese leek (*naganegi*) 長ねぎ 1本

5¼ oz. bacon ベーコン 150g

1 knob *shōga* ginger root しょうが 1かけ

1 large (6–oz.) can tuna ツナ大缶1 （185g）

2 Tbsp. saké 酒 大さじ2

2 Tbsp. *mirin* (sweet saké) みりん 大さじ2

2 Tbsp. soy sauce 醤油 大さじ2

1 tsp. salt 塩 小さじ1

1 Tbsp. sesame oil ごま油 大さじ1

5 cups water 水 カップ5

bacon

tuna naganegi

Hakusai ginger

saké soySauce mirin

salt

sesame oil
at the end

1. Cut *naganegi* leek into 1–in. (2½–cm.) slices, on the diagonal.

   長ねぎを、1〜3cmの厚さの斜め切りにする。

2. Cut bacon strips into 2–in. (5–cm.) lengths. Transfer to a colander and pour boiled water over them, to reduce their oil content. Peel the ginger root and cut it finely.

   ベーコンを5cm幅で切ってざるに入れ、上から熱湯をかけて脂ぬきをする。しょうがの皮をむき、薄く切る。

3. Cut Chinese cabbage leaves down the middle and then across in 1–in. (2½–cm.) strips. Place water, Chinese cabbage and ginger root in a soup pot and boil 4 or 5 minutes, till cabbage softens.

   白菜を縦半分に切り、それを横から2〜3cm幅にざくざくと切る。鍋の中に水、しょうがと入れて4〜5分、白菜がやわらかくなるまで煮る。

4. Add *naganegi* leek, bacon and tuna and boil 2 or 3 minutes. Add saké, *mirin* and soy sauce. Flavor with a dash of sesame oil.

   ④ に長ねぎ、ベーコン、ツナを入れさらに2〜3分煮る。酒、みりん、塩、醤油を入れ、最後に、ごま油で味を調える。

ONION GRATIN SOUP

オニオングラタンスープ

Serves 4　4人分　40 min.　40分　　　　　　　　　174 kcal

2 onions (*tamanegi*)　玉ねぎ　2個

2 Tbsp. butter　バター　大さじ2

5 cups water　水　カップ5

2 (beef-flavored) bouillon cubes　固形スープ　2個

pinch each, salt and pepper　塩、こしょう　少量

4 slices French bread　フランスパン　4切れ

mild cheese (cheddar, Swiss, etc.)　ナチュラルチーズ（溶ける
タイプ）　少量

1. Slice onions thin. Melt butter and add the onions. Brown them slowly over low heat.

   熱したフライパンにバターを溶かし、薄切りにした玉ねぎをあめ色になるまで弱火でゆっくりいためる。

2. Heat ①, water and bouillon cubes in a soup pot. Season with salt and pepper.

   鍋に ① と水と固形スープを入れ火にかけ、塩、こしょうで味を調える。

3. Divide ② among 4 ovenproof soup bowls. Add a piece of French bread and a small amount of cheese to the top of each bowl.

   ② を4つの耐熱容器に分けて、3cmくらいの厚さに切ったフランスパン、チーズを入れる。

4. Bake for 10 minutes in a 350°F (180°C) oven.

   180℃くらいのオーブンで10分焼く。

♥ **By the way:** This soup is warming and delicious. Try it for supper on a cold evening.
とても体が温まるので、寒い夜にはおすすめのスープ。

CHICKEN VEGETABLE STEW
鶏のけんちん汁

Serves 4 4人分 40 min. 40分   298 kcal

1 large chicken breast (7 oz.) 鶏胸肉 大1枚（200g）

½ 16–in. *daikon* radish 大根 ½本

2 7–in. carrots にんじん 2本（280g）

1 6–in. eggplant なす 1個

1 24–in. burdock root (*gobō*) ごぼう 1本

1 taro (*satoimo*) さと芋 1個

1 cake *konnyaku* ("devil's tongue jelly") こんにゃく 1丁
(250g)

1 block firm tofu (*momen-dōfu*) もめん豆腐 1丁

1 Tbsp. sesame oil ごま油 大さじ1

3 Tbsp. soy sauce 醤油 大さじ3

½ Tbsp. salt 塩 大さじ½

1. Cut the *daikon* radish, carrots and eggplant into 2–in. (5–6 cm.) quarter-slices. Shave the burdock root into thin strips and soak it in cool water about 1 minute. Peel the taro and cut it into thin half-moon slices. Rip the *konnyaku* into bite-sized pieces and boil it briefly. Cut chicken into bite-sized pieces.

   大根、にんじん、なすはそれぞれ5～6cm厚さのいちょう切りにする。ごぼうはささがきにして1分ほど水にさらす。さと芋は皮をむき7～8mm厚さの半月に切る。こんにゃくは食べやすい大きさに手でちぎり、さっとゆでておく。鶏肉は、一口大に切る。

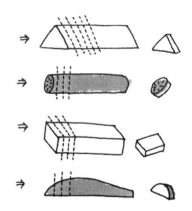

2. In a soup pot, sauté the vegetables, chicken and *konnyaku* in sesame oil.

   野菜と鶏肉とこんにゃくを鍋に入れごま油でいためる。

3. When chicken is cooked on the outside, add enough water to cover all ingredients. Simmer until vegetables soften and chicken is cooked through.

   鶏肉の表面の色が変わったら、材料がかぶるくらい水を入れ野菜がやわらかくなるまで煮る。

4. Crush the block of tofu with a fork and add it to ③.

   豆腐をくずし、③ に入れる。

5. Season with soy sauce and salt.

   醤油と塩で味つけする。

Note: For a richer flavor, add a little saké or a pinch of instant *dashi* powder at Step ③.

だしの素や酒を少々加えるとよりおいしい。

CHINESE CORN SOUP
中華風コーンスープ

Serves 4 4人分 **40 min.** 40分 **236 kcal**

1 can corn (cream-style) コーンのクリームスタイル缶詰 **1缶**
(450g)

1½ bouillon cubes 固形スープ **1½個**

3 cups water 水 カップ**3**

2 Tbsp. starch (*katakuriko*) 片栗粉 大さじ**2**

2 eggs 卵 **2個**

---

1. In a soup pot, bring water and bouillon cubes to a boil.
   鍋に水カップ3と固形スープを入れ沸騰させる。

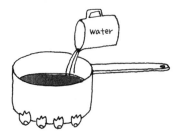

2. Add the creamed corn and simmer till mixture boils again.
   コーンの缶詰をスープごと加えて沸騰するまで煮る。

3. Dissolve starch in water (1 part starch to 2 parts water) and add to pot.
   片栗粉を2倍の水で溶き、鍋に加えて煮る。

4. Beat the eggs well, add them to pot and stir briefly. Soup is done when it returns to a simmer.
   卵を割り溶いてよくまぜ、鍋にそっと加えてかきまぜて煮立ったらできあがり。

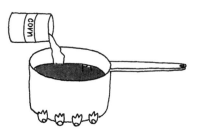

MISO SOUP WITH *DAIKON* RADISH

大根の味噌汁

Serves 4　4人分　15 min.　15分　　　　　　　**120 kcal**

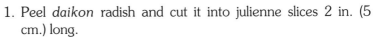

1 5–in. length *daikon* **radish　大根　120g**

1 deep-fried tofu pouch (*abura-age***)　油揚げ　1枚**

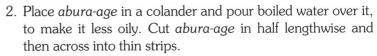

4 cups *dashi* **broth　だし　カップ4**

4 Tbsp. miso　味噌　大さじ4

1. Peel *daikon* radish and cut it into julienne slices 2 in. (5 cm.) long.

   大根は皮をむいて5cmのせん切りにする。

2. Place *abura-age* in a colander and pour boiled water over it, to make it less oily. Cut *abura-age* in half lengthwise and then across into thin strips.

   油揚げは、ざるにとり熱湯をかけて油抜きしたあと、縦長に2つに切り、7〜8mm幅に切る。

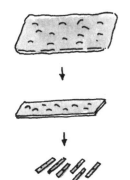

3. In a soup pot, bring *dashi* broth (page 222) to a boil.

   鍋にだし（222頁参照）を入れて、沸騰させる。

4. Add *daikon* radish and simmer on medium.

   沸騰したら大根を入れて中火で煮る。

5. When *daikon* radish softens, reduce the heat and add miso, stirring to help it dissolve.

   大根がやわらかくなったら、火を弱めおたまに味噌を取り、だしの中ではしなどで溶かしながらまぜる。

6. Heat until miso is completely dissolved (don't overcook), and pour into individual soup bowls.

   味噌がまざったら火を止め、おわんに盛る。

Note: Be sure to cook the radish thoroughly before adding the miso. Once you add miso, the radish will not get any softer.

大根は、味噌を入れる前によくやわらかくしないと、固いままになる。

MISO SOUP WITH TOFU AND SEAWEED

豆腐とワカメの味噌汁

Serves 4　4人分　20 min.　20分　　　　　　　　　　　　106 kcal

1 block "silken" tofu (*kinugoshi-dōfu*)　絹ごし豆腐　1丁

$\frac{1}{4}$ **cup dried *wakame* seaweed (*hoshi-wakame*)**　干しワカメ　カップ$\frac{1}{4}$　（5g）

3$\frac{1}{2}$ cups *dashi* broth　だし　カップ3$\frac{1}{2}$

3–4 Tbsp. miso　味噌　大さじ3–4

---

1. Dice the tofu.

   豆腐はさいの目に切る。

2. Reconstitute the dried seaweed by soaking it 10 minutes in about 2 cups cool water. Cut it into bite-sized pieces.

   干しワカメは10分ほどカップ2ぐらいの水につけて戻し、食べやすい大きさに切る。

3. In a soup pot, heat the *dashi* broth (page 222). When heated through, add the seaweed and miso. Stir the miso through well. Add the tofu and as soon as soup boils up, turn off the heat and serve.

   だし（222頁参照）を火にかけ、温まったらワカメを入れ、味噌を溶かし入れる。さらに豆腐を入れ、ぐらっと一煮立ちしたら火を止める。

Note: Cooking too long spoils tofu's soft texture. Cook only long enough to heat tofu through.

豆腐を入れたら煮すぎないこと。"す"が入ってしまう。

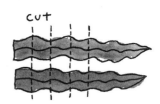

MISO SOUP VARIATIONS
その他の味噌汁

Mushroom-Tofu Miso Soup　なめこと豆腐の味噌汁

- 1 package *nameko* mushrooms　なめこ　1袋

  Place mushrooms in a colander and rinse briefly (rinsing too long will spoil their texture).

  ざるに入れて流水でさっと洗う。長く洗うとぬめりがとれてしまう。

- 1 block "silken" tofu (*kinugoshi-dōfu*)　絹ごし豆腐　**1丁**

  Dice the tofu.

  さいの目に切る。

Leek and Abura-age Miso Soup　ねぎと油揚げの味噌汁

- 1 16–in. length Japanese leek (*naganegi*)　長ねぎ　1本

  Cut the *naganegi* leek into half-inch (1–cm.) slices.

  1cmぐらいの小口切り。

- 1 deep-fried tofu pouch (*abura-age*)　油揚げ　1枚

  Place *abura-age* in a colander and pour boiled water over, to reduce its oil content. Cut *abura-age* in half lengthwise and then across into strips about $\frac{1}{3}$–in. (7–8mm.) wide.

  ざるにとり、熱湯をかけて油ぬきをしたあと、、。縦長に2つに切り、7～8mm幅に切る。

MISO SOUP WITH *SUITON* DUMPLINGS

すいとんの味噌汁

Serves 4   4人分   40 min.   40分   **271 kcal**

½ 24–in. burdock root (*gobō*)   ごぼう   ½本

½ 7–in. carrot   にんじん   ½本

1 4–in. length *daikon* radish   大根   ¼本

½ 16–in. Japanese leek (*naganegi*)   長ねぎ   ½本

¼ lb. chicken   鶏肉   100g

4–5 *shiitake* mushrooms   しいたけ   4〜5枚

4 cups *dashi* broth   だし   カップ4

1½ cups flour   小麦粉   カップ1½（200g）

4 cups water   水   カップ4

3⅓ Tbsp. miso   味噌   大さじ3⅓（60g）

---

1. Slice the burdock root and soak it in water for a few minutes, to mellow its flavor. Cut the carrot and *daikon* radish into quarter-slices. Cut the chicken and *shiitake* mushrooms into bite-sized pieces. Cut the *naganegi* leek into ½–in. (1–cm.) slices.

   ごぼうを輪切りにし、しばらくボールに入れた水にさらし、アクを抜く。にんじんと大根はいちょう切りにする。長ねぎは1cm幅の小口切り、鶏肉としいたけを1口大に切る。

2. In a soup pot, heat the *dashi* broth (page 222). When it comes to a boil, add the vegetables and chicken.

   鍋にだし（222頁参照）を入れ、沸騰したら野菜と鶏肉を入れる。

3. Mix water, a little at a time, into the flour, to form the dumpling dough. (It should be very soft, and enough for about 20 dumplings.)

   小麦粉に少しずつ水を加えてまぜ、耳たぶよりやわらかくする。

4. When vegetables are soft, use a spoon to cut off enough dough for one dumpling at a time, dropping them into the pot as you go.

   野菜が十分にやわらかくなったら、すいとんの種をスプーンですくって1口大に入れる。

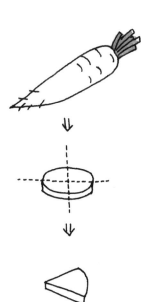

5. When dumplings float to the surface, add the shredded *naganegi* leek. Season with miso.

すいとんが浮き上がってきたら、長ねぎを加える。最後に味噌で味を調える。

CHILLED RICE SOUP
(*HIYASHIJIRU*)

冷やし汁

Serves 4　4人分　20 min.　20分　　　　　　　　　　250 kcal

3 perilla (*shiso*) leaves　青じそ（大葉）　3枚

a small amount of Japanese leek (*naganegi*)　長ねぎ　少量

1 8–in. cucumber　きゅうり　1本（100g）

4½ Tbsp. white sesame seeds　白ごま　40g

¼ cup miso　味噌　カップ¼（60g）

3 cups dashi　だし　カップ3

4 cups steamed rice（1lb）　ご飯　4人分（440g）

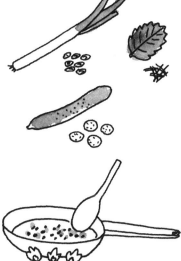

1. Mince the *shiso* leaves and *naganegi* leek. Slice the cucumber.
   しそと長ねぎをみじん切りにする。きゅうりを輪切りにする。

2. Toast the *sesame* seeds in a dry frying pan until a few begin to pop. Grind a portion of the seeds in a mortar, working the rest in gradually.
   弱火にかけたフライパンで2つ3つはじけるまでごまをいり、いったごまをすり鉢でする。

3. Add the miso little by little, mixing the seeds into it.
   味噌を加えて再びすりまぜる。

4. Add chilled *dashi* broth (page 222), stirring well.
   冷たいだし（222頁参照）を加えて味噌を溶く。

5. Add the sliced cucumbers, *shiso* leaves and *naganegi* leek, stir through.
   ① のきゅうりとしそと長ねぎを加える。

6. To serve, fill large soup bowls with rice and then scatter a few ice cubes on top of each, pour ⑤ over.
   冷たいご飯の上にでき上がった ⑤ をかけ、氷を2、3個のせて食べる。

AYU SWEETFISH SOUP

アユの吸い物

Serves 2 2人分   20 min. 20分   **89 kcal**

2 sweetfish (*ayu*) アユ 2尾

¼ bunch spinach ほうれん草 ¼わ

2 cups *dashi* broth だし カップ2

pinch salt 塩 少量

dash soy sauce 醤油 少量

4–6 thin slices *naruto* (pressed fish) なると 4～6切れ

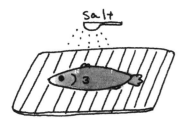

1. Lightly salt and broil the sweetfish, browning both sides.

   アユは両面にきれいなこげ目がつくように塩焼きにしておく。

2. Boil the spinach in lightly salted water 1 or 2 minutes, and soak in a bowl of water for a few minutes to mellow its flavor.

   ほうれん草は、塩を入れた熱湯で1～2分ゆで、水を入れたボールにつけてアクをぬいておく。

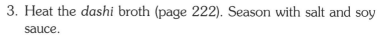

3. Heat the *dashi* broth (page 222). Season with salt and soy sauce.

   鍋にだし（222頁参照）を入れ、火にかけ塩、醤油で味を付け、吸い物の汁をつくる。

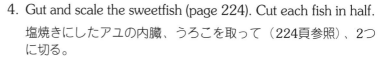

4. Gut and scale the sweetfish (page 224). Cut each fish in half.

   塩焼きにしたアユの内臓、うろこを取って（224頁参照）、2つに切る。

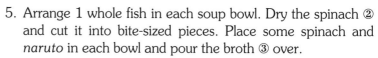

5. Arrange 1 whole fish in each soup bowl. Dry the spinach ② and cut it into bite-sized pieces. Place some spinach and *naruto* in each bowl and pour the broth ③ over.

   おわんにアユを入れ、なると、水気をとり食べやすい大きさに切ったほうれん草（②であくぬきしたもの）を加え、熱い汁を入れる。

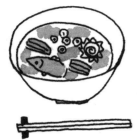

Vegetables

野菜

CABBAGE ROLLS WITH BACON BELTS
ロールキャベツ

Serves 4 4人分 60 min. 60分 669 kcal

8 large leaves cabbage キャベツ　葉8枚

1 lb. ground ham (lean cut) 豚ももひき肉（赤身）400g

1 egg 卵　1個

½ onion (*tamanegi*) 玉ねぎ　½個

½ carrot にんじん　½本

4 Tbsp. butter バター　大さじ4

1 cup bread crumbs パン粉　カップ1（50g）

8 strips bacon ベーコン　8枚

2 cups water 水　カップ2

1 (beef-flavored) bouillon cube 固形スープ1

3 Tbsp. flour (*komugiko*) 小麦粉　大さじ3

pinch each, salt and pepper 塩、こしょう　少量

5 Tbsp. ketchup ケチャップ　大さじ5

---

1. Shave the hard parts of the cabbage leaves down flat. Boil the leaves in lightly salted water till they soften. Drain.

   キャベツは葉の芯を平らにそぎ取り、やわらかくなるまで塩を少々入れた湯でゆでる。

2. Mince onion and carrot. Mix ground ham, egg, butter and bread crumbs. Season with salt and pepper.

   玉ねぎ、にんじんはみじん切りにし、ひき肉、卵、バター、パン粉とともにボールでまぜ、塩、こしょうする。

3. Form ② into 8 balls. Roll each ball inside 1 large cabbage leaf and belt with a strip of bacon.

   ②を8つに分け、それぞれをキャベツの葉でくるみ、ベーコンで帯をする。

4. Dissolve bouillon cube in boiling water to make 2 cups soup. Add ketchup. Drop cabbage rolls in and boil 20 minutes.

78

鍋に水カップ2を煮立て固形スープを溶かし、ケチャップを加えロールキャベツを20分ほど煮込む。

5. Melt butter in a small frying pan and mix flour in gradually. When golden brown, add about 1 Tbsp. of the soup from ④ and keep heating. When smooth, add to ④, to thicken the soup. Simmer on low for a few more minutes.

フライパンにバターを入れ、小麦粉が薄く色づくまでいためる。そこにスープ少量を ④ から取って加え、なめらかに溶けまざったところで鍋にもどし、数分弱火で煮る。

6. Serve, spooning a little sauce over each cabbage roll.

皿に盛りつけるときは、ロールキャベツにスプーンなどで煮汁をかけること。

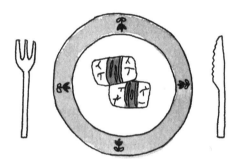

EGGPLANTS AND PEPPERS IN MISO

なすとピーマンの味噌いため

Serves 4　4人分　15 min.　15分　　　　　　　　　　86 kcal

5 6–in. eggplants　なす　5本（375g）

2 green peppers　ピーマン　2個

1 Tbsp. vegetable oil　サラダ油　大さじ1

1 Tbsp. miso　味噌　大さじ1

2 Tbsp. saké　酒　大さじ2

2 Tbsp. sugar　砂糖　大さじ2

1. Cut off the eggplant caps and both ends of the green peppers. Open peppers up lengthwise, remove seeds. Cut eggplants into half-moons, julienne the green peppers.

   なすはヘタを取り除き半月切りに、ピーマンは、縦に割り芯と種を除きせん切りにする。

2. Soak the eggplants in water about 5 minutes to mellow their flavor, drain.

   なすを水に5分ほど浸して、アクをぬいたら水気を切る。

5 minutes

3. Heat the oil in a frying pan and sauté the eggplants till tender.

   フライパンに油を熱し、なすをしんなりするまでいためる。

4. Add the green peppers and continue sautéeing about 1 more minute.

   ピーマンを加えて、さらに約1分いためる。

5. Combine and mix the saké, sugar and miso. Add them to ④, heat through.

   酒と砂糖と味噌を合わせておいたものを加え、さっと火を通す。

miso　sugar

Note: Sesame is the best type of oil to use in this dish, as it brings out the fragrance of the miso.

なすをいためるとき、ごま油を使うと、味噌をよりこうばしくし、味に深みが出る。

80

EGGPLANT CREAM CHEESE TEMPURA

なすのチーズサンド天ぷら

Serves 4　4人分　20 min.　20分　　　　　　　　　　398 kcal

---

4 6–in. eggplants　なす　4本（300g）

1½ cups cream cheese　クリームチーズ　カップ1½（250g）

½ cup flour (*komugiko*)　小麦粉　カップ½

1 tsp. curry powder　カレー粉　小さじ1

½ tsp. salt　塩　小さじ½

pinch pepper　こしょう　少量

¼ cup water　水　カップ¼

oil for deep frying　揚げ油

---

1. Cut off the caps of the eggplants. Cut each eggplant into 8 slices.

   なすはヘタを除き、（8つくらいの）輪切りにする。

2. Cut the cream cheese in half lengthwise and then into flat wafer-thin squares.

   クリームチーズは縦2つに切り、5mmほどの幅に切る。

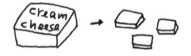

3. Place one square of cream cheese between every 2 eggplant slices.

   なす2枚でチーズをはさむ。

4. To make the batter, mix the flour, curry powder and salt and pepper. Gradually stir in the water.

   小麦粉にカレー粉、塩、こしょうをよくまぜる。少しずつ水を加えて溶きながら衣をつくる。

5. Coat ③ with the batter and deep fry.

   ③ に ④ の衣をつけ、油で揚げる。

WHOLE SIMMERED EGGPLANTS

なすの丸煮

Serves 4   4人分   20 min.   20分   120 kcal

8 small 6-in. eggplants, caps still on   なす   **8本**

A

| 2 cups *dashi* broth   だし   カップ2

| 5 Tbsp. soy sauce   醤油   大さじ5

| 4 Tbsp. saké   酒   大さじ4

| 1 generous Tbsp. sugar   砂糖   大さじ1強

1. With the tip of a knife, make 3 lengthwise cuts in each eggplant. Start near the cap and go almost to the bottom. Make cuts deepest in the middle.

   なすに縦に3本ほど包丁の先で切り込みをいれる。切り込みは真ん中あたりで一番深く。

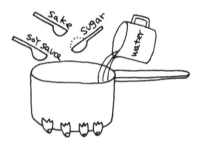

2. Combine Ⓐ in a fairly deep stew pot and heat till sugar dissolves. Add eggplants. Cover with a drop-lid (page 229) and bring to a boil over high heat.

   シチュー鍋のような深めの鍋にⒶの調味料を入れ、砂糖が溶けたところでなすを入れ、落とし蓋（229頁参照）をし強火で煮立たせる。

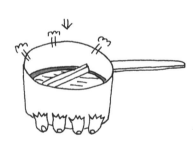

3. Lower heat to medium and simmer 15 minutes, turning eggplants every few minutes.

   煮立ったら中火にしてさらに15分ほど、なすをときおりひっくり返しながら煮る。

4. Cut through the neck of each eggplant, just below the cap, to make them easier to eat.

   できあがったら、食べやすくするためになすのヘタの部分を切り落とす。

Note: Serve hot, at room temperature, or chilled.
あたたかくても冷やして食べてもよい。

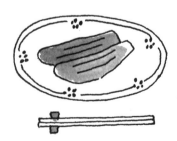

SPECIAL OKRA AND PICKLED PLUM GRAVY

オクラと梅干しの和えもの

Serves 4 4人分 5 min. 5分   11 kcal

5 okra オクラ 5本

3 pickled plums (*umeboshi*) 梅干し 3個

2 Tbsp. dried bonito shavings (*kezuribushi*) 削り節 大さじ2

1 Tbsp. soy sauce 醤油 大さじ1

---

1. Cut off okra stems. Slice okra thin.

   オクラはヘタを除いて、きざむ。

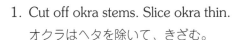

2. Remove the stones from the pickled plums and crush the fruit.

   梅干しは種を取り除き、フォークなどでよくつぶす。

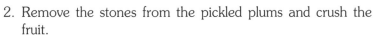

3. Combine the okra, pickled plums, dried bonito and soy sauce and mix well.

   オクラと梅干しと削り節と醤油をよくまぜる。

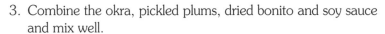

❤ **By the way:** Use as a flavorful topping for steamed rice or chilled tofu, or as a dip for raw vegetables.

あたたかいご飯にのせて食べる。冷やっこにのせたり、野菜のスティックにつけて食べてもおいしい。

SIMMERED MEAT AND POTATOES (*NIKUJAGA*)

肉じゃが

Serves 4 4人分 50 min. 50分   224 kcal

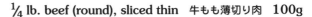

¼ lb. beef (round), sliced thin 牛もも薄切り肉 100g

3 potatoes (*jagaimo*) じゃがいも 3個

1 onion (*tamanegi*) 玉ねぎ 1個

1 Tbsp. vegetable oil サラダ油 大さじ1

½ Tbsp. sugar 砂糖 大さじ½

1 Tbsp. soy sauce 醤油 大さじ1

1 tsp. salt 塩 小さじ1

1 cup water 水 カップ1

⅓ cup green peas グリーンピース カップ⅓

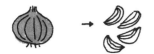

1. Cut the beef into bite-sized pieces.
   牛肉を食べやすい大きさに切る。

2. Peel the potatoes and cut them into fourths.
   じゃがいもは皮をむき4つに切る。

3. Cut the onion into eighths.
   玉ねぎを8等分する。

4. Heat oil in a soup pot and fry the beef, onion and potatoes together till meat changes color.
   鍋に油を熱し牛肉と玉ねぎとじゃがいもを一緒に肉の色が変わるまでいためる。

5. To ④, add the water and then the sugar, soy sauce and salt. Bring to a boil and skim the fat.
   ④に水を入れる。砂糖、醤油、塩を加え、煮立たせアクをとる。

6. Reduce heat and simmer 20 to 25 minutes, till tender.
   やわらかくなるまで20～25分煮る。

7. Sprinkle with green peas just before serving.
   食べる直前にグリーンピースを散らす。

SQUASH AND RED ADZUKI BEANS
かぼちゃのあずき煮

Serves 4 4人分 30 min. 30分   137 kcal

½ small Japanese squash (*kabocha*), or acorn squash (⅔ lb.)
かぼちゃ ½個（300g）

2 cups *dashi* broth だし カップ2

1 Tbsp. sugar 砂糖 大さじ1

2 tsp. soy sauce 醤油 小さじ2

1 (7–oz.) can boiled red adzuki beans (*yude-azuki*) ゆで
あずき 200g

1. Cut the squash into bite-sized pieces, peeling it here and there for the color contrast. Combine *dashi* broth, sugar, soy sauce and squash in a pot. Bring mixture to a boil.

   かぼちゃは食べやすい大きさに切り、ところどころ皮をむく。鍋にだし、砂糖、醤油、かぼちゃを入れて煮る。

2. When ① comes to a boil, cover with a drop-lid (page 229) and simmer until squash is soft enough to be pierced easily with a chopstick.

   沸騰したら、鍋に落とし蓋（229頁参照）をして、弱火でかぼちゃにすっとはしがささる位のやわらかさになるまで煮る。

3. Add adzuki beans to ② and cook until heated through.

   ②に、ゆであずきを加えて、あずきが温まるまで煮る。

SIMMERED TARO AND OCTOPUS

里芋とタコのうま煮

Serves 4　4人分　40 min.　40分　　　　　　　　　　　　146 kcal

---

1 lb. (about 8) taro (*satoimo*)　里芋　8個（500g）

5 oz. boiled octopus (*yudedako*)　ゆでダコ　150g

2 cups *dashi*　だし　カップ2

2 Tbsp. sugar　砂糖　大さじ2

2 Tbsp. saké　酒　大さじ2

3½ Tbsp. soy sauce　醤油　大さじ3½

1. Rinse taro well and boil briefly, in their skins. When they cool, peel the taro. Roughly cut the boiled octopus.

   里芋は皮の泥を水洗いし、皮つきのまま軽く数分下ゆでをし、冷めたら皮をむいておく。ゆでだこはぶつ切りにしておく。

2. Heat the *dashi* broth (page 222) and then add the peeled taro.

   里芋をだし（222頁参照）に入れ、中火で煮る。

3. Add sugar, saké and soy sauce. Cover, let simmer.

   ②に砂糖、酒、醤油を加え、蓋をして煮込む。

4. When the liquid is reduced, add octopus and cook till heated through.

   汁が少なくなってきたら、タコを入れてさっと煮る。

YAM WRAP
山芋の包み揚げ

Serves 4　4人分　15 min.　15分　　　　　　　　　　78 kcal

½ lb. Japanese yams (*yamaimo*)　山芋　200g

8 perilla (*shiso*) leaves　青じそ（大葉）　8枚

2 sheets dried, toasted *nori* seaweed (*yakinori*)　焼き海苔　2枚

pickled plum (*umeboshi*) paste　梅干しの裏ごし　少量

pinch flour　小麦粉　少量

dash water　水　少量

oil for deep frying　揚げ油

---

1. Cut each sheet of *nori* seaweed into eighths.

   焼き海苔を8等分にする。

2. Peel the Japanese yams and slice them into small rectangles, about 2 x 1 in. (5 x 3 cm.).

   山芋の皮をむき、5×3cm角ほどにスライスする。

3. Spread a little plum paste between every 2 pieces of yam.

   種をとり、フォークなどでつぶした梅干しを山芋の間にはさむ。

4. Wrap ③ with a *shiso* leaf and then a piece of *nori* seaweed. (Paste the edges down with a small amount of flour mixed with water.)

   ③ をしそをのせた海苔で巻く。巻き終わりを、小麦粉少々を水で溶いたものでとめる。

5. Deep fry ④ in oil heated to about 325°F (160°C).

   ④ を160℃の油で揚げる。

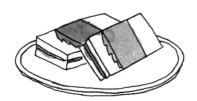

SPINACH WITH SESAME DRESSING

ほうれん草のごま和え

Serves 4　4人分　10 min.　10分　　　　　　　　　　　96 kcal

1 bunch spinach　ほうれん草　1わ（250g）

Ⓐ

| **3 Tbsp. white sesame seeds**　白ごま　大さじ3

| **1 Tbsp. soy sauce**　醤油　大さじ1

| **1 Tbsp. sugar**　砂糖　大さじ1

1. Boil spinach 2 minutes, then rinse and gently squeeze. Cut spinach into 1¼-in. (3-cm.) lengths.

   ほうれん草を熱湯で2分ほどゆでてから取り出し、水にさらし軽くしぼる。3cmくらいの長さに切る。

2. In a small frying pan, heat white sesame seeds till they turn light brown. Transfer to a mortar and grind, gradually adding the soy sauce and sugar.

   小さめのフライパンで白ごまを軽く焦げ色がつくくらいまでいり、すり鉢でていねいにすりながら醤油と砂糖を少しずつ加える。

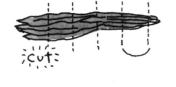

3. Toss lightly just before serving.

   食べる前に② をほうれん草に加え、和える。

❤ **By the way:** Try this with other vegetables, too, like green beans (*ingen*), bean sprouts (*moyashi*), or chrysanthemum leaves (*shungiku*).

いんげんやもやし、春菊などでもおいしい。

COOKED VEGETABLE SALAD
ゆで野菜サラダ

Serves 1   1人分   20 min.   20分   **202 kcal**

⅙ head cauliflower (about 2 oz.)　カリフラワー　50g

⅛ head broccoli (1 oz.)　ブロッコリー　30g

½ potato (*jagaimo*)　じゃがいも　½個（60g）

¼ 7–in. carrot　にんじん　⅕本強（30g）

generous Tbsp. canned or frozen corn　コーン（冷凍か缶詰）
大さじ1強

1 tsp. mayonnaise　マヨネーズ　小さじ1

1½ Tbsp. plain yogurt　プレーンヨーグルト　大さじ1½

1 tsp. lemon juice　レモン汁　小さじ1

pinch each, salt and pepper　塩、こしょう　少量

---

1. Cut the cauliflower and broccoli into small florets. Boil the two vegetables separately till tender.

   カリフラワーとブロッコリーは小さな房に分け、別々にやわらかくなるまでゆでる。

2. Slice potato and carrots very thin. Boil the two vegetables together till tender.

   じゃがいも、にんじんを4～5mmくらいの厚さの輪切りにして、いっしょにやわらかくなるまでゆでる。

3. Heat corn.

   コーンは熱湯でさっとゆでる。

4. Combine mayonnaise, yogurt, lemon juice and salt and pepper to make the dressing. Arrange ①, ② and ③ on a serving plate and spoon dressing over.

   マヨネーズ、ヨーグルト、レモン汁、塩、こしょうをまぜて器に盛った野菜にかける。

Note: To cut calories, use more plain yogurt and no mayonnaise.
カロリーを減らしたい場合はマヨネーズを少なくしてプレーンヨーグルトを増やす。

SAUTÉED BURDOCK (*KINPIRA GOBŌ*)

きんぴらごぼう

Serves 4　4人分　30 min.　30分　118 kcal

1 24–in. burdock root (*gobō*)　ごぼう　1本（200g）

1 7–in. carrot　にんじん　1本（130g）

1 cup *dashi*　だし　カップ1

2 Tbsp. saké　酒　大さじ2

2 Tbsp. soy sauce　醤油　大さじ2

2 Tbsp. *mirin* (sweet saké)　みりん　大さじ2

1 Tbsp. sugar　砂糖　大さじ1

1 Tbsp. sesame oil　ごま油　大さじ1

"seven-flavored" red pepper (*shichimi tōgarashi*)　七味唐がらし

1. Julienne the burdock root and carrot. Soak burdock in a small bowl of water to mellow its flavor.

   ごぼう、にんじんをせん切りにし、ごぼうは水につけ、アクぬきをする。

2. Sauté burdock and carrot together in sesame oil.

   ごぼう、にんじんをごま油でよくいためる。

3. Add *dashi* broth (page 222), saké, soy sauce, *mirin* and sugar, and cook until burdock root and carrot soften.

   だし（222頁参照）、酒、醤油、みりん、砂糖を入れ、ごぼう、にんじんがやわらかくなるまで煮る。

4. Arrange in small dishes and season to taste with hot and spicy "seven-flavored" red pepper.

   煮えたごぼうとにんじんを小鉢に盛る。好みで七味唐がらしをふる。

♥ **By the way:** Burdock root is rich in fiber and helps to prevent constipation. *Tōgarashi* red pepper speeds up the production of gastric juices, which improves digestion.

ごぼうの繊維が体中をそうじし、便秘予防に効果がある。唐がらしは、胃液の分泌を促して消化をたすける。

Eggs

たまご

SCRAMBLED EGGS WITH COD ROE
たらこのいりたまご

Serves 4 4人分 15 min. 15分   104 kcal

1 *tarako* cod roe sac たらこ ½腹

3 eggs 卵 3個

⅔ 16-in. Japanese leek (*naganegi*) 長ねぎ ⅔本

3 *shiitake* mushrooms しいたけ 3枚

1 Tbsp. vegetable oil サラダ油 大さじ1

dash soy sauce 醤油 少量

---

1. Slit the cod roe sac open with a fork. Scrape out the roe, discard the thin skin.

   たらこの皮を取り除く。

2. Mince the *naganegi* leek and the *shiitake* mushrooms (discard just the hard bottom part of the stem; use both cap and stem).

   石づきを除いたしいたけと長ねぎをみじん切りにする。

3. Break eggs into a medium-sized bowl.

   卵をボールに割り入れる。

4. Add the cod roe, *naganegi* leek and *shiitake* mushrooms to ③ and mix.

   たらこの身と長ねぎとしいたけを③のボールに加え、かきまぜる。

5. Lightly oil a frying pan and stir-fry ④ with a fork or pair of chopsticks.

   熱して油をひいたフライパンに④の具を入れ、ほろほろになるまで箸でかきまぜる。

6. Sprinkle with soy sauce.

   醤油をかけてできあがり。

CHINESE-STYLE SCRAMBLED EGGS
中華風いりたまご

Serves 4 4人分 20 min. 20分   241 kcal

$3\frac{1}{2}$ oz. pork (shoulder butt), sliced thin 豚肉肩ロース薄切り 100g

$\frac{1}{2}$ 16–in. Japanese leek (*naganegi*) 長ねぎ $\frac{1}{2}$本

10 snow peas (*sayaendō*) さやえんどう 10枚

4 tree clouds (*kikurage*) きくらげ 10g

5 eggs 卵 5個

2 tsp. saké 酒 小さじ2

dash soy sauce 醤油 少量

dash oil 油 少量

pinch salt 塩 少量

---

1. Cut the pork into bite-sized pieces and slice the *naganegi* leek thin. Cut the snow peas in half on a diagonal.

   豚肉を一口大に切り、長ねぎは小口から薄く切り、さやえんどうはななめに切る。

2. Lightly boil the snow peas and set them in a colander to cool.

   さやえんどうをゆで、ざるに上げて冷ましておく。

3. Add a pinch of salt to the eggs and beat them.

   卵をボールに割り入れ、少量の塩を入れてよく溶く。

4. In a small, lightly-oiled frying pan, scramble the eggs. Remove from pan and set aside.

   油をひいたフライパンで ③ をいり、皿にうつしておく。

5. Lightly oil the pan again and sauté the pork, tree clouds and *naganegi* leek.

   再び油をフライパンにひき、豚肉、きくらげ、長ねぎをいためる。

6. When pork turns whitish, add 2 tsp. saké, dash soy sauce and scrambled egg.

   豚肉の色が変わったら、酒、醤油少量を入れ、いためておいた卵をまぜあわせる。

7. Add the snow peas. Heat through and serve.

   ⑥ に ② のさやえんどうを入れ、さっとあわせる。

SCRAMBLED EGGS WITH *NAMEKO* MUSHROOMS AND *NATTO*

なめこと納豆のたまご焼き

Serves 4 4人分 20 min. 20分   161 kcal

7 oz. *nameko* mushrooms なめこ 200g

1 pack (3½ oz.) *natto* (fermented soybeans) 納豆 100g

4 eggs 卵 4個

pinch each, salt and pepper 塩、こしょう 少量

dash vegetable oil サラダ油 少量

1. Break eggs into a bowl. Add *nameko* mushrooms and *natto*. Beat all three together.

   ボールに卵を割り入れ、なめこと納豆を加えて、かきまぜる。

2. Oil and heat a frying pan, scramble ① on medium.

   フライパンにサラダ油をひいて熱し、①を流し込み、中火で焼く。

3. Cook to taste and sprinkle with salt and pepper.

   好みの固さになるまで焼き、塩とこしょうをふりかける。

♥ **By the way:** *Natto* is high in protein and is a good all-around health food. It's full of vitamin B$_2$, which helps keep the skin clear. Natto is said to be effective in keeping blood pressure down and building strong bones.

納豆はタンパク質、ビタミンB$_2$を多量に含んでいる。ビタミンB$_2$は肌荒れなどに効果的。このほか血圧を下げたり、骨を丈夫にするなど納豆は優れた健康食品。

POTATO EGG OMELETTE

スペイン風オムレツ

Serves 4　4人分　30 min.　30分　　　　　　　**172 kcal**

1–2 potatoes (*jagaimo*)　じゃがいも　**1〜2個**

4 eggs　卵　**4個**

pinch each, salt and pepper　塩、こしょう　少量

2 tsp. vegetable oil　サラダ油　小さじ2

---

1. Peel the potatoes and cut them into half-inch dice.

   じゃがいもの皮をむき、さいの目に切る。

2. Heat oil in a medium-sized frying pan. Add potatoes and sauté on medium, stirring occasionally, till golden brown. Season with salt and pepper.

   フライパンに油を熱し、じゃがいもを入れ、きつね色になるまで、ときどきかきまぜながら、できたら塩、こしょうする。

3. Beat the eggs and add them to the frying pan, over the potatoes.

   卵を溶いて、いためたじゃがいもをまぜる。

4. Turn heat down to low and cook eggs and potatoes together.

   ③ を、フライパンで弱火で焼く。

♥ **By the way:** Try putting in, with the potatoes at Step ②, any combination of these optional ingredients: 1 tsp. minced onion, 2 Tbsp. grated cheese, 1 Tbsp. chopped parsley, garlic powder to taste, 1 tsp. lemon juice. Serving with ketchup is another option.

ステップ ② でじゃがいもをいためるとき、玉ねぎのみじん切り（小さじ1）、粉チーズ（大さじ2）、パセリみじん切り（大さじ1）、ガーリックパウダー、レモン汁（小さじ1）、ケチャップなどを加えるとひと味ちがう味わいがでる。

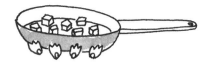

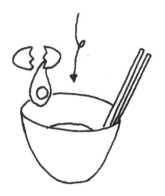

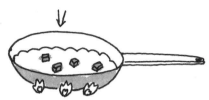

BUDGET SCRAMBLE

豆腐とたまごのいり煮

Serves 2 2人分 20 min. 20分　　　　　　　　150 kcal

2 eggs 卵 2個

1 block firm tofu (*momen-dōfu*) もめん豆腐 1丁

2 Tbsp. sugar 砂糖 大さじ2

3 Tbsp. soy sauce 醤油 大さじ3

dash vegetable oil サラダ油 少量

1. Place tofu in a mixing bowl and break it up with a fork.

   豆腐をボールに入れ、フォークなどでくずす。

2. Heat vegetable oil in a small frying pan. Add the tofu and scramble till it has the same consistency as moist scrambled eggs.

   小さめのフライパンにサラダ油を少々熱し、くずした豆腐の水気がなくなるまでいためる。

3. Add the eggs and scramble 2 more minutes.

   水気がなくなったら溶いた卵を加え、さらに2分ほどいためる。

4. Season with sugar and soy sauce.

   砂糖と醤油で味つけする。

FRIED EGG SURPRISE

ハムエッグ

Serves 1 1人分 8 min. 8分   143 kcal

1 egg 卵 1個

slice boneless roast ham ボンレスハム 1切れ（20g）

salt and pepper 塩、こしょう

1 tsp. vegetable oil サラダ油 小さじ1

1. Coat a medium-sized frying pan lightly with oil. Cook roast ham on low until heated through, turning once.

   中ぐらいのフライパンに油を熱し、ハムをひっくり返しながら中火で火が通るまでいためる。

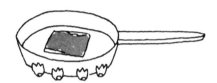

2. Crack an egg directly over the slice of ham. Season to taste and fry the egg sunny–side up.

   ハムの上で卵を割り、目玉焼きにする。塩、こしょうは好みに応じて使う。

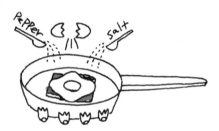

3. Slide onto the plate as is, with ham hidden beneath the egg.

   そのまま皿に盛ってできあがり。

SUGOMORI EGG NEST

巣ごもりたまご

Serves 4 4人分 20 min. 20分   131 kcal

4 eggs 卵 4個

4 leaves cabbage キャベツ 葉4枚

½ 8–in. carrot にんじん ½本

1 Tbsp. vegetable oil サラダ油 大さじ1

1 Tbsp. saké 酒 大さじ1

1 tsp. salt 塩 小さじ1

pinch pepper こしょう 少量

1. Shave any hard parts of the cabbage leaves down flat and cut cabbage into rather thick julienne slices. Cut carrots into thin half-moons.

   キャベツは芯を取り除き、太めのせん切りにし、にんじんは薄く半月切りにする。

2. In a frying pan, heat vegetable oil. Add the carrot and sauté. When carrot begins to soften, add cabbage, mix well.

   フライパンにサラダ油を熱し、にんじんをいため、多少しんなりし始めたらキャベツを入れ、まぜる。

3. When cabbage softens, season with saké, salt and pepper. In the frying pan, form cabbage mixture into the shape of bird's nests.

   キャベツがしんなりしたところで、調味料で味をつけ、フライパンの中で鳥の巣のように形づくる。

4. Crack eggs gently, without breaking yolks, directly over the cabbage nests. Heat in a frying pan on low, covered, till surface of eggs just begins to turn white.

   卵をそっとこわさないように ③ に割り入れ、フライパンに蓋をして火を弱め、卵の表面がうっすらと白くなるまで蒸し焼きにする。

Note: Many people find this dish especially good when eggs are soft enough to mix through cabbage.

卵のかたさは好みだが、半熟を野菜にからめて食べるのがおいしい。

Tofu

豆腐

TOFU-VEGETABLE SCRAMBLE

いり豆腐

Serves 4　4人分　20 min.　20分　　　　　　　　　155 kcal

1 block firm tofu (*momen-dōfu*)　もめん豆腐　1丁

2 fresh *shiitake* mushrooms　生しいたけ　2枚

1 7-in. carrot　にんじん　小1本

6 snow peas　さやえんどう　6枚

2 eggs　卵　2個

1 Tbsp. vegetable oil　サラダ油　大さじ1

Ⓐ

　½ cup *dashi* broth　だし　カップ½

　1 Tbsp. soy sauce　醤油　大さじ1

　2 tsp. sugar　砂糖　小さじ2

　1½ Tbsp. saké　酒　大さじ1½

　pinch salt　塩　少量

1. Drain the tofu (*see* next page). Transfer to a mixing bowl and crush by hand.

   豆腐の水気を切り、ボールに移し手で適当にくずす。

2. Remove stems from the *shiitake* mushrooms, cut caps up thin. Julienne the carrot.

   生しいたけは軸を取り除き、細く切る。にんじんはせん切りにする。

3. Remove the strings from the snow peas. Boil in the pod, till soft, and cut up small, on the diagonal.

   さやえんどうは筋をていねいに取り除き、やわらかくゆでて、斜めに細かく切る。

4. Heat oil in a saucepan, add the *shiitake* mushrooms and carrots and sauté. When heated through, add Ⓐ and simmer.

   鍋にサラダ油を熱し、しいたけ、にんじんをいため、火が通ったらⒶを入れて煮る。

5. Add ① and beaten eggs to ④. Stir-fry till mixture has consistency of moist scrambled eggs. Add ③ and serve.

④ に ① と溶き卵を加え、手早くまぜながらポロポロになるまでゆっくり火にかけ、③ を加えてできあがり。

❤ **By the way:** This side dish is inexpensive and easy to make. You can use any vegetables you happen to have on hand!
If you like, try adding 1 cup ground chicken at Step 4.

Tofu is very nutritious. It contains proteins that are easily broken down, unsaturated fat, essential amino acids and vitamins including B_1, B_2 and E. So it's great for fighting fatigue, making skin lustrous and improving circulation. It's also low-calorie.

これはとても手軽で安上がりなレシピ。台所にある適当な野菜を使ってもよし、またバリエーションとして鶏のひき肉などを加えると（Step 4）おいしい。

豆腐はとてもヘルシー。栄養価が高く、ばつぐんに消化のよいタンパク質、コレステロールの心配がいらない脂肪、人体に不可欠なアミノ酸、そしてビタミンB$_1$、B$_2$、Eなどが含まれているため、疲労を回復させ、美肌を保ち、血行をよくする。ダイエットにも効果的。

■ HOW TO DRAIN TOFU
豆腐の水の切り方

These are several ways to drain tofu. The fourth is probably the most effective.
豆腐の水を切るにはいくつかの方法がある。下の4つの中では、最後の方法が一番効果的。

- Cut tofu into 1–in. cubes and place in boiled water 3 minutes, then set in colander to drain.

  ふきんに包み、傾めにしたまな板などの上に20分くらいおく。

- Wrap tofu in a clean dishtowel and set on a pair of chopsticks stretched across a plate. Toast 3 minutes in a microwave.

  ふきんで包み、皿に割りばしを渡して、その上におき、3分ほどレンジにかける。

- Wrap tofu in a clean dishtowel or paper towels and set 20 minutes on a slanted cutting board.

  ふきんに包み、傾めにしたまな板などの上に20分くらいおく。

- Wrap tofu in a clean dishtowel and place a plate or other weight (twice as heavy as the tofu) on top. Let sit 30 minutes.

  ふきんに包み、豆腐の倍くらいの重石（皿など）をのせ30分くらいおく。

← Use this method.

TOFU STEAK

豆腐のステーキ

Serves 4 4人分 20 min. 20分   154 kcal

2 blocks firm tofu (*momen-dōfu*) もめん豆腐 2丁

½ clove garlic にんにく ½かけ

½ knob ginger root しょうが ½かけ

1 Tbsp. vegetable oil サラダ油 大さじ1

2 Tbsp. soy sauce 醤油 大さじ2

1. Drain blocks of tofu (page 101) and cut each into fourths. Grate ginger root and press or mince garlic.

   豆腐の水切りをし（101頁参照）、4等分に切る。にんにく、しょうがをすりおろす。

2. In a frying pan, heat the oil. Add tofu and cook well, turning once, till golden brown.

   フライパンに油を熱し、豆腐がきつね色になるまで両面を焼く。

3. Place ginger root and garlic on a small dish, alongside tofu. Sprinkle tofu with soy sauce.

   醤油をかけ、すりおろしたにんにくとしょうがをそえて食べる。

EASY TOFU DUMPLINGS

豆腐だんご

Serves 4　4人分　15 min.　15分　　　　　　　　　　　359 kcal

½ block firm tofu (*momen-dōfu*)　もめん豆腐　½丁

1 small boiled bamboo shoot (1⅔ oz.)　ゆでたけのこ　小1本 (50g)

⅔ lb. ground fresh ham　豚ももひき肉　300g

1 Japanese leek (*naganegi*)　長ねぎ　1本

5 fresh *shiitake* mushrooms　生しいたけ　5枚

1 tsp. salt　塩　小さじ1

1 Tbsp. starch (*katakuriko*)　片栗粉　大さじ1

oil for deep frying　揚げ油

1. Drain the tofu (page 101).

   豆腐の水切りをする（101頁参照）。

2. Mince the bamboo shoot and *naganegi* leek. Discard the hard bottom part of the *shiitake* mushroom stems and mince both caps and stem.

   ゆでたけのこ、長ねぎ、しいたけは石づきを除いて、それぞれみじん切りにする。

3. In a mixing bowl, crush tofu with a fork. Add ② and the ground ham, mix.

   豆腐をボールでくずし、そこに②とひき肉を加え、よくまぜる。

4. Add 1 tsp. salt and 1 Tbsp. starch to ③. Form mixture into 1–in. balls.

   ③に塩少々と大さじ1の片栗粉を加え、肉団子を作る。

5. Deep fry until golden brown.

   きつね色になるまで揚げる。

Note: This dish is nice with soy sauce or the dipping sauce for tempura (page 127).

醤油や天つゆ（127頁参照）につけて食べる。

DICED TOFU IN SPICY SAUCE (*MABŌDŌFU*)

麻婆豆腐

Serves 4 4人分 15 min. 15分   301 kcal

½ lb. ground ham 豚ももひき肉 200g

2 blocks firm tofu (*momen-dōfu*) もめん豆腐 2丁

2 16–in. Japanese leeks (*naganegi*) 長ねぎ 2本

1 Tbsp. starch (*katakuriko*) 片栗粉 大さじ1

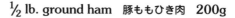

Ⓐ

2 Tbsp. *tōbanjan* (red, spicy Chinese miso) トウバンジャン
大さじ2

2 Tbsp. saké 酒 大さじ2

2 Tbsp. soy souce 醤油 大さじ2

1 Tbsp. sugar 砂糖 大さじ1

½ Tbsp. vegetable oil サラダ油 大さじ½

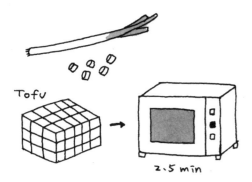

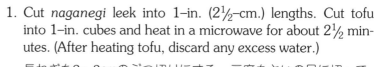

1. Cut *naganegi* leek into 1–in. (2½–cm.) lengths. Cut tofu into 1–in. cubes and heat in a microwave for about 2½ minutes. (After heating tofu, discard any excess water.)

   長ねぎを2〜3cmのぶつ切りにする。豆腐をさいの目に切って、電子レンジで2分半温める（温めたときに出る水は捨てる）。

2. In a large frying pan, sauté the ground ham. When browned, combine and add Ⓐ.

   ひき肉をいためる。色が変わったら、Ⓐを入れる。

3. Add *naganegi* leek and tofu to ②. Sauté well, then dissolve starch in water (1 part starch to 2 parts water), add.

   長ねぎと豆腐を加え、よくいためたら片栗粉を2倍の水で溶き入れ、できあがり。

COUNTRY-STYLE *DAIKON* RADISH AND TOFU

田舎風豆腐と大根の煮物

Serves 4　4人分　30 min.　30分　　　　　　　　　　155 kcal

½ 16–in. *daikon* radish　大根　½本（600g）

1 block firm tofu (*momen-dōfu*)　もめん豆腐　1丁

2 Tbsp. sesame oil　ごま油　大さじ2

½ Tbsp. sugar　砂糖　大さじ½

1 tsp. *mirin* (sweet saké)　みりん　小さじ1

3 Tbsp. soy sauce　醤油　大さじ3

---

1. Peel the *daikon* radish. Cut lengthwise into 4 equal parts, and then into quarter-slices. Drain tofu (page 101).

   大根の皮をむいて縦に4等分し、いちょう切りにする。豆腐をよく水切りする（101頁参照）。

2. Heat sesame oil in a sturdy saucepan. Add tofu, heat.

   鍋の中にごま油を入れて、よく熱する。豆腐を入れて、焦げめがつくまでいためる。

3. Add the *daikon* radish and continue heating till the radish softens.

   さらに大根を加えてよくいためる。弱火で大根の水分が出るまで煮る。

4. Add sugar, *mirin* and soy sauce and simmer. When radish absorbs the pan juices, it's done.

   砂糖、みりん、醤油を加えてさらに煮る。大根に味がしみたら、できあがり。

Note: This is one example of the kind of plain, nutritious dish that people usually learn how to make from their grandmothers.

これは"おばあちゃんの手料理"。今では、母の十八番となったヘルシーメニュー。

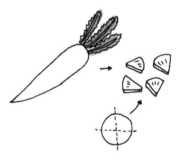

TOFU-CHEESE FRITTERS
チーズ入りひりょうず

Serves 4　4人分　70 min.　70分　　　　　　　　295 kcal

2 *nama-age* (fried blocks of tofu)　生揚げ　2丁

5 fresh *shiitake* mushrooms　生しいたけ　5枚

1 carrot　にんじん　1本

5 perilla (*shiso*) leaves　青じそ（大葉）　5枚

1 egg　卵　1個

1 tsp. salt　塩　小さじ1

oil for deep frying　揚げ油

3 oz. processed cheese　プロセスチーズ　80g

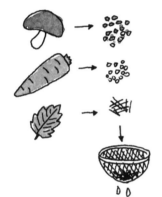

1. Place the *nama-age* in a colander. Pour boiled water over, to make them less oily. Cut into large dice and crush in a mortar.

   生揚げに熱湯をかけて油ぬきをしたらさいの目に切り、すり鉢でする。

2. Remove any hard parts from the bottom of the stems of the *shiitake* mushrooms. Mince the *shiitake* (caps and stems) and the carrot. Cut the *shiso* leaves in half lengthwise, then mince them finely crosswise.

   生しいたけは石づきを除き、にんじんとともにみじん切りにする。しそは縦に2等分して、せん切りにする。

3. Add ② and the egg and salt to ①, and mix.

   ①に②と卵と塩を入れ、まぜる。

4. Form the mixture into dumpling-sized balls. Cut cheese into half-inch dice, put one square of cheese in the center of each ball and flatten balls slightly.

   手のひらでまるめ、中心にさいの目切りにしたチーズを入れ、球を少しつぶした形に整える。

5. Fry slowly in oil heated to 325°F (160°C).

   中温（160℃）の揚げ油でゆっくり揚げる。

TUNA–MAYO TOFU GRATIN
豆腐とツナ・マヨグラタン

Serves 4　4人分　40 min.　40分　　　　　　　　359 kcal

2 blocks firm tofu (*momen-dōfu*)　もめん豆腐　2丁

1½ small cans tuna (4½–oz.)　ツナ（缶詰）　小1½缶（135g）

1 onion (*tamanegi*)　玉ねぎ　1個

6 Tbsp. mayonnaise　マヨネーズ　大さじ6

2 Tbsp. vegetable oil　サラダ油　大さじ2

1 stalk parsley　パセリ　1茎

1. Drain tofu (page 101) and cut it into half-inch (1–cm.) dice.
   豆腐の水気を切り（101頁参照）、1cm幅に切る。

2. Heat oil in a frying pan and grill tofu on both sides, till golden. Place in an ovenproof dish.
   フライパンに油を熱し、豆腐の両面を焼いたら耐熱皿に移し、並べる。

3. Mince the onion. Combine tuna, minced onion and mayonnaise, mix.
   ツナと玉ねぎのみじん切りをマヨネーズとまぜる。

4. Add ③ to ② and bake in a toaster oven for 5 minutes.
   ③ を ② にかけて、オーブントースターで約5分焼く。

5. Sprinkle minced parsley over ④.
   パセリのみじん切りを ④ にかける。

LOW-CAL TOFU SALAD

豆腐、糸こんにゃく ダイエットサラダ

Serves 4　4人分　20 min.　20分　　　　　　　140 kcal

4 leaves lettuce　レタス　4枚（80g）

1 whole fresh tomato　トマト　1個

1 8–in. cucumber　きゅうり　1本

¼ 7–in. carrot　にんじん　¼個

¼ *daikon* radish　大根　¼本（300g）

2 Tbsp. dried *wakame* seaweed (*hoshi-wakame*)　干しわかめ　4g

1 block firm tofu (*momen-dōfu*)　もめん豆腐　1丁

1 package thick *konnyaku* strands (*ito-konnyaku*)　糸こんにゃく　1袋分（180g）

2 Tbsp. canned corn　コーン（缶詰）　大さじ2

4 Tbsp. *Wafū* Dressing　和風ドレッシング　大さじ4

Boiled

TOFU

1. Tear lettuce into bite-sized pieces. Quarter the tomato and slice the cucumber thin, on the diagonal. Peel the carrot and *daikon* radish, julienne both. Reconstitute the seaweed. Prepare the *ito-konnyaku* by boiling it briefly. Cut tofu into eight pieces.

   レタスは適当な大きさにちぎる。トマトは縦4つに切る。きゅうりは薄く斜め切りにする。にんじんと大根はともに皮をむいてせん切りにする。わかめは水でもどす。糸こんにゃくはゆでる。それぞれ食べやすい大きさに切る。豆腐は8つに切る。

2. Mix all the ingredients. Sprinkle with *Wafū* Dressing (page 55).

   全部の材料をまぜる。和風ドレッシング（55頁参照）をかけるとおいしい。

Note: Reconstitute seaweed by soaking it in 2 cups cold water about 10 minutes.

干しわかめは、水カップ2に10分浸してもどす。

❤ **By the way:** *Konnyaku* is a starchy root available as a block or cake and in thinner and thicker filaments (*shirataki* and *ito-konnyaku* respectively). In all its forms it is completely noncaloric.

こんにゃく、糸こんにゃく、糸こんにゃくをさらに細くしたしらたき、すべてカロリーはゼロ。

TOFU BURGERS
豆腐ハンバーグ

Serves 4　4人分　50 min.　50分 396 kcal

⅔ lb. ground fresh ham　豚ももひき肉　300g

1⅓ blocks firm tofu (*momen-dōfu*)　もめん豆腐　1⅓丁

1 egg　卵　1個

1 onion (*tamanegi*)　玉ねぎ　1個

½ rib celery　セロリ　½本

1 tsp. salt　塩　小さじ1

pinch pepper　こしょう　少量

1 Tbsp. vegetable oil　サラダ油　大さじ1

soy sauce, grated *daikon* radish, grated ginger root　醤油、
大根おろし、おろししょうが

1. Drain tofu (page 101).

   豆腐の水切りをする（101頁参照）。

2. Mince onion and celery.

   玉ねぎとセロリをみじん切りにする。

3. Combine ground ham, tofu, egg, onion, celery and salt and
   pepper in a large mixing bowl. Knead mixture until sticky.

   ボールにひき肉、豆腐、卵、玉ねぎ、セロリ、塩、こしょうを
   入れ、ねばりがでるまでよくこねる。

4. Divide into 4 patties. Lightly oil a frying pan and fry patties
   over a low flame. Sprinkle with a dash of soy sauce and set
   out small dishes of grated *daikon* radish and ginger root
   beside each plate.

   材料を4等分にして丸め、フライパンにサラダ油をひき、弱火
   で焼く。醤油を少々かけ、大根おろしやおろししょうがをそえ
   て食べるとおいしい。

TOFU TOPPED WITH MISO AND CITRON

豆腐のゆず味噌かけ

Serves 1　1人分　**20 min.**　20分　　　　　　　　**26 kcal**

½ block firm tofu (*momen-dōfu*)　もめん豆腐　½丁

small section of *yuzu* citron peel　ゆずの皮　少量

1⅓ tsp. miso　味噌　小さじ1⅓

⅔ tsp. sugar　砂糖　小さじ⅔

1 tsp. saké　酒　小さじ1

2 tsp. *dashi* broth　だし　小さじ2

1. Cut tofu into 2 squares. Place in a pan of water and boil gently, till heated through.

   豆腐を半分に切り、軽くゆでる。

2. In a small bowl, combine miso, sugar, saké and *dashi* broth (page 222) and mix well. Microwave at 500W for 30 seconds. Alternatively, place the mixture into a small saucepan on medium and, while stirring with a wooden spoon or spatula, heat until mixture thickens and has the same basic consistency as miso.

   小さめのボールを用意し練り味噌をつくる。味噌、砂糖、酒、だし（222頁参照）をよくまぜ合わせ、電子レンジ（500W）に30秒ほどかける。レンジを使わない場合は、小さい鍋に上の材料を入れ、中火にかけながら、木のへらなどでよくまぜ、もとの味噌の堅さになったら火を止めて冷ます。

3. Drain tofu (page 101) and place on a plate. Pour ② over and arrange a few thin slices of citron peel on top.

   豆腐の水気を切り（101頁参照）、小皿にとったら、練り味噌②を豆腐にかける。ゆずの皮のせん切りをその上にのせる。

Pasta & Noodles

パスタ・ヌードル

NOODLE SAUCES AND SOUPS
そば・うどんのつゆ

These are many different ways to prepare Japanese *soba* or *udon* noodles. In some, noodles are dipped into a small cup of sauce and in others they are placed in a bowl of soup. Either way they are made from *dashi* broth (page 222) and soy sauce and *mirin*.

そば・うどんの「つけつゆ」も「かけつゆ」も、だし（222頁参照）＋醤油＋みりんでつくる。

Dipping sauce (*tsuketsuyu*): 3–4 parts *dashi* broth / 1 part soy sauce / 1 part *mirin* (sweet saké)

つけつゆ：だし3〜4・醤油1・みりん1

Soup (*kaketsuyu*): 7–8 parts *dashi* broth / 1 part soy sauce / 1 part *mirin* (sweet saké)

かけつゆ：だし7〜8・醤油1・みりん1

■ HOW TO MAKE SAUCE OR SOUP FOR JAPANESE NOODLES　つゆの作り方

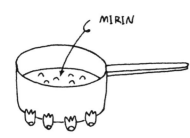

1. In a saucepan, bring *mirin* to a simmer.
   鍋にみりんを煮立たせる。

2. Add *dashi* broth and soy sauce and bring to a simmer once more.
   だし、醤油を加え、もうひと煮立ちさせる。

■ HOW TO COOK DRIED JAPANESE NOODLES　乾めんのゆで方

1. In a large pot, bring water to a boil.
   鍋にたっぷりの湯を沸騰させる。

2. Add *soba* (or *udon*) noodles, fanning them out around the rim of the pot to help keep them from sticking.
   そば（うどん）を鍋の縁に沿って平均的に入れる。

3. Boil gently, stirring periodically, with chopsticks.
   おだやかに沸騰させながら、箸でめんをほぐす。

4. When water is just about to boil up, add $\frac{1}{2}$ cup of cool water and again bring nearly to a boil.
   ふきこぼれそうになったらカップ$\frac{1}{2}$ほどの水を差し水として入れ、沸騰させる。

5. Test noodles for doneness. Their strands should be flexible and their centers no longer solid. Set them in a colander and rinse right away.
   めんを数本取り、白い芯が消え、全体に透き通る感じになっていたらすぐざるにあげ流水で洗う。

SOBA NOODLES WITH DEEP-FRIED TOFU (*KITSUNE SOBA*)

きつねそば

Serves 4 4人分   30 min. 30分   469 kcal

---

4 packs fresh (precooked) *soba* noodles (1¾ lb.) ゆでそば
4玉（720g）

4 deep-fried tofu pouches (*abura-age*) 油揚げ 4枚

½ roll *naruto* (pink spiral–patterned cake of pressed fish)
なると ½本

1 4–in. length Japanese leek (*naganegi*) 長ねぎ 10cm

½ cup *dashi* だし カップ½

7 cups *soba* broth (*kaketsuyu*) かけつゆ カップ7

---

1. Cut each *abura-age* into 4 triangles. Place them in a colander and pour boiled water over, to reduce their oil content. Place them in a pot with the *dashi* broth and cover with a drop-lid (page 229). Simmer until liquid cooks off.

   油揚げは各1枚ずつ4つの三角に切り、熱湯をかけ油ぬきしたら、だしカップ½といっしょに鍋に入れ、落とし蓋（229頁参照）をして汁がなくなるまで煮る。

2. Place *soba* noodles in a large pot of water till heated through (don't overcook).

   そばはたっぷりの湯で堅めにゆでておく（ゆですぎに注意）。

3. Bring soup for *soba* noodles (*kaketsuyu*, page 112) to a simmer.

   かけつゆ（112頁参照）をひと煮立ちさせる。

4. Cut the *naruto* into ¼–in. (6–mm.) slices, on the diagonal. Slice the *naganegi* leek very finely.

   なるとは斜めにスライスし、長ねぎは小口切りにし薬味にする。

5. Arrange boiled *soba* noodles in a large *donburi* bowl. Pour ③ over. Top with ① and place condiments ④ at the side of the plate.

   ゆでたそばを器に盛り、③を注ぎ、①、④の具と薬味をあしらう。

UDON NOODLES SIMMERED IN MISO

味噌煮込みうどん

Serves 4　4人分　30 min.　30分　　　　　　　405 kcal

2 portions dried *udon* noodles　うどん（乾燥）　小2束（330g）

1 chicken breast (skinless)　鶏胸肉（皮なし）　160g

1 3–in. length *daikon* radish　大根　200g

⅔ 7–in. carrot　にんじん　⅔本

⅓ bunch spinach　ほうれん草　⅓わ（60g）

½ 16–in. Japanese leek (*naganegi*)　長ねぎ　½本

6 cups *dashi* broth　だし　カップ6

⅔ Tbsp. miso　味噌　大さじ⅔

6–7 Tbsp. *mirin* (sweet saké)　みりん　大さじ6〜7

spicy "seven-flavored" red pepper　七味唐がらし

---

1. Cook the dried *udon* noodles (page 112).

   うどんをゆでておく（112頁参照）。

2. Cut chicken into bite-sized pieces. Cut *daikon* radish and carrot into thin rectangular blocks. Boil the spinach briefly and cut it into bite-sized pieces.

   鶏肉は一口大にし、大根、にんじんは短冊切り、ほうれん草はゆでて食べやすい長さに切る。

3. Combine *dashi* broth (page 222), chicken, radish and carrot in a soup pot and bring to a simmer. Cook until vegetables soften. Season with miso and *mirin*.

   鍋にだし（222頁参照）、鶏肉、大根、にんじんを入れて中火で煮る。材料がやわらかくなったら味噌とみりんで味をつける。

4. Add ② to ③ and simmer briefly. If broth looks too light, add a little soy sauce. Transfer to deep-sided plates or bowls. Garnish with thin slices of *naganegi* leek.

   ③ にうどん、② のほうれん草を加えて、軽く煮立たせ味をみる。うすければ醤油を少々足す。器に盛り、小口切りにしたねぎを薬味にする。

SALAD-STYLE *UDON* NOODLES

サラダうどん

Serves 4　4人分　15 min.　15分　　　　　　　　　　661 kcal

---

4 packs fresh (precooked) *udon* noodles (2 lb.)　ゆでうどん
4玉

4 Tbsp. dressing　ドレッシング　大さじ4

1 8–in. cucumber　きゅうり　1本

½ 7–in. carrot　にんじん　½本

1 tomato　トマト　1個

½ head cabbage　キャベツ　½個

4 leaves lettuce　レタス　4枚

---

1. Cut the cucumber and carrot into thick slices. Cut tomato into eighths. Chop the cabbage into thin strips and tear lettuce into bite-sized pieces.

   きゅうりとにんじんは輪切り、トマトは8等分、キャベツはせん切り、レタスは手でちぎる。

2. Cook noodles in a pot of boiling water about 5 minutes. Transfer to a colander and rinse well with cold water. Set noodles out on glass plates. Arrange vegetables on top decoratively.

   うどんを鍋で約5分間ゆでる。ざるに上げ、流水でよく洗い水切りをしたらガラスの器に移し、上に野菜を盛りつける。

3. Sprinkle your favorite dressing over the entire salad.

   盛りつけた野菜の上から好みのドレッシングをかけてできあがり。

↓ 5 minutes

boiling water

CHILLED *SŌMEN* NOODLES WITH VEGETABLES

五目そうめん

Serves 1　1人分　30 min.　30分　　　　　　　　　416 kcal

---

2 portions dried *sōmen* noodles　そうめん（乾燥）　2束（80g）

dash vegetable oil　サラダ油　少量

1 slice boneless smoked ham　スライスハム　1枚（20g）

½ egg　卵　½個（25g）

⅕ 7–in. carrot　にんじん　⅕本（30g）

1 fresh *shiitake* mushroom　生しいたけ　1枚（10g）

⅕ 8–in. cucumber　きゅうり　⅕本（20g）

B
| Garnishes

| 2–in. length Japanese leek (*naganegi*)　長ねぎ　5cm

| 1 knob ginger root　しょうが　1かけ

---

1. Make dipping sauce (page 112).

    つけつゆを作る（112頁参照）。

2. Julienne the ham, cucumber and carrot. Beat the egg and scramble it lightly in a small oiled frying pan. Chop the egg into thin strips. Remove stems from the *shiitake* mushrooms and cut the caps up finely. Boil the carrots and *shiitake* mushrooms together briefly.

    ハム、きゅうり、にんじんはせん切り。溶き卵はフライパンでうす焼きし、焼けたら細く切る。しいたけは軸を除いてうすく切り、にんじんとともにゆでる。

3. Boil *sōmen* noodles (page 112). Drain and transfer to a plate. Arrange the five toppings in a colorful way on top of the noodles. Set dipping sauce out in small ceramic cups (*sobachoko*). Grate the ginger and mince the *naganegi* leek. Set these out together on very small plates.

    そうめんをゆでる（112頁参照）。水気が切れたら皿に盛り、5種類の具を彩りよくのせる。つけ汁をそば猪口に用意し、長ねぎの小口切りとしょうがのすりおろしを小皿にそえる。

116

FRIED NOODLES (*YAKISOBA*)
焼きそば

Serves 4　4人分　40 min.　40分　　　　　　　　　　890 kcal

4 packs fresh (precooked) Chinese-style noodles (*chūkamen*)
中華蒸しめん　4玉

½ lb. fresh ham, sliced thin　豚もも薄切り肉　250g

4 large cabbage leaves　キャベツ　葉4枚

½ 7–in. carrot　にんじん　½本

½ onion (*tamanegi*)　玉ねぎ　½個

1 boiled bamboo shoot (*takenoko*)　ゆでたけのこ　1本（50g）

4 fresh *shiitake* mushrooms　生しいたけ　4枚

2 Tbsp. vegetable oil　サラダ油　大さじ2

pinch salt　塩　少量

4 Tbsp. Worcestershire sauce　ウスターソース　大さじ4

pinch dried, powdered *aonori* seaweed　青海苔　少量

1. Cut the pork into bite-sized pieces.

   豚肉は一口大に切る。

2. Chop the cabbage and carrot into thin rectangular blocks. Cut onion in half and then slice it. Slice the bamboo shoots thin.

   キャベツ、にんじんは短冊切り、玉ねぎは半分に切りスライスする。たけのこは薄くスライスする。

3. Remove stems from the *shiitake* mushrooms, slice the caps thin.

   しいたけは軸を取り除き、薄切りに。

4. Heat the oil in a wok and stir-fry the ham. When the meat changes color, add cabbage, carrots, onions, bamboo shoots and *shiitake* mushrooms, in that order. When all ingredients have softened, add salt, mix well. Take from the wok and set aside.

   中華鍋（またはフライパン）にサラダ油を入れ、熱したところで肉をいためる。肉の色が変わったら、キャベツ、にんじん、玉ねぎ、たけのこ、しいたけの順で入れ、いためる。しんなり

したら塩を少々加えてよくまぜ、いったん皿などにすべて取り
出す。

5. Place steamed noodles in the wok and stir-fry lightly. Add 1
   Tbsp. hot water. Cover and let noodles steam 2 minutes.
   Return ④ to the wok and mix. Sprinkle with Worcestershire
   sauce. Arrange on a plate, garnish with powdered *aonori*
   seaweed.

中華めんを同じフライパンに入れ、軽くいためたら湯を大さじ
1杯入れて2分ぐらいいためる。皿にとっておいた具をすべて
中華めんにまぜ、ウスターソースで味を調え、皿に盛り、青の
りをかけてできあがり。

❤ **By the way:** Steamed, skinless chicken can be substituted for ham.
蒸した鶏肉（皮なし）を豚肉の代わりにしてもおいしい。

CHILLED SUMMER NOODLES (*HIYASHI CHŪKA*)

冷やし中華

Serves 4　4人分　30 min.　30分　　　　　　　　　　　　360 kcal

---

4 packs Chinese-style noodles (*chūkamen*)　生中華めん　4玉

A

Toppings　具

1 chicken breast skinned　鶏胸肉（皮なし）　1枚

2 cups water　水　カップ2

1 Tbsp. saké　酒　大さじ1

2 eggs　卵　2個

4 slices boneless smoked ham　ボンレスハム　4枚

½ package bean sprouts　もやし　½袋

½ carrot　にんじん　½本

1 cucumber　きゅうり　1本

B

Seasonings　調味料

¼ cup soy sauce　醤油　カップ¼

2 tsp. sugar　砂糖　小さじ2

2 tsp. sesame oil　ごま油　小さじ2

C

Condiments　薬味

dash Japanese-style prepared mustard　練りがらし　少量

pinch fresh parsley　パセリ　少量

---

1. Sprinkle the chicken with saké, place in a small pot. Add 2 cups water and boil chicken briefly, till heated through. Tear into thin strips. Set the water aside, to use as stock.

   鶏肉に酒をふって小鍋に入れ、水2カップを加えて肉に火が通るまでゆで、できあがったら細く裂く。ゆで汁はとっておく。

2. Scramble the *eggs* lightly in a small frying pan, and cut into thin strips.

   フライパンで薄焼き卵をつくり、細く切る。

3. Cut the ham into thin strips.

   ハムを細く切る。

4. Remove roots from the bean sprouts. Boil the sprouts very briefly.

   もやしは根を除き、手早くゆでる。

5. Julienne the carrots and cucumbers. Boil the carrots.

   にんじんときゅうりを細く切り、にんじんはゆでる。

6. To make the sauce, combine seasonings Ⓑ and 1 cup of the stock from Step ①.

   調味料Ⓑと①のゆで汁カップ1とをまぜ、かけ汁を作る。

7. Place noodles into a large pot of boiling water. Cook till almost soft (don't overboil). Rinse with cool water and drain.

   たっぷりと沸騰させた湯で中華めんをゆでる（ゆですぎに注意）。ゆだったら冷水ですすぎ、よく水をきる。

8. Place noodles on plate. Arrange the six toppings from Steps ① through ⑤ directly on top. Pour sauce Ⓑ on generously. Add condiments Ⓒ to the side of the plate.

   そばを皿に盛り、①〜⑤の具をそばの上にきれいにのせる。⑥をまんべんなくかけ、好みでⒸを添える。

SPAGHETTI CARBONARA
スパゲッティ・カルボナーラ

Serves 4 4人分 45 min. 45分   929 kcal

1 lb. bacon ベーコン 450g

½ onion (*tamanegi*) 玉ねぎ ½個

2 green peppers ピーマン 2個

1 lb. spaghetti スパゲッティ 400g

dash olive oil オリーブ油 少量

2 eggs 卵 2個

4 Tbsp. Parmesan cheese (or 3 Tbsp. Parmesan and 1 Tbsp. romano) パルメザンチーズ 大さじ4（またはパルメザン大さじ3とロマノ大さじ1）

pinch each, salt and pepper 塩、こしょう 少量

---

1. Mince the onion and green pepper. Grate the cheese.

   玉ねぎ、ピーマンをみじん切りにし、チーズはおろす。

2. Cook spaghetti (*see next page*). While pasta is cooking, go on to Steps ③–⑤.

   パスタをゆでる（次頁参照）。この間を利用してStep ③〜⑤ を進める。

3. Slice bacon thinly, crosswise. Sauté in a dry frying pan until crisp.

   ベーコンを薄く切り、多少堅くなるまで油をひかないフライパンでいためる。

4. Take bacon out of the pan and set it aside. Reserve just 3 Tbsp. of the bacon drippings. Discard the rest.

   ベーコンから出た汁は大さじ3杯分だけとっておいて、あとは捨てる。ベーコンはフライパンから取り出しておく。

5. Add onion and green pepper to reserved pan drippings and sauté until tender. Remove from heat and set aside.

   汁を残したフライパンで玉ねぎ、ピーマンを多少しんなりするまでいためたら、火からおろしておく。

6. When spaghetti is done, drain right away and return it to the pot (don't let it get cold).

パスタがゆだったら素早く水をきり、冷めないよう湯をあけた鍋にもどす。

7. Break eggs into the pot of noodles and sprinkle cheese, salt and pepper over. Stir through well.

パスタの鍋に卵を割り入れ、チーズ、こしょうを加えてよくまぜる。

8. Reheat the bacon from ④ and the vegetable mixture ⑤ and add them to the pot of pasta. Turn the heat back on under the pot, while stirring well, heat through.

⑤ を再び熱し、パスタに入れてよくかきまぜる。かきまぜながらパスタの鍋を熱する。

9. Set out a small bowl of grated cheese for garnish.

食べるときは、小ぶりのボールなどにおろしたチーズを入れて出すとよい。

■ HOW TO COOK PASTA

Cook pasta in a large pot of lightly salted water containing a dash of olive oil. The ratio of pasta to water should be about 1 to 10. Pasta is done when "al dente"—not too hard but not completely soft, either. It should be very flexible when you swirl it around in the water with a fork, but should still have some "bite" left to it, too. Test for doneness by biting a strand.

パスタのゆで方:

パスタは"アル・デンテ（歯ごたえ）"が勝負。噛んだとき、腰があることが大切、そのためゆで上がる少し前から噛むか指で切ってみてかたさ具合をチェックする。ゆでるときのパスタと水、塩などの目安は、パスタ1人分（約100g）＋水（1リットル）＋塩（小さじ2）。

COD ROE SPAGHETTI
たらこスパゲッティ

Serves 4　4人分　30 min.　30分　　　　　　　　　　　**509 kcal**

---

1 lb. spaghetti　スパゲッティ　**400g**

1 pair *tarako* cod roe sacs　たらこ　**1腹**

4 Tbsp. butter　バター　大さじ**4**

pinch salt　塩　少量

8 perilla (*shiso*) leaves　青じそ（大葉）　**8枚**

---

1. Mince the *shiso* leaves, set aside. Slit the cod roe sacs open with a fork. Scrape out the roe, discard the thin skin. Set roe aside. Soften butter to room temperature.

   しそは細く切り、たらこは皮をむいておく。バターは室温にもどしておく。

2. Cook and drain spaghetti (page 122). Transfer spaghetti to a large bowl, add the butter and mix.

   スパゲッティをゆでる（122頁参照）。水気を切ってボールに入れ、バターを加えてよくかきまぜる。

3. Add the cod roe from ① to ② and mix well.

   ① のたらこを ② に加え、よくまぜる。

4. Set spaghetti out on individual plates. Spoon ③ over and sprinkle with minced *shiso* leaves.

   ③ をお皿に盛り、しそのせん切りを上にのせる。

SPAGHETTI WITH SHORT-NECKED CLAMS

あさりのスパゲッティ

Serves 4 4人分 30 min. 30分 466 kcal

1 lb. spaghetti スパゲッティ 400g

7 oz. short-necked clams あさり 200g

1 green pepper ピーマン 1個

3 stalks asparagus グリーンアスパラガス ½わ (80g)

1 clove garlic にんにく 1かけ

pinch fresh parsley パセリ 少量

4 tsp. olive oil オリーブ油 小さじ4

½ cup white wine 白ワイン カップ½

pinch each, salt and pepper 塩、こしょう 少量

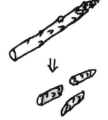

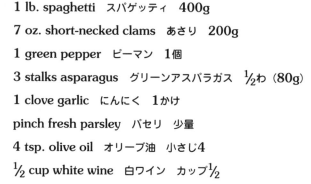

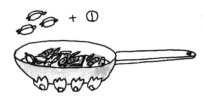

1. Cook spaghetti (page 122). While it's cooking, cut green peppers into long thin strips. Slice asparagus on the diagonal. Mince the garlic clove, or crush it under the blade of a heavy knife.

スパゲッティをゆで（122頁参照）、その間にピーマンは細長く、アスパラガスは斜めに切り、にんにくを潰しておく。

2. Heat olive oil in a large frying pan. Brown the garlic in it, stirring constantly. Add clams, asparagus and green pepper. Sauté several more minutes, till asparagus softens.

オリーブ油でにんにくをいため、あさりとアスパラガスとピーマンを加える。そして、アスパラガスがやわらかくなるまでいためる。

3. Add white wine to ②. Cover and heat 1 minute.

白ワインを ② に加え、ふたをして1分熱する。

4. Add spaghetti. Season with minced parsley, salt and pepper, and serve.

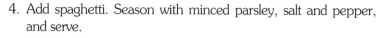

みじん切りにしたパセリとゆでたスパゲッティを③ に加え、塩、こしょうしよくまぜてできあがり。

124

Fried Foods

揚げ物

Serves 4　4人分　40 min.　40分　　　　　　　　200 kcal./1

1 whole squid　イカ　1杯（250g）

4 prawns　くるまエビ　4尾（200g）

1 lotus root (*renkon*)　れんこん　1節

1 sweet potato (*satsumaimo*)　さつまいも　1本

4 green peppers　ピーマン　4個

8 *shiitake* mushrooms　しいたけ　8枚

1 egg　卵　1個

1 cup flour (*komugiko*)　小麦粉　カップ1

1 cup water　水　カップ1

oil for deep frying　揚げ油

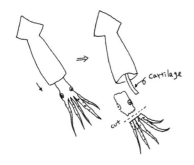

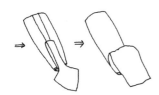

1. To prepare the squid, pull the head portion (which includes the legs) away from the body. Carefully pull out the sac containing the innards. Pull out the soft backbone (it looks like a transparent straw.) Grip the triangular mantle and pull it firmly away from the body. This leaves the tube-shaped body, open at just one end. Rinse the body well and make a few slashes lengthwise to prevent shrinkage as it cooks. Cut body crosswise into rings, each about 1 in. (2–3 cm.) wide. Cut the legs away from the head in groups of 2 or 3. Discard the head, innards, backbone and mantle. Pat pieces dry.

   イカは足と内臓を取り出し、軟骨を抜き取る。エンペラ（三角のところ）は下にひっぱって取り、皮をむき、水で洗い、包丁でタテに切り目を入れ、食べやすいように2～3cmの輪切りにする。足は、頭を取り除き、2～3本ずつ分けておき、いずれもよく水気を切る。

2. To prepare prawns, remove shells but leave tails on. Cut along the back of the shell of each prawn and take out the black vein. Pat prawns dry.

   エビは尾を残して殻をむく。背わたがあれば取っておく。水気をよくふき取る。

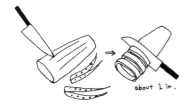

3. Peel and slice the lotus root. Without peeling it, cut the sweet potato into slices about half an inch (1 cm.) wide.

Soak lotus root and sweet potato in a small bowl of salted water.

れんこんは皮をむいて、さつまいもは皮ごと1cmくらいの厚さで輪切りにし、海水くらいの塩水に入れておく。

4. Cut green pepper in half and take out the seeds. Remove the stems from the *shiitake* mushrooms and lightly score a cross in each mushroom's cap.

ピーマンは縦半分に切り、種を除き、しいたけは軸を取り、軽く十字に包丁を入れる。

5. To make batter, combine egg, water (in summer, use ice water) and flour, mixing just until combined. Don't overmix.

衣をつくる。卵、水（夏は氷水）、小麦粉を軽くまぜ合わせる。

6. Place in oil heated to a moderate temperature (350°F/ 170–180°C). (Test the temperature by dropping in a small amount of batter. Temperature is right if batter sinks toward the middle of the pan and then rises.)

170〜180℃の中温。箸で落とした衣が途中まで沈んで上がれば適温。

7. Put ingredients into the wok in order, starting with the ones that will take longest to cook. When oil quiets down and tempura feels lighter when you pick it up with chopsticks, it's done. Drain well before serving.

火の通りにくいものから順に揚げる。油の音が小さくなり、材料を持ち上げて軽くなったら火が通った証拠。油をよく切る。

8. Tempura is best eaten right away. Serve with dipping sauce and grated *daikon* radish.

天ぷらは揚げたてがおいしい。天つゆに大根おろしなどで食べる。

Dipping sauce for tempura (*tentsuyu*)　天つゆ

Serves 4　4人分
1½ cups *dashi* broth　だし　カップ1½
3 Tbsp. soy sauce　醤油　大さじ3
4 Tbsp. *mirin* (sweet saké)　みりん　大さじ4

Bring the *dashi* broth to a simmer in a small saucepan. Add the soy sauce and *mirin*, bring to a simmer once more. Make sauce darker or lighter by adjusting the amount of *dashi*.

小ぶりの鍋にだしを煮立てたら、分量の調味料を加えもうひと煮立ちさせる。味は、だしの量で調節。

FRIED JUMBO SHRIMP
エビフライ

Serves 4   4人分   30 min.   30分   184 kcal

8 prawns   くるまエビ   8尾

4 Tbsp. flour (*komugiko*)   小麦粉   大さじ4

1 egg   卵   1個

½ cup bread crumbs   パン粉   カップ½

oil for deep frying   揚げ油

salt and pepper   塩、こしょう   少量

4 leaves cabbage   キャベツ   葉4枚

½ lemon   レモン   ½個

Worcestershire sauce   ソース

Japanese-style prepared mustard   練りがらし

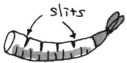

1. Remove the shells, legs and heads from the prawns, but leave the tails on. Cut along the back and rinse out the black vein. Make two or three slits on the belly of each prawn, to keep them from curling up in the frying pan.

   エビは、尾を残して殻、頭、背わたを取り、水洗いし、腹側に包丁で2、3か所の切り目を入れる。これは、揚げているときエビが曲がらないようにするため。

2. Sprinkle prawns with salt and pepper. Dip prawns into flour, beaten egg and breadcrumbs, in that order.

   エビに塩、こしょうをする。卵をボールに溶いておく。エビに小麦粉、卵、パン粉の順で衣をつける。

3. Heat oil to 350°F (180°C). Tap off any extra bread crumbs. Lower each prawn gently into the oil. Fry till golden brown, turning occasionally.

   油を180℃くらいに熱する。余分なパン粉を払い落とし、鍋のへりからゆっくりとすべらせるように入れ、ときどきひっくり返し、きつね色になるまで揚げる。

4. Serve a small mound of julienned cabbage alongside prawns. Garnish plate with lemon wedges and set out some Worcestershire sauce and Japanese-style prepared mustard.

   キャベツのせん切り、レモンを添えて盛りつける。ソースや練りがらしで食べるとおいしい。

BITE-SIZED PORK NUGGETS
一口カツ

Serves 4　4人分　30 min.　30分　　　　　　　　　　**560 kcal**

1 lb. pork (tenderloin)　豚ヒレ肉ブロック　**400g**

½ cup flour (komugiko)　小麦粉　カップ½

2 eggs　卵　**2個**

2 cups bread crumbs　パン粉　カップ**2**

salt and pepper　塩、こしょう

8–10 leaves cabbage　キャベツ　葉**8〜10枚**（**100g**）

Worcestershire sauce　ソース

Japanese-style mustard　練りがらし

1. Cut the pork tenderloin into bite-sized nuggets and sprinkle with salt and pepper. Dip pork nuggets into flour, beaten egg and bread crumbs, in that order.

   ヒレ肉を一口大に切り、塩、こしょうしたら小麦粉、溶き卵、パン粉の順に衣をつける。

2. Place pork nuggets into oil heated to 350°F (170–180°C) and heat, turning occasionally, till both sides are golden brown.

   170〜180℃に熱した油に衣をつけた肉を入れ、両面がきつね色になるまでときどきひっくり返しながら揚げる。

3. Drain nuggets well and arrange on plates.

   油を切り、皿に盛る。

4. Julienne the cabbage and soak in cold water to make it crispier. Mound cabbage beside pork nuggets. Sprinkle both cabbage and nuggets with Worcestershire sauce, and dip nuggets into Japanese-style mustard.

   キャベツをせん切りにし、冷水に浸けシャキッとさせてから、カツのつけ合わせとして皿に盛る。ソースや練りがらしで食べるとおいしい。

SQUASH AND CHEESE CROQUETTES

かぼちゃコロッケ

Serves 4　4人分　30 min.　30分　　　　　　262 kcal

½ small Japanese squash (*kabocha*), or acorn squash (1 lb.)
かぼちゃ　½個（400g）

1½ slices processed cheese　プロセスチーズ　1½切れ（30g）

2 Tbsp. flour (*komugiko*)　小麦粉　大さじ2

1 egg　卵　1個

2 cups bread crumbs　パン粉　カップ2

½ tsp. salt　塩　小さじ½

⅛ tsp. pepper　こしょう　小さじ⅛

ketchup　ケチャップ

1. Peel the squash and remove the seeds. Chop the pulp into bite-sized or larger pieces.

   かぼちゃの種を取り、皮をむき、一口大に切る。

2. In a saucepan, simmer squash till soft. Drain off the liquid and transfer to a mixing bowl. Mash and season with salt and pepper.

   やわらかくなるまで煮たあと、水を切り、ボールに移して潰し、塩、こしょうする。

3. Cut cheese into quarter-inch squares, add to ②.

   チーズを5〜6mm角に切り、② に加える。

4. Form ③ into 8 croquettes.

   ③ を8個に分け、コロッケの形にまとめる。

5. Dip ④ into the flour, beaten egg and bread crumbs, in that order.

   ④ に小麦粉、溶き卵、パン粉の順に衣をつける。

6. Deep fry, till golden, in oil heated to 350°F (170–180°C). Serve with ketchup.

   油を170〜180℃に温めておき、きつね色になるまで揚げる。ケチャップをつけて食べる。

SEAFOOD CROQUETTES

シーフードコロッケ

Serves 4 4人分 70 min. 70分   698 kcal

1 whole squid イカ 1杯

12 prawns エビ 12尾

12 scallops ホタテ貝柱 12個

3 Tbsp. butter バター 大さじ3

$1\frac{1}{3}$ cups flour (*komugiko*) 小麦粉 カップ$1\frac{1}{3}$

1 cup milk 牛乳 カップ1

pinch each, salt and pepper 塩、こしょう 少量

1 egg 卵 1個

$\frac{1}{2}$ cup bread crumbs パン粉 カップ$\frac{1}{2}$

oil for deep frying 揚げ油

1. Cut the squid (page 126), prawns and scallops into quarter-inch (5–6 mm.) dice. In a frying pan, sauté and season with salt and pepper.

   イカ（126頁参照）、エビ、ホタテ貝柱を5〜6mm角に切り、フライパンでいため、塩、こしょうする。

2. Combine butter and 1 cup of the flour in a large, heavy skillet. Heat slowly, stirring continuously. Add milk a little at a time, till sauce is smooth and creamy. Add ① to the skillet and mix.

   厚手の鍋にバターと小麦粉カップ1を入れ、こがさないようにへらでまぜながらいため、さらさらにする。牛乳を少しずつ加え、なめらかになるように弱火にかけながらホワイトソースをつくる。塩とこしょうで味を調え、① をまぜる。

3. Form ② into 12 balls. Dip them into the remaining $\frac{1}{3}$ cup flour, the beaten egg and the bread crumbs, in that order.

   ② を12個に分けて丸め、とっておいた小麦粉カップ$\frac{1}{3}$、溶き卵、パン粉の順に衣をつける。

4. Deep fry till golden brown.

   180℃に熱した油できつね色になるまで揚げる。

CLASSIC CHINESE PORK DUMPLINGS (*GYŌZA*)
餃子

Serves 4　4人分　30 min.　30分　　　　　　　　　　36 kcal

---

24 wrapping sheets for *gyōza* dumplings　餃子の皮　24枚

¼ lb. fresh ground ham　豚ももひき肉　100g

4 leaves cabbage　キャベツ　葉4枚

½ bunch scallions (*nira*)　にら　½わ

1 clove garlic　にんにく　1かけ

1 knob ginger root　しょうが　1かけ

pinch each, salt and pepper　塩、こしょう　少量

dash of soy sauce　醤油　少量

1 Tbsp. vegetable oil　サラダ油　大さじ1

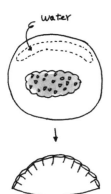

water

1. Rinse the cabbage leaves and scallions, pat dry and mince finely. Grate ginger root and press or mince the garlic. Combine all with the ground ham in a mixing bowl. Add salt, pepper and soy sauce, mix well by hand. Place 1 tsp. of the mixture in the middle of each dumpling wrapping sheet.

   キャベツ、にらをみじん切りにして水気をしぼる。にんにく、しょうがをおろす。これらをボールでひき肉と調味料を加えて手でまぜ、できた具を皮の真ん中に小さじ1のせる。

2. Spread a little water out on each wrapping sheet, as in illustration. Fold over and form the edge into accordion pleats.

   図のように指で水をつけて、ひだをよせながら包む。

3. Spread dumplings out on a good-sized, lightly oiled frying pan and sauté on medium till nicely browned.

   フライパンに油を熱し、餃子を並べて、中火で焼く。

4. Add enough water to cover just the bottom of the *gyōza* dumplings. Cover pan and steam till water cooks off. Eat dumplings while they're hot, with either Mustard Soy Sauce or Vinegar Soy Sauce (page 133).

   具の¼くらいまで水を入れてふたをし、水がなくなるまで蒸し焼きにする。温かいうちに、からし醤油か酢醤油（次頁参照）で食べる。

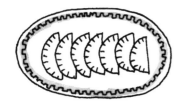

FRIED *GYŌZA* STUFFED WITH CHICKEN AND VEGETABLES

鶏肉と野菜の揚げ餃子

Serves 4　4人分　20 min.　20分　　　　　　　　264 kcal

7 oz. ground chicken　鶏のひき肉　**200g**

½ lb. mixed vegetables　ミックスベジタブル　**250g**

12 wrapping sheets for *gyōza* dumplings　餃子の皮　**12枚**

1 Tbsp. butter　バター　**大さじ1**

⅓ tsp. salt　塩　**小さじ⅓**

⅓ tsp. pepper　こしょう　**小さじ⅓**

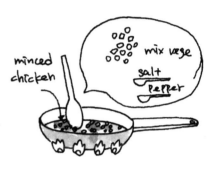

1. Heat butter in a frying pan. Add chicken and sauté on low until meat turns white.

   フライパンにバターを熱し。鶏肉を弱火で白っぽくなるまでいためる。

2. Mince and add the mixed vegetables, continue heating till they soften. Season with salt and pepper.

   ミックスベジタブルをみじん切りにして鶏肉に加えやわらかくなるまでいため、塩、こしょうする。

3. Wrap a small amount of ② into each *gyōza* sheet. Press the edges down with a fork and secure them with a little flour and water. Fry *gyōza* dumplings in oil heated to 350°F (180°C), until golden brown.

   それを餃子の皮で包み、端をフォークで押さえつけるようにして閉じ、180℃に熱した油できつね色になるまで揚げる。

■ How To Make Mustard Soy Sauce and Vinegar Soy Sauce
Combine in about these ratios:
Mustard: Soy sauce 1 + Japanese-style prepared mustard 1 + dash Chinese-style red chili pepper oil (*rayu*)
Vinegar: Soy sauce 1 + vinegar 1 + dash *rayu*

からし醤油と酢醤油のつくり方
それぞれの材料をおよそ次のような割合でまぜてつくる。
からし醤油：醤油1 + 練りがらし1 + ラー油　少量
酢醤油：醤油1 + 酢1 + ラー油　少量

HOME-STYLE *GYŌZA* DUMPLINGS WITH CORNED BEEF

手作り餃子

Serves 4　4人分　15 min.　15分　　　　　　　　　277 kcal

³⁄₄ cup corned beef　コンビーフ　カップ³⁄₄（180g）

20 wrapping sheets for *gyōza* dumplings　餃子の皮　20枚

2 Tbsp. mayonnaise　マヨネーズ　大さじ2

2 Tbsp. ketchup　ケチャップ　大さじ2

pinch flour　小麦粉　少量

dash water　水　少量

oil for deep frying　揚げ油

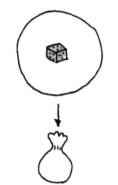

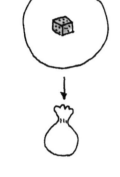

1. Dice corned beef.

   コンビーフをさいの目に切る。

2. Place a small amount of beef onto each *gyōza* sheet. Run a little flour mixed with water around the edge of the wrapping sheet, so it will close better. Pull edges up into a pouch shape, twist shut.

   ① を餃子の皮で包む。皮の周囲に小麦粉を水で溶いてぬると、のりの役目をする。

3. Deep fry ② in oil heated to 350°F (180°C) till golden brown.

   油が180℃になったら ② をきつね色になるまで揚げる。

4. Dip into a sauce of mayonnaise and ketchup.

   マヨネーズとケチャップをまぜ、ソースをつくる。

SPRING ROLLS (*HARUMAKI*)
春巻き

Serves 4 4人分 50 min. 50分   621 kcal

12 wrapping sheets for spring rolls 春巻きの皮 12枚

½ lb. pork (picnic shoulder), sliced thin 豚肩薄切り肉 200g

1 bunch Japanese scallions (*nira*) にら 1わ

5 *shiitake* mushrooms しいたけ 5枚

1 package bean sprouts もやし 1パック

pinch starch (*katakuriko*) 片栗粉 少量

pinch each, salt and pepper 塩、こしょう 少量

dash saké 酒 少量

dash soy sauce 醤油 少量

1 Tbsp. sesame oil ごま油 大さじ1

dash vinegar 酢 少量

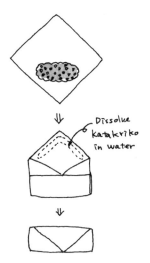

Dissolve katakriko in water

1. Cut pork up finely and soak in a mixture of soy sauce and saké. Cut Japanese scallions into 1½-in. lengths. Remove stems from the *shiitake* mushrooms and slice caps thin.

   肉は細かく切り、醤油と酒につけておく。にらは3〜4cmの長さに切り、しいたけは軸を除いて薄く切る。

2. Dust pork with starch and sauté in an oiled frying pan till browned through. Remove it from the pan and set aside.

   豚肉に片栗粉をまぶしていため、お皿に取り出しておく。

3. In the same pan, fry the scallions and *shiitake* from ① and the bean sprouts. Season with salt, pepper, saké, soy sauce and sesame oil.

   ① の野菜ともやしをいためて、塩・こしょう・酒・醤油・ごま油を加える。

Deep fry

4. Mix pork with ③ and divide into 12 portions. Wrap the mixture up in spring roll sheets and deep fry.

   肉と ③ を合わせて、12に分け、春巻きの皮で包み、揚げる。

5. Set out individual small plates of Mustard Soy Sauce or Vinegar Soy Sauce (page 133).

   からし醤油か酢醤油（133頁参照）で食べる。

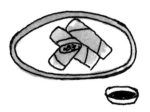

BEAN SPROUT SPRING ROLLS
もやし春巻き

Serves 4   4人分   40 min.   40分   295 kcal

$3\frac{1}{2}$ oz. pork (picnic shoulder), sliced thin   豚肩薄切り肉   100g

1 Tbsp. soy sauce   醤油   大さじ1

dash saké   酒   少量

1 Tbsp. vegetable oil   サラダ油   大さじ1

$\frac{1}{2}$ 7–in. carrot   にんじん $\frac{1}{2}$本

3 *shiitake* mushrooms   しいたけ   3枚

1 package bean sprouts   もやし   1パック

8 wrapping sheets for spring rolls   春巻きの皮   8枚

pinch each, salt and pepper   塩、こしょう   少量

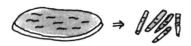

1. Cut pork up small, soak in soy sauce and saké.

   肉を細切りにし、醤油と酒で下味をつける。

2. Julienne the carrot. Remove stems from the *shiitake* mushrooms and slice caps thin.

   にんじんはせん切り、しいたけは軸を除いて薄く切る。

3. Heat oil in a frying pan. Sauté meat until browned throughout. Add ② and the bean sprouts, continue to sauté.

   フライパンに油を熱して肉をいため、色が変わったら、②ともやしを加えていためる。

4. Correct the seasoning with salt and pepper.

   いためた肉や野菜の味を、塩、こしょうで調える。

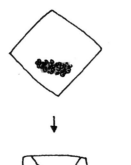

5. Divide ④ into 8 portions and wrap up in the spring roll sheets.

   ④を8つに分けて、春巻きの皮で巻く。

6. Deep fry ⑤ in oil heated to 350°F (180°C). Serve hot, with some Mustard Soy Sauce or Vinegar Soy Sauce (page 133) on the side.

   包んだ肉や野菜を180℃の油で揚げる。からし醤油か酢醤油（133頁参照）で食べる。

Rice

ご飯

SWEET POTATO RICE
さつまいもご飯

Serves 4　4人分　120 min.　120分　　　　　　　　　440 kcal

---

1 (*satsumaimo*) sweet potato (½ lb.)　さつまいも　1本（250g）

2 cups uncooked rice　米　カップ2（320g）

2 ¾ cups water　水　カップ2¾

3 Tbsp. saké　酒　大さじ3

2 Tbsp. salt　塩　大さじ2

1 Tbsp. black sesame seeds　黒ごま　大さじ1

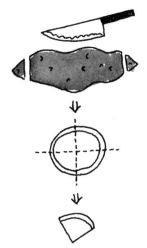

1. Prepare the rice (page 220).

   米をといでおく（220頁参照）。

2. Wash the sweet potato and cut off both ends. Cut into quarter-slices about half an inch (1 cm.) thick. Soak sweet potato in water to mellow its flavor, then transfer to a colander and drain.

   さつまいもを水洗いして、両端を切る。約1cmの厚さに切ってから、いちょう切りにする。すぐに水に放し、アク抜きをして、ざるにあげ、水気を切る。

3. Add the sweet potatoes to ①. Season with saké and salt, then mix and cook as you would any other rice. When rice is finished cooking, let it steam about 10 minutes, then stir gently.

   ① の米に、さつまいも、酒、塩を加えてまぜ、炊きあげる。10分ほど蒸らしてから、ふんわりまぜる。

4. Arrange in rice bowls and sprinkle with black sesame seeds.

   器に盛り、黒ごまを散らす。

❤ **By the way:** 1 cup uncooked rice yields just over 2 cups steamed rice (enough to fill 3 small *chawan* rice bowls).

カップ1（160g）の米は炊き上がると340g。これはおよそご飯茶碗3杯分。

RICE WITH *DAIKON* RADISH AND GROUND CHICKEN

大根と鶏ひき肉の炊き込みご飯

Serves 4　4人分　90 min.　90分　　　　　　　　438 kcal

washed rice

daikon

Ⓐ saké
sweet rice wine
soy sauce

chicken

②

chicken

1 3½–in. length *daikon* radish　大根　250g

3½ oz. ground chicken　鶏ひき肉　100g

2 cups uncooked rice　米　カップ2 （320g）

2 cups water　水　カップ2

Ⓐ

　2 Tbsp. saké　酒　大さじ2

　2 Tbsp. *mirin* (sweet saké)　みりん　大さじ2

　3 Tbsp. soy sauce　醤油　大さじ3

　1 Tbsp. shredded *nori* seaweed　焼き海苔（細く切ったもの）
　大さじ1

1. Prepare the rice for cooking (page 220).

   米をといでおく（220頁参照）。

2. Peel and cut the *daikon* radish into very thin strips 1–in.
   long.

   大根の皮をむき、細めの拍子木切りにする。

3. Combine and mix Ⓐ in a small bowl. Add ground chicken
   and mix again.

   ボールで鶏ひき肉とⒶをまぜる。

4. Lay ② and ③ into the rice cooker or pot, on top of the rice.
   When rice is finished cooking, let it steam about 10 minutes
   and mix. Place rice in individual *chawan* bowls and sprinkle
   shredded *nori* over the top.

   炊飯器に②と③を入れて、炊く。炊きあがったら約10分蒸ら
   し、かきまぜる。茶碗によそって、海苔をかける。

CHESTNUT RICE
栗ご飯

Serves 4　4人分　70 min.　70分　378 kcal

12 chestnuts, in the shell (6 oz.)　栗　12個（180g）

3⅓ oz. *shimeji* mushrooms　しめじ　1パック（100g）

½ deep-fried tofu pouch (*abura-age*)　油揚げ　½枚

1½ cups uncooked rice　米　カップ1 ½（240g）

½ cup *mochigome* (uncooked glutinous rice)　もち米
カップ½（80g）

2 cups *dashi* broth　だし　カップ2

2 tsp. saké　酒　小さじ2

2 tsp. soy sauce　醤油　小さじ2

½ tsp. *mirin* (sweet saké)　みりん　小さじ½

pinch salt　塩　少量

---

1. Shell the chestnuts (page 141). Soak 5 minutes in lightly salted water, transfer to a colander and drain.

   栗は鬼皮と渋皮をむき（次頁参照）、薄い塩水に5分くらい漬け、ざるに入れ水気を切る。

2. Cut off the hard bottom part of the *shimeji* mushroom stems and cut mushrooms into small clusters. Cut *abura-age* into thin rectangular strips.

   しめじは石づきを除き小分けにし、油揚げは横半分に切ってから短冊切りにする。

3. Heat the *dashi* broth (page 222). Add saké, soy sauce and *mirin*, bring to a boil.

   だし（222頁参照）に酒、醤油、みりんを加えて煮立たせる。

4. Add ② to ③, heat over a moderate flame about 5 minutes.

   ③に②を入れ、中火で5分くらい煮る。

5. Combine the two kinds of rice in a large bowl or pan. Wash and drain (page 220).

   米ともち米は、一緒にまぜて大きめのボールでとぎ、水を捨てる（220頁参照）。

6. In a thick-sided pot or an electric rice cooker, mix ⑤ and the liquid only from ④ well. Arrange mushrooms, *abura-age* and chestnuts on top. Cook as you would any other other rice.

炊飯器に ⑤ と、④ の煮汁だけを入れてまぜ、上に ④ で煮たしめじと油揚げ、そして ① を入れて炊く。

■ HOW TO SHELL CHESTNUTS
栗の皮のむき方

1. Soak chestnuts in boiled water 20 minutes.

   栗を熱湯に20分浸ける。

2. Insert a knife into the border between the dark, rougher bottom part and the smooth top part of the chestnut. Cut a narrow strip upward. Work the top part of the shell off first, then remove the bottom.

   底のザラザラしているところの境から包丁を入れ、縦に皮をむいていき、底のザラザラしているところを最後にむく。

3. The thin skin inside the shell also needs to be removed. Insert knife into the flat area and work it up toward the pointed tip. Remove the skin, starting from the top.

   渋皮は、平らな面から先に、底から縦方向にむき、最後に底をむく。

RICE WITH *SHIMEJI* MUSHROOMS AND TUNA

しめじとツナの炊き込みご飯

Serves 4 4人分 90 min. 90分   **394 kcal**

5 oz. *shimeji* mushrooms しめじ 1½パック（150g）

1 small (3–oz.) can tuna ツナ缶 小1缶（90g）

2 cups uncooked rice 米 カップ2（320g）

2 cups water 水 カップ2

3 Tbsp. soy sauce 醤油 大さじ3

1½ Tbsp. saké 酒 大さじ1½

1½ Tbsp. *mirin* (sweet saké) みりん 大さじ1½

pinch salt 塩 少量

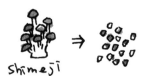

shimeji

tuna

1. Prepare the rice for cooking (page 220).

   米をといでおく（220頁参照）。

2. Cut off the hard bottom part of the *shimeji* mushroom stems. Cut mushrooms up fine.

   しめじは石づきを除き細かく切る。

3. Drain off the tuna oil, flake the tuna.

   ツナの油を捨てて、細かくほぐす。

4. Add *shimeji* mushrooms and tuna to the rice and mix. Season with soy sauce, saké, *mirin* and salt. Let mixture sit for 1 hour in a pot or electric rice cooker.

   しめじとツナと調味料を炊飯器のかまの中に入れて、1時間おく。

5. Cook rice. Afterward, let rice steam about 15 minutes.

   炊けたら、15分ほど蒸らす。

②＋③

soy sauce
rice wine
sweet sake
salt

leave for an hour

HEALTHY TEA RICE (*CHAMESHI*)
茶めし

Serves 4 4人分 60 min. 60分   361 kcal

2 Tbsp. green tea (*sencha*) leaves 煎茶 大さじ2 (10g)

2½ cups dried bonito shavings (*kezuribushi*) 削り節
カップ2½

2 cups uncooked rice 米 カップ2 (320g)

2 cups water 水 カップ2

pinch salt 塩 少量

dash soy sauce 醤油 少量

1. Prepare the rice for cooking (page 220).
   米をといでおく（220頁参照）。

2. Grind the green tea leaves and bonito shavings together in a mortar.
   煎茶の葉と削り節をすり鉢ですりつぶす。

3. Add ② to ①, season with salt and soy sauce and mix.
   洗った米に ② を入れる。塩としょうゆで味を調える。

4. Cook as you would any other rice.
   炊き方は通常どおり。

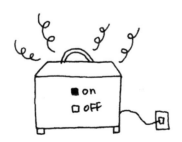

RED RICE AND BEANS (*SEKIHAN*)
赤飯

Serves 4 4人分   90 min. 90分   346 kcal

¼ cup uncooked red adzuki beans あずき カップ¼ (40g)

2 cups uncooked glutinous rice (*mochigome*) もち米 カップ 2 (320g)

2 cups water 水 カップ2

2 Tbsp. black sesame seeds 黒ごま 大さじ2

1 tsp. salt 塩 小さじ1

1. Rinse and pick over the adzuki beans. Place them in a pot with 1 cup water and bring to a simmer, then lower heat and cook 1 more minute. Discard the water and drain. Add 1 cup of new water and bring to a simmer again, then turn heat to low and simmer 20–25 minutes. Strain through a colander lined with a clean dampened kitchen cloth, reserving the liquid. Stir a spoon through the liquid, to circulate air through and deepen its red color.

   あずきを水洗いし、ごみなどきれいに取り除いておく。あずきの4～5倍の水で強火で煮立たせ、沸騰したら、弱火にして1分煮る。ゆで汁を捨て、よく水をきり、新たに同じ量の水で煮立て、煮立ったら弱火にして20～25分くらい煮る。ざるにあげ、ぬれぶきんをかけ、ゆで汁はこし、スプーンなどですくい上げ、空気に触れさせ色を出す。

2. Rinse and drain the rice (page 220). Place it in the reserved bean water from ① and leave it to soak overnight. This will give rice a pretty pink color. Next morning, drain in a sieve for at least 30 minutes. Mix rice and beans together.

   米をとぎ、水気をきり（220頁参照）、ゆで汁に浸けて一晩おく。米はピンク色になる。蒸す30分くらい前に浸けてあった米をざるにあげ、よく水をきり、ゆでてあるあずきを加え、へらなどでよくまぜあわせる。

3. Fill the bottom part of a steamer with water. Add the rice and bean mixture and pat it smooth. Poke about 5 holes here and there in rice with your fingers, to help it steam better. Drape a clean dishtowel over the top and then fit the lid on over the cloth. Steam on high for 40 to 50 minutes, until both rice and beans are done.

蒸し器と蓋の間にふきんをはさみ、蒸し器の底に水を入れる。
中底に米とあずきを入れ、平らにならし、指で5か所くらい穴
をつくっておく。40〜50分あるいは米とあずきが蒸し上がるま
で強火で蒸す。

4. Toast sesame seeds in a small frying pan till they start to
   crackle. Transfer them to a small bowl and mix the salt in.

   小さなフライパンでごまをはぜるまでいり、小さなボールに移
   し、塩とまぜる。

5. Serve rice in bowls or on plates, sprinkling it with the
   sesame seed mixture. Or form it into rice balls. This dish
   can also be heated up again later, or eaten cold.

   赤飯は茶碗や皿に盛り、ごま塩をふりかけてできあがり。好み
   でおむすびにしてもおいしい。温めなおして食べても、冷えた
   ままでもよい。

❤ **By the way:** *Sekihan* is often served at celebrations like a birthday, the
first day at a new school, an entrance exam. passed, etc. (It's also served
on ordinary occasions!)

赤飯はお祝いごと（誕生日、入学、合格の祝いなど）には欠かせない大事な主役。

RICE WITH *AYU* SWEETFISH

アユの炊き込みご飯

Serves 4　4人分　60 min.　60分　　　　　　　　　　463 kcal

---

4 sweetfish (*ayu*)　アユ　4尾

2 cups uncooked rice　米　カップ2 （320g）

2 cups water　水　カップ2

1 3–in. length kelp (*konbu*)　こんぶ　1枚 （8cm）

1 Tbsp. saké　酒　大さじ1

dash soy sauce　醤油　少量

pinch salt　塩　少量

a small amount of red vinegared ginger (*benishōga*)　紅しょうが　少量

---

1. Clean and scale the sweetfish (page 224).

   アユの内臓をていねいに除く（224頁参照）。

2. Prepare rice for cooking (page 220). Add water, salt, soy sauce, saké and kelp to the rice cooker or pot.

   米をとぎ（220頁参照）炊飯器に入れ、水と塩、醤油、酒、切れめを入れたこんぶを加える。

3. When water begins to boil, add sweetfish and cook well.

   沸騰しはじめたら、アユを入れ炊きあげる。

4. When rice is finished cooking, turn off heat and let steam 10 minutes. Take out the kelp and sweetfish. Remove fish head and bones. Return fish to the pot and mix with the rice.

   10分蒸らし、こんぶとアユを取り出す。アユは頭と骨を取り除き、炊飯器に戻してご飯とまぜる。

Note: At Step ②, make a few cuts in the kelp with scissors to allow it to flavor the rice better.
After heaping rice into *chawan* bowls, sprinkle each with red ginger root, for additional flavor and color.

好みで紅しょうがを加える。

FULL MOON RICE (*TSUKIMIDON*)

月見丼

Serves 4　4人分　15 min.　15分　　　　　　225 kcal

4 bowls (1 lb.) chilled steamed rice　冷えたご飯　4人分（440g）

4 egg yolks　卵黄　4個分

4 *chikuwa* (tube-shaped cakes of pressed fish)　ちくわ　4本

½ cup *agedama* (bits of tempura batter skimmed from the hot oil)　揚げ玉　カップ½

1 7–in. carrot　にんじん　1本

1 green pepper　ピーマン　1個

1 onion (*tamanegi*)　玉ねぎ　1個

1½ cups dipping sauce for soba (*tsuketsuyu*)　そばつゆ　カップ1½

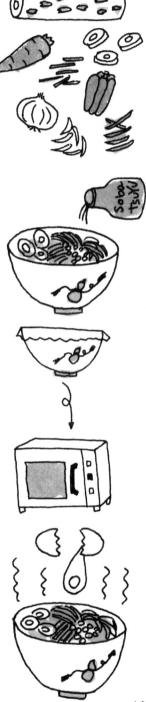

1. Cut *chikuwa* into thick slices. Julienne the carrot, green pepper and onion. Divide all into 4 portions.

   ちくわは輪切り、にんじん、ピーマン、玉ねぎはせん切りにして、すべて4人分に分ける。

2. Scatter 1 portion of ingredients from ① and a sprinkling of *agedama* over each large *donburi* bowl of steamed rice. Pour *soba* broth (page 112) over.

   小さめのどんぶりに冷えたご飯を盛り、その上にちくわ、にんじん、ピーマン、揚げ玉、玉ねぎをのせ、そばつゆ（112頁参照）をかける。

3. Cover each bowl with plastic wrap and heat in a microwave about 2 minutes.

   どんぶりにラップをかけて、電子レンジで約2分加熱する。

4. Remove from the microwave and garnish with the yolk of a single raw egg.

   電子レンジから取り出し、卵黄をのせる。

❤ **By the way:** This is a delicious and simple way to serve leftover rice.
こうすれば冷えたご飯も素早くおいしく調理できる。

147

PORK CUTLET BOWL (*KATSUDON*)
カツ丼

Serves 1   1人分   40 min.   40分   1090 kcal

1 (loin) pork chop   豚ロース   1枚

salt, pepper and garlic to taste   塩、こしょう、にんにく

1 Tbsp. flour (*komugiko*)   小麦粉   大さじ1

1 egg   卵   1個

2 Tbsp. bread crumbs   パン粉   大さじ2

oil for deep frying   揚げ油

½ onion (*tamanegi*)   玉ねぎ   ½個

1 Tbsp. canned green peas   グリーンピース（缶詰）   大さじ1

1 cup steamed rice   ご飯   1人分（110g）

Ⓐ

| Broth for simmering pork: つゆの材料

½ cup *dashi* broth   だし   カップ½

½ Tbsp saké   酒   大さじ½

1 tbsp. sugar   砂糖   小さじ1

1 Tbsp. soy sauce   醤油   大さじ1

1. Trim excess fat from pork chop and rub meat with salt, pepper and garlic. Dust pork chop with flour, dip it into the beaten egg and coat it with bread crumbs. Deep fry it in a wok or heavy pan in vegetable oil heated to 350°F (180°C) 5 to 7 minutes, turning once or twice and skimming fat from the oil occasionally. When pork chop is golden brown, remove it from wok and drain well.

   豚肉は余分なあぶら身を除き、塩、こしょう、にんにくなどを少々すり込んで、小麦粉、溶き卵、パン粉の順で衣をつけ、180℃くらいに熱したサラダ油で5〜7分くらい、両面がきつね色になるまで揚げる。揚がったらペーパータオルにとり油を切る。油かすは鍋から取り除き、きれいに揚げる。

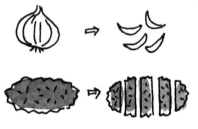

2. Chop onion finely. Cut breaded pork chop crosswise into strips ¾ in. (2 cm.) wide.

   玉ねぎを薄切りにし、カツは2cm幅くらいに切る。

3. In a small saucepan combine Ⓐ to make the sauce (for *dashi* broth, *see* page 222). Bring to a simmer or medium.

   小さめのフライパンにつゆの材料 Ⓐ（だし：222頁参照）を入れ中火で煮立たせる。

4. Add onion and pork chop from ② to ③ and simmer.

   ③ に ② を加えて煮る。

5. When onion softens, crack beaten egg into the pan and swirl it around. When egg is half-cooked, add the green peas and cook 30 seconds longer.

   玉ねぎがやわらかくなってきたら卵を割りほぐして回しかけ、卵が半ば煮えたところで、グリーンピースを適当に加え、30秒ほどそのまま火にかける。

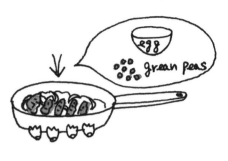

6. Place a large helping of rice in a big bowl. Ladle mixture ⑤ over the rice.

   どんぶりにご飯を盛り、⑤ を汁ごとすべらせるようにのせる。

❤ **By the way:** For the similar and equally popular dish *tonkatsu* (pork cutlet), do only Step 1. Serve the deep-fried pork chop as is, arranged on a plate with a mound of shredded cabbage and dab of mustard alongside, and with the rice in a separate bowl.

おいしくて人気のあるカツフライは、Step ① でつくる。皿にカツ、キャベツのせん切り、練りがらしを添えて食卓へ。

CHICKEN AND EGG OVER RICE (*OYAKODON*)

親子丼

Serves 4　4人分　60 min.　60分　　　　　　　　**493 kcal**

2 chicken breasts (skinned)　鶏胸肉（皮なし）　2枚（250g）

1 onion (*tamanegi*)　玉ねぎ　1個

12 trefoil leaves (*mitsuba*)　みつば　12本

2⅓ cups *dashi* broth　だし　カップ2⅓

4 Tbsp. soy sauce　醤油　大さじ4

4 tsp. sugar　砂糖　小さじ4

2 Tbsp. *mirin* (sweet saké)　みりん　大さじ2

4 eggs　卵　4個

4 Tbsp. shredded *nori* seaweed　焼き海苔（細く切ったもの）大さじ4

4 cups steamed rice　ご飯　4人分（440g）

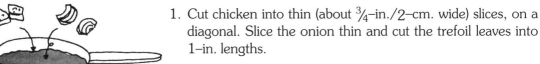

1. Cut chicken into thin (about ¾-in./2-cm. wide) slices, on a diagonal. Slice the onion thin and cut the trefoil leaves into 1-in. lengths.

   鶏肉はそぎ切り（2cm幅）にし、玉ねぎは5mmの厚さに切り、みつばは3cmに切る。

2. In a saucepan, combine *dashi* broth (page 222), soy sauce, sugar and *mirin*.

   鍋にだし（222頁参照）、醤油、砂糖、みりんを合わせる。

3. Heat ② on high. Add the chicken and onion, cook 4–5 minutes more.

   ② を火にかけ、鶏肉と玉ねぎを入れ、強火にかけて4〜5分煮る。

4. Beat the eggs and add them to ③. Scatter trefoil leaves into the pot. When eggs are half-cooked, turn off heat.

   ③ に溶き卵を流し入れ、みつばを散らし、卵が半熟になったら火を止める。

5. Place rice in a *donburi* bowl and arrange ④ attractively on top. Garnish with seaweed.

   どんぶりにごはんを盛り、上に ④ を形よくのせ、海苔をかける。

BEEF BOWL (*GYŪDON*)

牛丼

Serves 1 1人分 20 min. 20分   875 kcal

2 oz. beef (round), sliced thin 牛もも薄切り肉 **60g**

¼ onion (*tamanegi*) 玉ねぎ **¼個**

¼ pack *shirataki* (thin strands of *konnyaku*) しらたき **¼玉**

½ Tbsp. vegetable oil サラダ油 大さじ½

½ Tbsp. sugar 砂糖 大さじ½

½ Tbsp. saké 酒 大さじ½

1 Tbsp. soy sauce 醤油 大さじ1

½ cup *dashi* だし カップ½

a small amount of red, vinegared ginger (*benishōga*) 紅しょうが 少量

1 cup steamed rice ご飯 **110g**

---

1. Cut meat into bite-sized pieces. Slice onion thin. Cut *shirataki* into 2–in. (5–cm.) lengths and boil them briefly.

   肉は一口大に切り、玉ねぎは薄切り、しらたきは食べよい長さに切り、さっと湯がいておく。

2. Heat oil on low. Add onions, sauté until tender. Add beef.

   サラダ油を鍋に熱し、玉ねぎをいためる。しんなりしてきたら、肉を加える。

3. When beef changes color, add sugar, saké, soy sauce and *dashi*, in that order. Add *shirataki* noodles, cook about 5 minutes more.

   肉の色が変わったら、調味料を砂糖、酒、醤油、だしの順で入れ、しらたきを加えて5分くらい煮る。

4. Place hot rice in a large *donburi* bowl and arrange beef, onion and *shirataki* from ③ on top. Then spoon sauce from ③ over generously. Add a few pieces of vinegared ginger for color and flavoring.

   ご飯をどんぶりに盛り、③ をその上にのせる。上から煮汁をまんべんなくかけ、最後に紅しょうがをそえる。

SALMON-SESAME RICE BALLS (*ONIGIRI*)

サケとごまのおにぎり

2 rice balls 2個 15 min. 15分   **241 kcal**

2 cups cooked rice (*gohan*) ご飯　カップ2人分（220g）

1 salmon steak (2 oz.) 生ザケ　1切れ（60g）

1 sheet toasted *nori* seaweed 焼き海苔　1枚

1 Tbsp. white sesame seeds 白ごま　大さじ1

1 Tbsp. dried bonito shavings (*kezuribushi*) 削り節　大さじ1

1½ Tbsp. soy sauce 醤油　大さじ1½

1. Broil salmon well. Flake it with a fork or chopsticks.

   サケを焼き、身を細かくほぐす。

Salmon

Yakinori

2. Cut seaweed in half, crosswise. Leave one half whole and cut the other half up small.

   海苔はおにぎりにつける分をとっておいて残りを細かくちぎる。

3. Add the salmon, white sesame seeds, toasted seaweed and dried bonito to the steamed rice and mix.

   ご飯に、ほぐしたサケ、白ごま、焼き海苔、削り節を加えてまぜる。

4. Add soy sauce, mix again. Form into 2 rice balls. Flatten each ball into a triangle shape about 3 inch thick. Wrap some *nori* seaweed around each ball.

   醤油を加えて再びまぜ、2つの三角おにぎりを作り、海苔を巻く。

♥ **By the way:** Or try eating simply as mixed rice, without forming into balls.

おにぎりにせず、まぜご飯で食べてもよい。

white sesame

KATUOBUSHI

Add soy sauce

SALMON SUSHI

鮭ずし

Serves 4　4人分　40 min.　40分　　　　　　　　　　379 kcal

3 salted salmon steaks　塩ザケ　3切れ（180g）

1 cucumber　きゅうり　1本

1 oz. pickled *daikon* radish (*takuan*)　たくあん　6切れ（30g）

2 cups (uncooked) rice　米　カップ2（320g）

Ⓐ

　Mixed vinegar for sushi　合わせ酢

　$4\frac{1}{3}$ Tbsp. rice vinegar (*kome-su*)　米酢　カップ$\frac{1}{4}$

　1 Tbsp. sugar　砂糖　大さじ1

　1 tsp. salt　塩　小さじ1

1. Prepare rice for cooking (page 220).

　米をといでおく（220頁参照）。

2. Cook the rice and transfer to a mixing bowl. In a separate small bowl combine and mix Ⓐ. Pour the mixture generously over rice. Mix and let cool.

　米を炊いたらボールに移し、Ⓐ の材料をまぜて合わせ酢をつくり、まんべんなくかけてよくまぜ、冷ます。

3. Julienne the *takuan* and the cucumber.

　たくあんときゅうりをせん切りにする。

4. Grill the salmon steaks and flake with a fork or chopsticks.

　サケを焼き、身を細かくほぐす。

5. Add ③ and ④ to the rice and mix.

　③ と ④ をすしめしにまぜる。

❤ **By the way:** As a rule of thumb, the ratio of mixed vinegar ingredients to steamed rice is vinegar, 6–7% of rice; sugar, 1–1.4%; and salt, 0.7–0.8%.

すしの合わせ酢は、炊き上がったご飯の重量に対して、酢6〜7％、砂糖1〜1.4％、塩0.7〜0.8％の量が基本。

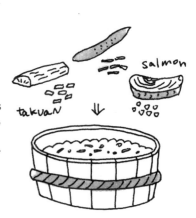

GREEN TEA OVER RICE (OCHAZUKE)

お茶漬け

Serves 4 4人分 5 min. 5分   226 kcal

---

4 cups steamed rice　ご飯　4人分（440g）

1 salted salmon steak (3½ oz.)　塩ザケ　1切れ（100g）

a small amount of (shredded) *nori* seaweed　焼き海苔（細く切ったもの）　少量

a small amount of Japanese horseradish (*wasabi*)　わさび　少量

2 Tbsp. green tea leaves (*sencha*)　煎茶　大さじ2（10g）

6 cups hot water　湯　カップ6

---

1. Cook salmon steak in a small frying pan, turning once. Flake it, remove any bones.

   塩ザケを小ぶりのフライパンで焼いて、焼けたら身をほぐす。

2. Place steamed rice in a *chawan* rice bowl and sprinkle ① over.

   茶碗にご飯を盛り、① をのせる。

3. Place tea leaves in a teapot, add hot water. Let steep about 10 seconds. Strain, and pour over ②.

   きゅうすにお茶葉を入れ、熱湯を注ぎ、10秒ほどおいて ② にかける。

4. Grate *wasabi* horseradish into a small bowl and put a dab of it inside the rice bowl, up near the rim. (Or use prepared horseradish, from a tube.) Sprinkle *nori* seaweed over.

   わさびをおろし（チューブ入りのものでもよい）、茶碗のふちに少しのせ、海苔をかける。

♥ **By the way:** This dish has many variations. A popular one is Umeboshi Ochazuke, or Green Tea Over Rice with Pickled Plums. Plums are used instead of salmon, making this a light dish, good for times when you're not too hungry.

お茶漬けにもいろいろな種類があって、中でも「梅干し茶漬け」はポピュラー。これは、塩ザケの代わりに梅干しを使うもので、さっぱりしていて食欲のないときにもOK。

LETTUCE AND EGG FRIED RICE

レタスと卵のチャーハン

Serves 4　4人分　30 min.　30分　　　　　　　　　330 kcal

4 cups steamed rice　ご飯　4人分　（440g）

4 leaves lettuce　レタス　4枚（80g）

3 eggs　卵　3個

½ Japanese leek (*naganegi*)　長ねぎ　½本

1 knob ginger root　しょうが　1個

2 Tbsp. vegetable oil　サラダ油　大さじ2

2 Tbsp. saké　酒　大さじ2

pinch each, salt and pepper　塩、こしょう　少量

1 tsp. sesame oil　ごま油　小さじ1

1. Tear lettuce into bite-sized pieces. Slice the *naganegi* leek and mince the ginger root.

   レタスは食べやすい大きさにちぎり、長ねぎは斜め切り、しょうがはみじん切りにする。

2. Beat the eggs and season with a little salt. In a wok, heat half the vegetable oil (1 Tbsp.) and add the eggs. Scramble eggs briefly, removing them when about half-done.

   ボールに卵を割り溶き、塩を少々まぜ、大さじ1のサラダ油をフライパンに熱して卵をいため、半熟状で取り出す。

3. Heat the remaining 1 Tbsp. oil and sauté the minced ginger root. When ginger is soft and aromatic, fragrant, add the steamed rice and *naganegi* leek.

   残りのサラダ油を熱してしょうがをいため、香りが出たら、ご飯と長ねぎを入れる。

4. Add the eggs from ② to the rice mixture and continue to sauté. Season to taste with saké, salt and pepper.

   まぜたご飯に ② の半熟卵を加えて、いためる。それに酒、塩、こしょうを加える。

5. Add lettuce and sesame oil to ④, mix.

   ④ に、レタスとごま油を入れてまぜる。

MUSHROOM PILAF
きのこピラフ

Serves 4　4人分　30 min.　30分　　　　　　　484 kcal

4 cups steamed rice　ご飯　4人分　（440g）

12 mushrooms　マッシュルーム　12個　（180g）

7 oz. *shimeji* mushrooms　しめじ　2パック　（200g）

½ lb. pork (tenderloin)　豚ヒレ肉ブロック　200g

5 Tbsp. butter　バター　大さじ5

1 Tbsp. vegetable oil　サラダ油　大さじ1

pinch each, salt and pepper　塩、こしょう　少量

1. Slice the mushrooms. Remove the hard bottom part of the *shimeji* mushroom stems. Pull the mushrooms apart with your hands.

   マッシュルームを薄切りにし、しめじは石づきを除き、ほぐしておく。

2. Cut the pork into bite-sized pieces. Dust with salt and pepper.

   豚ヒレ肉を一口大に切り、塩、こしょうする。

3. Heat 1 Tbsp. of the butter and the vegetable oil in a good-sized frying pan. Add ① and ② and sauté till fragrant.

   フライパンに大さじ1のバターとサラダ油を熱し、① と ② をいためる。

4. Place the remaining 4 Tbsp. of butter and the steamed rice in a separate, large frying pan and sauté briefly. Sprinkle with salt and pepper.

   別のフライパンにバター大さじ4とご飯を入れ、手早くいため、塩、こしょうをふる。

5. Add ③ to ④ and mix.

   ③ の具を ④ に入れまぜる。

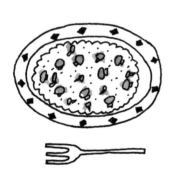

MINCED MEAT CURRY
ひき肉カレー

Serves 4　4人分　40 min.　40分　　　　　　　　191 kcal

½ lb. ground pork　豚ひき肉　200g

1 onion (*tamanegi*)　玉ねぎ　1個

1 clove garlic　にんにく　1かけ

1 Tbsp. vegetable oil　サラダ油　大さじ1

1 cup water　水　カップ1

1 cup tomato juice　トマトジュース　カップ1

2½ oz. block curry roux　カレールウ　80g

pinch each, salt and pepper　塩、こしょう　少量

---

1. Mince onion and garlic.

   玉ねぎ、にんにくはみじん切り。

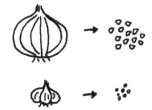

2. Heat vegetable oil in a frying pan. Add onions and garlic, sauté. Add ground meat and sauté well.

   フライパンにサラダ油を熱し玉ねぎ、にんにくをいため、ひき肉を加えて、よくいためる。

3. Add water and tomato juice, simmer on medium 7–8 minutes, skimming fat occasionally.

   ② に水カップ1とトマトジュースを加え、アクを取り除きながら7～8分中火で煮る。

4. Turn off the heat and add curry roux, stir through well. When roux is dissolved, turn heat back on, to low. Season with salt and pepper. Serve when heated through.

   ③ の火をいったん止めて、カレールウを加える。ルウが溶けたら数分弱火にかける。塩、こしょうで味を調える。

BEEF CURRY
ビーフカレー

Serves 4　4人分　70 min.　70分　　　　　　　　978 kcal

---

1 lb. beef (round)　牛もも肉のかたまり　400g

1 onion (*tamanegi*)　玉ねぎ　1個

2 cloves garlic　にんにく　2かけ

1 clove ginger root　しょうが　1かけ

½ 1–in. carrot　にんじん　½本

3 Tbsp. curry powder　カレー粉　大さじ3

1 can whole tomatoes　トマトの水煮缶　大1缶（160g）

5 cups water　水　カップ5

1 bouillon cube　固形スープ　1個

½ apple　りんご　½個

½ banana　バナナ　½本

2 bay leaves　ローリエ　2枚

½ cup white wine　白ワイン　カップ½

2 Tbsp. flour　小麦粉　大さじ2

2 Tbsp. butter　バター　大さじ2

½ cup milk　牛乳　カップ½

dash vegetable oil　サラダ油　少量

2 oz. block curry roux　カレールウ　60g

salt and pepper　塩、こしょう　少量

---

1. Cut beef into bite-sized pieces, sprinkle with salt and pepper.
   牛肉は一口大に切り、塩、こしょうする。

2. Mince onion, garlic and ginger root.
   玉ねぎ、にんにく、しょうがはみじん切りにする。

3. Grate carrot and apple.
   にんじんとりんごはすりおろす。

4. Cut the banana into half-inch (12–mm.) dice.
   バナナはさいの目切り。

5. Heat butter and vegetable oil in a small frying pan. Add beef and sauté.

   フライパンにバター、サラダ油を熱し、牛肉をいためておく。

6. Heat the butter in a saucepan. Add the minced onion and brown.

   鍋にバターを溶かし、玉ねぎをきつね色になるまでいためる。

7. When onion is browned, add garlic and ginger root, sauté until fragrant.

   ⑥に、にんにく、しょうがを加え、さらにいためる。

8. Add carrot and apple, heat until liquid is reduced.

   すりおろしたにんじん、りんごを加え、水分がなくなるまでいためる。

9. Add curry powder, continue heating.

   カレー粉を加えて、さらにいためる。

10. Turn flame down to low and continue heating.

    弱火にして小麦粉を加え、いためる。

11. Pour in the white wine. Seed the tomatoes, chop them up roughly. Add the tomatoes with the liquid from the can. Add the water and the bouillon cube.

    白ワイン、種を取り粗くほぐしたトマトと缶汁、水、固形スープを入れ、のばす。

12. Add the banana from ④ and the beef from ⑤.

    ④のバナナと⑤の牛肉を加える。

13. Add bay leaves and correct the seasoning with a little salt. Simmer over low heat for about one hour.

    ローリエを入れ、塩を少し加え、1時間くらい弱火で煮込む。アクが出たら取り除く。

14. Turn off the heat and add the curry roux and stir it through. Add the milk and turn the heat back on to low, simmer 5 or 6 minutes. serve.

    いったん火を止め、カレールウを入れて溶かし、牛乳を加えてさらに弱火で5〜6分煮てできあがり。

EGGPLANT CURRY

なすのカレー

Serves 4　4人分　40 min.　40分　　　　　　　　　213 kcal

4 or 5 6–in. eggplants　なす　4〜5個

2 tomatoes　トマト　2個

1 onion (*tamanegi*)　玉ねぎ　1個

$\frac{1}{4}$ lb. ground pork　豚ひき肉　100g

1 Tbsp. vegetable oil　サラダ油　大さじ1

4 cups water　水　カップ4

2 oz. block curry roux　カレールウ　60g

ground pork

1. Cut eggplants into half-inch (1–cm.) slices. Soak briefly in cool water, to mellow the flavor.

   なすを1cmくらいの輪切りにし、水につけ、アク抜きをする。

2. Cut tomatoes and onion into half-inch (1–cm.) wedges.

   トマトと玉ねぎを1cm幅のくし形に切る。

3. Heat oil in a frying pan and sauté the onion, ground pork, eggplants and tomatoes in it, in that order. Heat until meat is no longer sticky, turn off the flame.

   フライパンに油を熱し、玉ねぎ、ひき肉、なす、トマトの順にいためて、ひき肉がパラパラになったら火を止める。

solid curry sauce

water

4. In a soup pot, bring 4 cups water to a boil. Add ③ and simmer 10 minutes on medium, skimming the fat occasionally.

   鍋にカップ4の水を沸騰させ、③ を入れ、アクを除きながら、中火で10分ほど煮る。

5. Turn heat off for a moment, add curry roux to the pot and stir to help it dissolve. Turn heat back on, to low, and simmer a few minutes more, till heated through.

   ④ の火をいったん止めて、カレールウを入れて溶かし、溶けたら、弱火で数分煮る。

Note: Be sure to turn off the heat in Step ⑤, since the curry roux won't dissolve properly otherwise.

Step ⑤ で、火を止めてからでないと、ルウがだまになってよく溶けない。

HASHED BEEF RICE

ハヤシライス

Serves 4　4人分　120 min.　120分　　　　　　　　**771 kcal**

⅓ lb. beef (chuck), sliced thin　牛肩ロース薄切り　300g

1½ onions (*tamanegi*)　玉ねぎ　1½個

1 clove garlic　にんにく　1かけ

1 Tbsp. butter　バター　大さじ1

Ⓐ

   1½ onions (*tamanegi*)　玉ねぎ　1½個

   ½ rib celery　セロリ　½本

   ¼ 7–in. carrot　にんじん　¼本

   ½ cup wine　赤ワイン　カップ½

   ¼ cup tomato purée　トマトピュレー　カップ½

   ½ cup ketchup　ケチャップ　カップ½

   1 can (10–oz.) demiglace sauce　デミグラスソース　1缶（290g）

   1–2 bay leaves　ローリエ　1〜2枚

   pinch each, salt and pepper　塩、こしょう　少量

---

1. Make sauce from ingredients Ⓐ: Mince the 1½ onions and the celery and carrot. Sauté all in butter until golden. Add red wine, tomato purée, ketchup, demiglace sauce and bay leaf. Simmer on low heat 30–40 minutes, stirring occasionally.

　Ⓐ の材料でソースをつくる。玉ねぎ、セロリ、にんじんはみじん切りにし、バターでうっすら色づくまでいためる。赤ワイン、トマトピュレー、ケチャップ、デミグラスソース、ローリエを加え、時々かきまぜながらとろ火で30〜40分煮る。

2. Slice the other 1½ onions thin and mince the garlic. Heat butter in a frying pan and lightly brown the onions and garlic together.

　残りの玉ねぎは薄切り、にんにくはみじん切りにしてバターでいっしょにきつね色になるまでゆっくりいためる。

3. Cut beef into bite-sized pieces, season with salt and pepper and add to ②. Continue sautéeing.

牛肉は1口大に切り、塩、こしょうをして、② に入れ、さらに
いためる。

4. Combine ③ and ① and simmer on low for 20–30 minutes, watching to be sure it doesn't burn. Correct the seasoning with salt, as necessary.

① でつくっておいたソースと ③ を合わせて、弱火で20〜30分こがさないように煮る。味をみて、足りないようなら塩を足す。

5. Serve over rice.

ご飯にかけて食べる。

Meat

SHABU-SHABU

しゃぶしゃぶ

Serves 4　4人分　20 min.　20分　　　　　　　　　918 kcal

1 lb. beef (sirloin), sliced paper thin　牛サーロイン薄切り　400g

2 block firm tofu (momen-dōfu)　もめん豆腐　2丁

2 16–in. Japanese leeks (naganegi)　長ねぎ　2本

4 large leaves Chinese cabbage (hakusai)　白菜　葉4枚

½ lb. spring chrysanthemums (shungiku)　春菊　1わ

6 cups dashi broth　だし　カップ6

Ⓐ

   Lemon–Soy Sauce　醤油だれ

   4 Tbsp. lemon juice　レモン汁　大さじ4

   3 Tbsp. soy sauce　醤油　大さじ3

   6 Tbsp. dashi broth　だし　大さじ6

Ⓑ

   Sesame–Mayonnaise Sauce　マヨネーズだれ

   6–8 Tbsp. mayonnaise　マヨネーズ　大さじ6~8

   4 Tbsp. white sesame seeds (ground roasted)　すり白ごま　大さじ4

---

1. Slice Japanese leek into 2–in. lengths, on the diagonal. Cut tofu and Chinese cabbage into bite-sized pieces. Cut *shungiku* leaves in half.

   長ねぎは5cmくらいの長さで斜めに切る。豆腐、白菜は食べやすい大きさ、春菊は半分の長さに切っておく。

2. Make dipping sauces Ⓐ and Ⓑ and set them out in very small individual bowls.

   それぞれのたれをめいめいの小皿に用意。

3. Arrange meat, tofu and vegetables attractively on a platter. Set the platter next to an electric skillet or hot pot, at the dining table.

   大皿に肉、豆腐、野菜をきれいに並べ、しゃぶしゃぶの鍋の近くに置く。

4. Heat *dashi* broth (page 222) in the skillet. When it comes to a simmer, drop some of the vegetables in. After a few minutes, these can be dipped into sauce and eaten, and more vegetables added to the broth.

鍋にだし（222頁参照）を入れ、煮立ったら肉以外の材料を適当に入れ、火が通ったらたれをつけて食べる。

5. Simply swish pieces of meat through the broth very briefly, till they change color, and then dip them into a sauce and eat.

肉はそのつどだしにつけてしゃぶしゃぶとすすいで、火を通し、たれをつけて食べる。

6. When meat and vegetables are gone, use up the broth by adding some precooked *udon* noodles or steamed rice. Heat a few minutes and serve.

肉、野菜などすべて食べ終えたところで、鍋に残っただしを利用し、うどんやご飯をそのだしであたためて食べるととてもおいしい。

COLD *SHABU-SHABU* FOR SUMMER

豚の冷たいしゃぶしゃぶ

Serves 4 4人分 30 min. 30分   274 kcal

---

1 lb. pork (picnic shoulder), sliced thin 豚肩薄切り肉 **400g**

4 8–in. cucumbers きゅうり **4本**

1 clove garlic にんにく **1かけ**

5 Tbsp. soy sauce 醤油 **大さじ5**

1 Tbsp. sesame oil ごま油 **大さじ1**

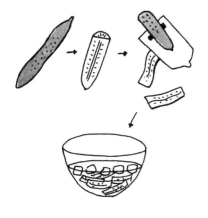

1. Cut cucumbers in half crosswise and slice each half thin, lengthwise.

   きゅうりを半分の長さに切り、縦長に薄切りにする。

2. Soak cucumbers in ice water.

   氷水にきゅうりをひたす。

3. Boil pork 1 minute, then plunge into a separate bowl of ice water and set in a colander to drain.

   豚肉を1分ゆで、別の氷水にくぐらせ、ざるに上げる。

4. Mince or press garlic. For the sauce, combine and mix garlic with soy sauce and sesame oil.

   にんにくをすり下ろし、醤油、ごま油をまぜる。

5. Drain cucumbers, transfer to a plate.

   きゅうりの水切りをし、皿にひく。

6. Drain boiled pork and place it on top of the cucumbers. Pour the sauce from ④ over.

   豚肉を⑤の上にのせ、上から④をかける。

BEEF AND BOK CHOY

チンゲン菜と牛肉のオイスターソース炒め

Serves 4   4人分   40 min.   40分   **217 kcal**

1 bundle bok choy (*chingensai*)   チンゲン菜   **1株**

1 7–in. carrot   にんじん   **1本**

½ lb. beef (round), sliced thin   牛もも薄切り肉   **200g**

6 *shiitake* mushrooms   しいたけ   **6枚**

1 cup water   水　カップ**1**

3 tsp. Chinese-style powdered soup base   中華風スープの素
小さじ**3**

½ Tbsp. starch (*katakuriko*)   片栗粉　大さじ½

3 Tbsp. sesame oil   ごま油　大さじ**3**

2½ Tbsp. oyster sauce   オイスターソース　大さじ2½

1. Julienne the carrot. Remove stems from the *shiitake* mushrooms and cut caps up small. Cut beef and bok choy into bite-sized pieces.

   にんじんはせん切り、しいたけは軸を除いて細切り、チンゲン菜は食べやすい大きさ、牛肉は一口大にする。

2. Sauté carrot in sesame oil, till soft. Add beef and brown both sides.

   にんじんをやわらかくなるまでごま油でいためる、火が通ったら牛肉を加えてさらにいためる。

3. Add bok choy, *shiitake* mushrooms and water.

   ②にチンゲン菜、しいたけ、水を加える。

4. Season with Chinese-style powdered soup base, cook 3–5 minutes more.

   中華風スープの素で味をつけ、さらに3〜5分煮る。

5. Season with oyster sauce. Add dissolved starch and stir through.

   オイスターソースで味つけをし、片栗粉を2倍の水で溶いてから流し入れる。

SUKIYAKI

すき焼き

Serves 4   4人分   30 min.   30分   420 kcal

1 lb. beef (round), slice thin   牛もも薄切り肉   400g

1 Japanese leek   長ねぎ   1本

1 pack *shirataki* (thin strands of *konnyaku*)   しらたき   1玉

1 block grilled tofu (*yaki-dōfu*)   焼き豆腐   1丁

8 *shiitake* mushrooms   しいたけ   8枚

½ lb. spring chrysanthemums (*shungiku*)   春菊   1わ

1 Tbsp. vegetable oil   サラダ油   大さじ1

Ⓐ

> ½ cup soy sauce   醤油   カップ½
>
> ½ cup *mirin* (sweet saké)   みりん   カップ½
>
> 4–5 Tbsp. sugar   砂糖   大さじ4〜5
>
> 1 cup *dashi* broth   だし   カップ1

---

1. Combine and heat Ⓐ in a saucepan, to make the soup for the pot. (For *dashi* broth, see page 222.)

   小鍋にⒶをまぜ、煮立たせて割り下をつくる。だし（222頁参照）。

2. Cut tofu into rectangular blocks about 2 in. long. Slice *naganegi* leeks thin, on the diagonal. Remove stems from the *shiitake* mushrooms and cut each cap into two or three pieces. Prepare *shirataki* by pouring boiled water over them. Cut spring chrysanthemums into bite-sized pieces.

   焼き豆腐は四角く、ねぎは斜めに薄く切り、しいたけは軸を取り除いて 2〜3 にスライスし、しらたきはあらかじめ熱湯をかけて臭みを除いておき、春菊は食べやすい大きさにカットしておく。

3. Put a thick-sided pot onto a moderate flame (cast-iron is best). Add a dash of oil.

   鉄のすき焼き鍋を中火で熱し、サラダ油を少量ひく。

4. When oil is heated, add the *naganegi* leeks, which will take longest to cook. Sauté leeks briefly, then pour ① over and let pot start to simmer. Add meat, grilled tofu, *shirataki* and

spring chrysanthemums, in that order. When all ingredients are heated through, carry pot to the table (or cook right at the table in an electric skillet.)

鍋が熱くなったところで、ねぎを入れ、① を加え、肉、豆腐、しらたき、春菊といった順で煮て、火が通るころ鍋を食卓に運ぶ。テーブル用コンロで料理しながら食べるのもおいしい。

❤ **By the way:** *Shirataki* are made from *konnyaku* and like it, have no calories. *Shiitake* mushrooms are another completely noncaloric food.

しらたきは、こんにゃくを糸状にしたもの。カロリーゼロは、しいたけと同じ。

HAMBURGERS WITH TOMATO GRAVY

煮込みハンバーグ

Serves 4　4人分　60 min.　60分　　　　　　　　　　　405 kcal

⅔ lb. ground beef　牛ひき肉　300g

1 onion (*tamanegi*)　玉ねぎ　1個

3 Tbsp. milk　牛乳　大さじ3

1 egg　卵　1個

⅔ cup bread crumbs　パン粉　カップ⅔

½ tsp. salt　塩　小さじ½

pinch pepper　こしょう　少量

pinch nutmeg　ナツメグ　少量

1 Tbsp. vegetable oil　サラダ油　大さじ1

1½ Tbsp. butter　バター　大さじ1½

2½ Tbsp. flour (*komugiko*)　小麦粉　大さじ2½

1 cup ketchup　トマトケチャップ　カップ1

2 cups water　水　カップ2

1 bouillon cube　固形スープ　1固

1. Mince the entire onion. Heat vegetable oil in a frying pan, add and brown half the onion. Pour milk over the bread crumbs, to plump them.

   玉ねぎをみじん切りにし、その半分をフライパンにサラダ油を熱していため、冷ましておく。パン粉は牛乳でふやかす。

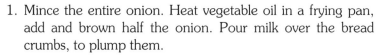

2. Season ground beef with salt, pepper, nutmeg, egg and the bread crumbs and browned onion from ①. Mix by hand till sticky and form into 4 patties.

   ボールにひき肉、塩、こしょう、ナツメグ、卵、①のパン粉といためた玉ねぎを入れ、手のひらでねばりがでるまでよくまぜ、4つのハンバーグをつくる。

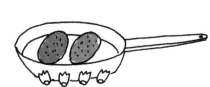

3. Heat vegetable oil in a frying pan and sauté patties till brown on both sides and heated through.

   サラダ油をフライパンに熱し、②の両面をよく焼き、皿に取り出しておく。

4. Heat butter in a saucepan and brown the other half of the onion from ①. When heated through, add flour, ketchup, water and bouillon cube.

バターを鍋に熱して ① で残った玉ねぎをいため、小麦粉、トマトケチャップ、水、固形スープを加える。

5. Add ③ to ④ and simmer about 10 minutes. Correct seasoning with salt and pepper.

④ の中に ③ をハンバーガー入れ、10分ほど煮込み、塩とこしょうで味を調える。

KOREAN ONE-POT DINNER
韓国鍋

Serves 4　4人分　30 min.　30分　　　　　　　　　　　414 kcal

½ lb. beef (round), sliced thin　牛もも薄切り肉　200g

1 block firm tofu (*momen-dōfu*)　もめん豆腐　1丁

1 package (8.75 oz.) bean sprouts　もやし　1袋（250g）

3 packs fresh (precooked) *udon* noodles　ゆでうどん　3玉

4 cups water　水　カップ4

1 clove garlic　にんにく　1かけ

1 generous Tbsp. red miso (*akamiso*)　赤味噌　大さじ1強

2 scant Tbsp. Korean mustard (*kochujan*)　コチュジャン　大さじ2弱

2 Tbsp. bottled flowering fern (*zenmai*)　ぜんまいの水煮　大さじ2

1. Cut the beef into bite-sized pieces and the tofu into cubes. Rinse the bean sprouts and set them in a colander to drain. Boil *udon* noodles briefly.

   牛肉は食べやすい大きさに、とうふは角切りにする。もやしは水で洗いざるに上げておき、うどん玉はさっと熱湯でゆでておく。

2. Heat the water in a large soup pot. Mince the garlic. Stir red miso, Korean mustard and minced garlic into the pot.

   鍋にお湯を沸騰させ、その中に赤味噌とコチュジャンと、すりおろしたにんにくを入れる。

3. Add the other ingredients and cook till all are heated through.

   残りの材料を適量ずつ入れ、煮えたところから食べる。

Note: Skim the fat from the surface once in a while.
ときどきアクをすくう。

GINGER PORK

豚肉のしょうが焼き

Serves 4 4人分 50 min. 50分   242 kcal

1 lb. fresh ham, sliced thin 豚もも薄切り肉 400g

2 large cabbage leaves キャベツ 葉2枚（100g）

1 tomato トマト 1個

2 Tbsp. vegetable oil サラダ油 大さじ2

6 Tbsp. soy sauce 醤油 大さじ6

3 Tbsp. *mirin* (sweet saké) みりん 大さじ3

1 knob ginger root しょうが 大1かけ

1. Grate the ginger root. Combine and mix the soy sauce, *mirin* and grated ginger in a good-sized mixing bowl. Spread slices of pork out flat and lay them, one by one, into the mixture. Marinate about 30 minutes.

   しょうがを下ろし、醤油、みりんと合わせてつけ汁をつくる。豚肉を一枚一枚広げて、つけ汁をよくしみこませるため、ときどき表裏を返しながら30分ぐらいおく。

2. Heat vegetable oil in a frying pan. Sauté the pork, turning once, till heated through.

   フライパンにサラダ油を熱したら、肉を中火色が変わるまで両面焼く。

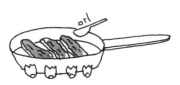

3. Chop cabbage into thin strips about 1 in. (2½ cm.) long and cut tomato into wedges.

   キャベツは細かく、トマトはくし形に切っておく。

4. Place ② on a plate and add ③ alongside as garnish.

   皿に肉を盛り、キャベツとトマトを添えてできあがり。

Note: Don't marinate the meat too long, or it will get very spicy! If fresh ginger root is not available, try the paste form that comes in a tube.

肉をつけ汁につけすぎると辛くなるので注意。しょうがが手に入らないときは、チューブ入りしょうがでよい。

STEWED PORK AND VEGETABLES
豚肉と野菜の煮込み

Serves 4 4人分 60 min. 60分   379 kcal

½ lb. pork (flank) 豚ばら肉 200g

½ lb. *shirataki* (thin strands of *konnyaku*) しらたき 1玉

2 potatoes (*jagaimo*) じゃがいも 2個

1 onion (*tamanegi*) 玉ねぎ 1個

1 block firm tofu (*momen-dōfu*) もめん豆腐 1丁

3 Tbsp. green peas グリーンピース 大さじ3

3 Tbsp. sugar 砂糖 大さじ3

3 Tbsp. saké 酒 大さじ3

5 Tbsp. soy sauce 醤油 大さじ5

1½ cups water 水 カップ1½

1. Cut the pork into bite-sized pieces and pour boiled water over, to reduce their oil content. Prepare the *shirataki* by boiling them 3 or 4 minutes, then cut into 2–in. (5–cm.) lengths.

   肉は食べやすい大きさに切り、熱湯に通して脂ぬきをする。しらたきは3〜4分ゆでて臭みをぬき、流水で洗ってから5cmくらいの長さに切る。

2. Peel and quarter the potatoes, soak them in cold water. Cut onion into eighths.

   じゃがいもは皮をむいて、4つ割りにして水にさらす。玉ねぎを8つ割りにする。

3. Lay *shirataki* in the bottom of a soup pot and scatter meat over them. Add potatoes and onion. And water and bring to a simmer.

   鍋底にしらたきを敷き、ばら肉を散らし、じゃがいも、玉ねぎを入れ、水を加えてひと煮立ちさせる。

4. Add sugar and saké and simmer 5 minutes more. Add soy sauce and simmer again 5 minutes. When liquid boils down, tear the tofu and add it to the pot. Mix all ingredients and simmer on low until liquid boils down again.

砂糖、酒を入れて約5分煮て、醤油を入れる。煮詰まったら豆
腐をちぎって入れ、汁を弱火で煮詰める。

5. Arrange on a plate, scatter green peas over for color.

器に盛って、グリーンピースを彩りよく散らす。

SPICY PINEAPPLE PORK

豚肉とカリフラワーのパイナップル煮

Serves 4　4人分　30 min.　30分　　　　　　　　　　280 kcal

---

²⁄₃ lb. pork (picnic shoulder)　豚肩肉かたまり　300g

1 head cauliflower　カリフラワー　1個

¼ cup canned pineapple, in juice　パイナップル（缶詰）　3切れ
汁　カップ¼

½ onion (*tamanegi*)　玉ねぎ　½個

1 green pepper　ピーマン　1個

1 clove garlic　にんにく　1かけ

2 Tbsp. vegetable oil　サラダ油　大さじ2

2 Tbsp. lemon juice　レモン汁　大さじ2

1 can (5¼ oz.) whole tomatoes　トマト（水煮缶詰）　大1缶
(160g)

1 Tbsp. ketchup　ケチャップ　大さじ1

2 tsp. Worcestershire sauce　ウスターソース　小さじ2

1 tsp. *tōbanjan* (red, spicy Chinese miso)　トウバンジャン
小さじ1

---

1. Dice the pork and sprinkle it with salt and pepper. Cut cauliflower into florets and pineapple into bite-sized pieces. Mince the onion and cut the green pepper into 1–in. squares. Cut garlic finely.

   豚肉はさいころ大にして塩、こしょうをし、カリフラワーは小房に分け、パイナップルは食べやすい大きさにし、玉ねぎはみじん切り、ピーマンは2cm角にし、にんにくは薄く切っておく。

2. Heat oil in a small frying pan and sauté the pork only.

   小ぶりのフライパンに油を熱し、① の豚肉を焼く。

3. Heat oil in a large saucepan and sauté the onion and garlic from ①. When onion and garlic soften, add the lemon juice, ketchup, Worcestershire sauce, *tōbanjan* and pineapple juice. Crush the canned tomatoes by hand and add.

   大きめの鍋に油を熱して、① の玉ねぎとにんにくをいためたら、レモン汁、トマトケチャップ、ウスターソース、トウバンジャン、パイナップルの汁、缶詰のトマトを手で潰して加える。

4. Add the sautéed pork and the cauliflower to ③. Cover and simmer 5–10 minutes. Add pineapple and simmer 10 more minutes. Add green pepper and bring to a simmer once more. Correct seasoning with salt.

③ に ② とカリフラワーを加えてまぜ、蓋をして5〜10分煮る。パイナップルを加えてさらに10分煮て、ピーマンを加えてもうひと煮立ちさせる。味がうすければ塩で加減する。

BROILED MARINATED SPARERIBS

スペアリブの網焼き

Serves 2 2人分 210 min. 210分 825 kcal

4 spareribs スペアリブ 4本（正味380g）

Ⓐ

> Marinade つけ汁
>
> ¼ cup each: red wine, tomato purée, soy sauce 赤ワイン、トマトプレー、醤油 各カップ¼
>
> 1 Tbsp. Worcestershire sauce ウスターソース 大さじ1
>
> 2 Tbsp. onion (*tamanegi*), minced very fine おろし玉ねぎ 大さじ2
>
> 4 Tbsp. vegetable oil サラダ油 大さじ4
>
> 2 tsp. grated ginger root おろししょうが 小さじ2
>
> 1 clove garlic, pressed or minced にんにく すりつぶしたもの 1かけ分
>
> pinch each, salt and pepper 塩、こしょう 少量
>
> prepared mustard 練りからし

· 10 - 15 minutes

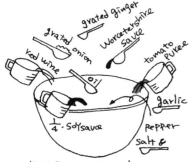

· marinate for 2 hours.

1. Rub spareribs with salt and pepper. Let stand 10 to 15 minutes.

   スペアリブに塩とこしょうをよくまぶし、10～15分おいておく。

2. In a deep bowl, combine and mix Ⓐ to make the marinade. Marinate ribs for 2 hours, turning them occasionally.

   深めのボールにつけ汁 Ⓐ の材料を入れ、よくまぜてからスペアリブを漬け、ときおり肉をひっくり返しながら2時間くらいそのままにしておく。

3. Lift ribs from the marinade and set them on a rack in a shallow pan. Bake about 40 minutes at 350°F (180°C), brushing the marinade from ② over occasionally. Lower heat to 300°F (150°C) and bake another 30 minutes.

   オーブン皿に網をのせ、その上に Ⓐ から取り出したスペアリブをおく。180℃に熱したオーブンで40分くらい、ときおりスペアリブにつけ汁をぬりながら焼く。さらに温度を150℃くらいにして30分ほど焼く。

4. If any marinade from ② is left over, boil it till it thickens, and pour it over the ribs as sauce. Serve with a dab of mustard on the side.

　スペアリブを皿に取る。残った漬け汁は煮立て、粘りが出てきたら火を止め、スペアリブにかける。練りからしを少々添えてできあがり。

STEWED CABBAGE AND PORK

だんだんキャベツ

Serves 4   4人分   60 min.   60分   356 kcal

---

1 lb. ground fresh ham   豚ももひき肉   400g

10 cabbage leaves   キャベツ　葉10枚

1 onion (*tamanegi*)   玉ねぎ　1個

dash vegetable oil   サラダ油　少量

½ egg   卵　½個

a small amount of bread crumbs   パン粉　少量

pinch each, salt and pepper   塩、こしょう　少量

1 (beef-flavored) bouillon cube   固形スープ　1個

2 cups water   水　カップ2

cut core flat

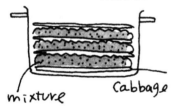

Pile up cabbage and mixture

mixture   cabbage

soup

1. Cut away any harder parts of the cabbage leaves, then boil leaves, till tender.

   キャベツは葉の芯を取り除き、やわらかくなるまでゆでる。

2. Mince the entire onion finely. Sauté half.

   玉ねぎをみじん切りにし、その半分を十分にいためる。

3. In a large bowl combine the minced pork, onion (both cooked and uncooked), egg and bread crumbs. Sprinkle with salt and pepper and knead well.

   ひき肉、玉ねぎ（残っている半分といためたもの）のみじん切り、卵、パン粉をボールに入れ、塩、こしょうをし、よく練る。

4. Layer the cabbage from ① and mixture ③ alternately into a greased soup pot. When liquid has completely cooked off, add the soup and water and bouillon cube and bring to a boil, covered. Reduce heat and simmer about 20 minutes.

   鍋に油をひき、① のキャベツと ③ を交互に重ねていためる。水気がなくなったら水と固形スープを加えて沸騰させ、沸騰したら、弱火で20分ほど蒸し煮する。

Note: This dish is good with bread (especially sourdough, rye or pumpernickel). As seasonings, try ketchup or mustard.

パンによく合う。ケチャップやマスタードを添えると一層おいしい。

CHINESE GINGER CHICKEN
中華風ゆで鶏

Serves 4　4人分　30 min.　30分　　　　　　143 kcal

2 chicken legs with thigh meat　鶏もも肉　2枚

1 Japanese leek (*naganegi*)　長ねぎ　1本

3 knobs ginger root　しょうが　3かけ

8 leaves lettuce　レタス　8枚

12 cherry tomatoes　プチトマト　12個

¼ cup saké　酒　カップ¼

dash soy sauce　醤油　少量

dash red chili pepper oil　ラー油　少量

---

1. In a soup pot, combine the minced ginger root, the *naganegi* leek chopped roughly into 2–in. (5 cm) lengths and the chicken. Add enough water to cover, season with saké. Simmer on medium 20 minutes.

   鍋にしょうがの薄切り、長ねぎのぶつ切り（5cmくらい）、鶏肉、たっぷりかぶるくらいの水、酒を入れ、中火で約20分ゆでる。

2. When meat is soft enough to be pierced easily with a chopstick, turn off the heat. When chicken cools, cut into bite-sized pieces.

   肉は箸を刺してみてすっと通ったら、火を止めてそのまま冷まし、冷めたら食べやすい大きさに薄切りにする。

3. Serve on a bed of lettuce and garnish with cherry tomatoes. Set out small dishes of soy sauce mixed with a dash of red chili pepper oil.

   ② を皿に盛り、レタス、プチトマトを添える。小皿に醤油とラー油を少々加え、つけて食べる。

❤ **By the way:** Add some spices to the water from ① and serve it as soup
ゆで汁は、調味料で味をつければ、スープになる。

181

CHICKEN *TERIYAKI*

チキン照り焼き

Serves 4　4人分　30 min.　30分　　　　　　　　　355 kcal

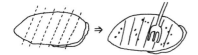

4 chicken breasts　鶏胸肉　4枚

3 Tbsp. vegetable oil　サラダ油　大さじ3

1 Tbsp. sugar　砂糖　大さじ1

1 Tbsp. *mirin* (sweet saké)　みりん　大さじ1

Ⓐ

> Marinade　つけ汁
>
> 3 Tbsp. soy sauce　醤油　大さじ3
>
> 1 Tbsp. saké　酒　大さじ1
>
> 1 Tbsp. *mirin* (sweet saké)　みりん　大さじ1

Ⓑ

> Garnishes　つけ合わせ
>
> orange slices　オレンジ輪切り
>
> *daikon* radish shoots (*kaiwarena*)　貝割れ菜
>
> cucumbers or carrot, cut into thin rectangular blocks　きゅうりかにんじんの短冊切り

1. Cut deep lines in the chicken to let heat pass through evenly. Pierce both sides of the meat with a fork to help it absorb the marinade better.

   平均して焼けるように鶏肉に包丁で深く切り目を何本か入れ、汁がよく浸み込むようフォークなどで肉を刺しておく。

2. To make marinade, mix Ⓐ in a large bowl. Add chicken and let it sit for 30 minutes, turning it occasionally.

   深めのボールに Ⓐ を入れ、よくまぜ合わせてから鶏肉をつけ、時折ひっくり返しながらそのまま30分ほどしみ込ませる。

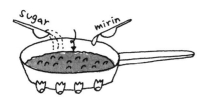

3. Remove the chicken. Heat oil in a skillet. Add the chicken, skin side down. Cook on medium till skin is crispy and brown. Turn chicken, cover the skillet and reduce heat to low for another 4–5 minutes. When meat is tender and juices are clear, remove from heat.

   フライパンにサラダ油をひいて熱し、用意のできた鶏肉を皮を

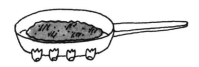

底にして鍋に入れ、皮にうっすらと焦げめがつくまで中火で4〜5分焼く。

4. Remove chicken and wipe skillet clean. Combine sugar, *mirin* and  and bring to a simmer. Add sautéed chicken, skinless side down, and heat 1 minute. Turn meat and heat another 30 seconds.

鶏肉を取り出し、フライパンをペーパータオルでふき、そこに砂糖、みりん、Ⓐ をまぜながら煮立てる。鶏肉を皮のない方を下にして入れ、1分ほど火を通してひっくり返し、30秒ほどでまた裏返し、火をよく通す。

5. Cut chicken into slices ¾-in. (2–cm.) wide and arrange on a plate. Pour the remaining pan juices over. Garnish with Ⓑ.

煮えたところで肉を取り出し、2cmくらいに切ってきれいに皿に盛りつける。付け合わせには、Ⓑ がよくあう。

FRIED POTATO-COATED CHICKEN

ポテト衣のフライドチキン

Serves 4　4人分　15 min.　15分　　　　　　　　　　**75 kcal**

**2 chicken *sasami* (inner breast fillets), or 1 chicken breast
cut in half lengthwise**　鶏ささみ　2本（80g）

1 potato (*jagaimo*)　じゃがいも　1個

½ tsp. salt　塩　小さじ½

pinch pepper　こしょう　少量

pinch starch (*katakuriko*)　片栗粉　少量

oil for deep frying　揚げ油

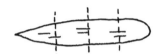

1. Cut chicken into 2–in. (4–cm.) lengths.
   ささみを4cmぐらいの長さに切る。

2. Season with salt and pepper. Dust lightly with starch.
   切ったささみに塩、こしょうをして、うすく片栗粉をまぶして
   おく。

3. Peel potato and cut it into thin julienne slices. Do not rinse.
   じゃがいもの皮をむき、細いせん切りにする。切ったじゃがい
   もは洗わない。

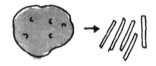

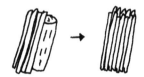

4. Place the potato strips against the sides of the chicken,
   press together firmly.
   じゃがいもをささみに手で握るようにして、しっかりつける。

5. Deep fry coated chicken till golden brown in oil heated to
   350°F (180°C).
   180℃の油できつね色になるまで揚げる。

♥ **By the way:** Also try soaking the chicken at Step ① for about 10 minutes in a mixture of soy sauce, saké and ginger juice (or garlic powder).
切ったささみに少量の醤油、酒、しょうがのしぼり汁（あるいはガーリックパ
ウダー）などで、10分程下味をつけておくと、また違う味が楽しめる。

FRIED CHICKEN STUFFED WITH PICKLED PLUM

梅干し入りささみのフライ

Serves 4 4人分 40 min. 40分   344 kcal

8 chicken *sasami* (inner breast fillets), or 4 chicken breasts cut in half lengthwise 鶏ささみ 8本（320g）

7 pickled plums (*umeboshi*) 梅干し 7個

15 perilla (*shiso*) leaves 青じそ（大葉） 15枚

2½ Tbsp. flour (*komugiko*) 小麦粉 大さじ2½

1 egg 卵 1個

2 cups bread crumbs パン粉 カップ2

oil for deep frying 揚げ油

Mix!

1. Remove the stone from the pickled plums.

   梅干しのたねを取り出す。

2. Chop the *shiso* leaves up finely. Combine them with plum fruit, crush the two together.

   しそを細かくきざみ、梅干しにたたきまぜる。

3. Without severing meat, cut along the length of each fillet (or half-breast) so that meat opens like a pocket. Spread ② inside the meat pockets, and press them closed again.

   ささみを切り開き、中に ② をぬり、しっかりと閉じる。

4. Dust ③ with flour, then dip them into the beaten egg and coat them with bread crumbs.

   ③ に小麦粉、溶き卵、パン粉の順で衣をつける。

5. Fry ④ in oil heated to about 350°F (170–180°C).

   ④ を170〜180℃で揚げる。

flour

↓

↓

bread crumbs

❤ **By the way:** Tart pickled plums and minty shiso leaves contrast nicely with the milder taste of chicken.

鶏肉は味が淡泊なので、酸味や香りの強いものと組み合わせるとおいしくなる。

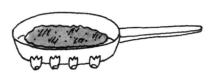

CHICKEN CHEESE POCKETS
イタリア風フライドチキン

Serves 4　4人分　30 min.　30分　　　　　　　　　324 kcal

8 chicken *sasami* (inner breast fillets), or 4 chicken breasts cut in half lengthwise　ささみ　8本

2 slices cheese　スライスチーズ　2枚

½ bunch spinach　ほうれん草　½わ

1 egg　卵　1個

4 Tbsp. flour (*komugiko*)　小麦粉　大さじ4

½ cup bread crumbs　パン粉　カップ½

oil for deep frying　揚げ油

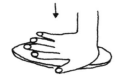

1. Cut the cheese slices finely. Boil the spinach, and cut it into 1½–in. lengths.

   スライスチーズは細かく切り、ほうれん草はゆでて3〜4cmほどの長さに切っておく。

2. Without severing the meat, cut along the length of each fillet so that meat opens like a pocket.

   ささみを縦に4〜6cm、切りはなさないようにして半分になるように包丁をいれる。

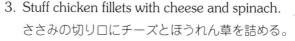

3. Stuff chicken fillets with cheese and spinach.

   ささみの切り口にチーズとほうれん草を詰める。

4. Press chicken pockets shut with your hands. Dip into flour, beaten egg, and bread crumbs, in that order.

   ③ を手でよく押さえつけて形を整え、小麦粉、溶き卵、パン粉の順に衣をつける。

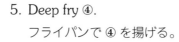

5. Deep fry ④.

   フライパンで ④ を揚げる。

Fish

SALT-GRILLED MACKEREL (*AJI NO SHIOYAKI*)

アジの塩焼き

Serves 1　1人分　20 min.　20分　　　　　　　　　137 kcal

1 whole horse mackerel (*aji*)　アジ　1尾

pinch salt　塩　少量

2 Tbsp. grated *daikon* radish　大根おろし　大さじ2

soy sauce　醤油

---

1. Scrape off the row of tough scales from each side of the fish, remove entrails (page 224). Rinse well.

   アジは、うろことぜいご（側面のギザギザ）とはらわたを除き、水でよく洗う。（224頁参照）

2. Pat fish dry, sprinkle with salt and let sit about 10 minutes.

   アジの水気をよくふきとり、塩をふったら10分ぐらいおいておく。

3. Grill until nicely browned.

   焼き色がつくまで焼く。

4. Place a small mound of grated *daikon* radish alongside fish. Sprinkle soy sauce over fish and *daikon*.

   アジを皿にとり、大根おろしを添え、醤油を少々かける。

♥ **By the way:** Salt-grilling also works nicely with other kinds of fish, like saury or sardine.

アジの代わりに、サンマやイワシを塩焼きにしてもおいしい。

KETCHUP GINGER FISH FRY
アジのケチャップ煮

Serves 4   4人分   30 min.   30分   232 kcal

4 whole horse mackerel (*aji*)   アジ   4尾

$\frac{2}{3}$ cup flour (*komugiko*)   小麦粉   カップ$\frac{2}{3}$

4 Tbsp. ketchup   ケチャップ   大さじ4

1 Tbsp. sugar   砂糖   大さじ1

1 Tbsp. *mirin* (sweet saké)   みりん   大さじ1

$1\frac{1}{2}$ Tbsp. Worcestershire sauce   ウスターソース   大さじ$1\frac{1}{2}$

1 Tbsp. soy sauce   醤油   大さじ1

1 tsp. grated ginger   おろししょうが   小さじ1

1. Remove horse mackerel heads. Clean and scale the fish (page 224). Score a couple of diagonal cuts in the body (*see* illustration).

   包丁でアジの頭を切りおとし、うろことぜいご、はらわたを取り除き（224頁参照）、図のように切れ目を入れる。

deep fry

2. Coat with flour and deep fry in oil heated to 350°F (170–180°C).

   ① に薄く小麦粉をまぶし、170〜180℃の油で揚げる。

3. Combine ketchup, sugar, *mirin*, Worcestershire sauce, soy sauce and grated ginger in a frying pan, heat.

   フライパンにケチャップ、砂糖、みりん、ウスターソース、醤油、おろししょうがを入れ火にかけ、まぜる。

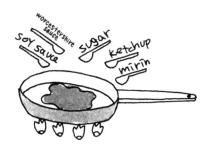

Worcestershire sauce   soy sauce   sugar   ketchup   mirin

4. Add the fried horse mackerel to ③ and continue to heat, while stirring, 1 minute.

   ③ の中に揚がったアジを入れて、1分ほどからめる。

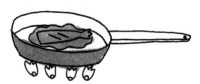

1 minute.

SARDINE MISO PATTIES
イワシの味噌ハンバーグ

Serves 4　4人分　40 min.　40分　　　　　　　　　255 kcal

8 whole fresh sardines　イワシ　8尾

½ onion (*tamanegi*)　玉ねぎ　½個

½ carrot　にんじん　½本

1 egg　卵　1個

1 tsp. flour (*komugiko*)　小麦粉　小さじ1

1 Tbsp. white miso (*shiromiso*)　白味噌　大さじ1

1 Tbsp. ginger juice　しょうが汁　大さじ1

4 Tbsp. grated *daikon* radish　大根おろし　大さじ4

1 Tbsp. vegetable oil　サラダ油　大さじ1

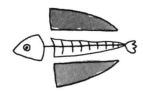

1. Fillet each sardine (page 225). Grind fillets in a mortar.

   イワシを三枚におろし（225頁参照）、身をすり鉢でよくする。

2. Mince the onion and carrot.

   玉ねぎとにんじんはみじん切りにしておく。

3. Add onion and carrot from ②, as well as the white miso, ginger juice, flour and egg to the mortar. Mix well.

   ① に ② の玉ねぎとにんじん、白味噌、しょうが汁、小麦粉、卵を加えよくまぜる。

4. Form ③ into 4 patties. Heat oil in a frying pan and sauté patties till both sides are nicely done.

   ③ を4つに分け、だ円形にする。フライパンに油を熱し、両面をよく焼く。

5. Add a small mound of grated *daikon* radish to the side of the plate.

   大根おろしを添えて、皿に盛る。

Note: For ginger juice, grate some fresh ginger root, and squeeze.
しょうが汁はすりおろしたしょうがをしぼってつくる。

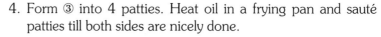

SARDINE ROLLS

イワシロール

Serves 4　4人分　30 min.　30分　　　　　　　　　157 kcal

4 whole fresh sardines　イワシ　4尾

pinch each, salt and pepper　塩、こしょう　少量

2 Tbsp. miso　味噌　大さじ2

½ Tbsp. white sesame seeds　白ごま　大さじ½

1 Tbsp. minced onion (*tamanegi*)　玉ねぎのみじん切り　大さじ1

½ tsp. ginger juice　しょうが汁　小さじ½

8 perilla (*shiso*) leaves　青じそ（大葉）　8枚

2 Tbsp. flour (*komugiko*)　小麦粉　大さじ2

1 Tbsp. vegetable oil　サラダ油　大さじ2

---

1. Fillet each sardine (page 225).

   イワシを三枚におろし（225頁参照）、塩、こしょうする。

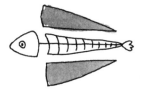

2. Add miso, sesame seeds, minced onion and ginger juice, mix.

   味噌、白ごま、玉ねぎのみじん切り、しょうが汁を合わせてまぜる。

3. Cover each sardine fillet with 1 *shiso* leaf, and flavor it by dipping it into ②. Roll and secure with a toothpick.

   イワシの身の上にしそをのせ、②をのせる。それを巻いて、ようじでとめる。

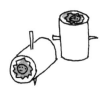

4. Dust with flour. Heat oil in a frying pan and sauté the sardine rolls.

   ③に小麦粉をまぶし、油を熱しフライパンで焼く。

WHITE FISH WITH PICKLED PLUM SAUCE

梅干しあんかけ揚げ魚

Serves 4 4人分 30 min. 30分   281 kcal

1 lb. white fish 白身の魚 400g

A

	Seasoning:

Seasoning:

1 tsp. ginger juice しょうが汁 小さじ1

2 tsp. saké 酒 小さじ2

pinch salt 塩 少量

B

Pickled plum sauce: 梅干しあん

10 pickled plums (*umeboshi*) 梅干し 10個

6 Tbsp. sugar 砂糖 大さじ6

½ cups water 水 カップ½

dash soy sauce 醤油 少量

1 Tbsp. *mirin* (sweet saké) みりん 大さじ1

2 Tbsp. starch 片栗粉 大さじ2

C

Coating for fish: 衣

1 egg 卵 1個

3 Tbsp. water 水 大さじ3

5 Tbsp. flour (*komugiko*) 小麦粉 大さじ5

oil for deep frying 揚げ油

1. Remove bones from white fish and cut fish, on the diagonal, into slices ¾-in. (2 cm.) wide.

   白身の魚の骨を除き、2cmくらいの大きさのそぎ切りにする。

2. Combine Ⓐ and mix to make the seasoning. Sprinkle over fish.

   Ⓐ の調味料を切った魚の上にふりかける。

3. Remove the stones from the pickled plums and crush the

fruit into a paste. Combine and mix Ⓑ to make the plum sauce. Add the crushed fruit to the plum sauce. Bring fruit and sauce to a simmer in a small saucepan. Thicken the sauce with a little starch mixed with water (1 part starch to 2 parts water).

梅干しの種を取り除き、実をよくつぶす。Ⓑ の調味料をまぜ合わせ煮立てる。そこに2倍の水で溶いた片栗粉を加えて、梅干しあんを作る。

4. Pat white fish dry with paper towels and dust with flour. Combine and mix Ⓒ to make the coating. Coat fish with Ⓒ and deep fry.

魚の水気をペーパータオルでふきとり、小麦粉をまぶしてからⒸの衣にくぐらせ、180℃の油で表面がからっとするまで揚げる。

5. Arrange ④ on a plate and spoon the hot plum sauce from ③ over.

④ を器に盛り、③ の温かい梅干しあんをかける。

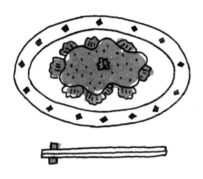

PEPPER SALMON
ピーマンとサケの変わり揚げ

Serves 4　4人分　20 min.　20分　　　　　　　　259 kcal

4 salmon steaks　サケ　4切れ

2 green peppers　ピーマン　2個

a small amount of red chili pepper (*tōgarashi*)　赤唐がらし　少量

pinch each, salt and pepper　塩、こしょう　少量

1 Tbsp. saké　酒　大さじ1

2 Tbsp. flour (*komugiko*)　小麦粉　大さじ2

1 egg, beaten　卵　1個

2 Tbsp. bread crumbs　パン粉　大さじ2

oil for deep frying　揚げ油

Worcestershire or soy sauce　ウスターソースか醤油

1. Mince both the green and the dried chili peppers. Combine peppers in a small mixing bowl, sprinkle with salt and saké.

   ピーマンと赤唐がらしをみじん切りにしてボールに入れ、塩、酒を加えてまぜ合わせる。

2. Cut each salmon steak into thirds. Cut almost all the way through the middle of each piece, horizontally, so that the salmon folds open. Lift fold, and sprinkle some pepper inside.

   切り身は3等分にし、厚みの半分に切り、こしょうをふる。

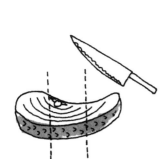

3. Place a small amount of mixture ① into the pocket of each piece.

   切り込みの中に ① を少量入れる。

4. Coat stuffed salmon pieces with flour, beaten egg and bread crumbs, in that order.

   切り身に小麦粉、溶き卵、パン粉の順で衣をつける。

5. Deep fry in oil heated to 350°F (180°C), till light brown.

   サケを180℃に熱した油で、きつね色になるまで揚げる。

❤ **By the way:** Sprinkle with Worcestershire or soy sauce, as you prefer.
ウスターソースや醤油など好みでつけてたべる。

Seafood

海産物

BUTTER SHRIMP

エビのバター焼き

Serves 4　4人分　20 min.　20分　　　　　　　　　　　134 kcal

8 raw jumbo shrimp in the shell (1¼ lb.)　くるまエビ　8尾（殻つき 560g）

4 Tbsp. butter　バター　大さじ4

2 garlic cloves　にんにく　2かけ

2 Tbsp. lemon juice　レモン汁　大さじ2

salt and pepper　塩、こしょう

1 stalk parsley　パセリ　1茎

bread crumbs　パン粉

1. Rinse shrimp. Remove shells, legs and heads, but leave tails on. Devein.

   エビは背わたを抜き、尾はつけたままにして殻とひげ、足、頭を取り除き、よく水洗いする。

2. In a skillet, melt butter over medium heat. Stir in pressed or minced garlic and sauté very briefly (do not brown).

   フライパンにバターを中火で溶かす。みじん切りにしたにんにくをすばやくいためる（焦がさないようにする）。

3. Add shrimp and sauté 1–2 minutes each side, till flesh turns pink.

   ② にエビを入れ、1、2分いため、全体がピンク色になったら火からおろす。

4. Pour lemon juice over, sprinkle with salt and pepper. Remove shrimp only and place on a plate.

   レモン汁をかけ、塩、こしょうし、エビだけを皿に盛る。

5. Quickly raise the heat under the skillet and boil juices till syrupy. Sprinkle with minced parsley.

   ④ を火にかけ、手早く熱して汁が濃くなったところで刻んだパセリとバターでいためたパン粉をまぜる。

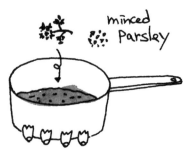

6. Pour ⑤ over shrimp. Serve immediately.

   ⑤ をエビにかけ、冷めないうちに食卓へ。

Note: At Step ⑤ you may also want to sprinkle over some bread crumbs sautéed in butter.

Step ⑤ でバターでいためたパン粉をふりかけるとこうばしい。

❤ **By the way:** If you prefer, use scallops in place of shrimp.

エビの代わりにホタテ貝柱でもどうぞ。

QUICK CRAB PLATE

とろみカニのレタス添え

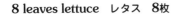

Serves 4　4人分　20 min.　20分　　　　　　　　　192 kcal

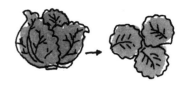

8 leaves lettuce　レタス　8枚

3½ oz. canned crab meat　カニの缶詰　100g

1 egg white　卵白　1個

1 bouillon cube　固形スープ　1個

1 cup hot water　熱湯　カップ1

2 tsp. vegetable oil　サラダ油　小さじ2

1½ Tbsp. starch　片栗粉　大さじ1½

½ tsp. salt　塩　小さじ½

⅛ tsp. pepper　こしょう　小さじ⅛

1. Tear lettuce leaves into fairly large pieces and place them in a pot of boiling water containing 1 tsp. oil. Boil about 10 seconds.

   油小さじ1を入れた沸騰湯に、大きめにちぎったレタスを10秒ゆでる。

2. Drain lettuce leaves and spread them out on a plate.

   ゆでたレタスの水気をとり、皿に並べておく。

3. Sauté the crab meat in an oiled frying pan.

   油をひいたフライパンでカニをいためる。

4. Dissolve the bouillon cube in 1 cup hot water and pour over the sautéed crab meat, season with salt and pepper.

   固形スープとカップ1の湯を ③ に加え、塩、こしょうで味を調える。

5. Dissolve starch in a little water (1 part starch to 2 parts water) and add to ④.

   ④ が熱くなったら片栗粉を2倍の水に溶いて加え、とろみをつける。

6. Add the egg white to ⑤. When egg white just begins to harden, arrange ⑤ on top of the boiled lettuce.

   ⑤ に卵白を加える。卵白がふわっと固まったら、レタスの上にのせる。

FRIED STUFFED SQUID

イカの香り焼き

Serves 4　4人分　45 min.　45分　　　　　　　308 kcal

2 whole squid　イカ　2杯

¼ onion (*tamanegi*)　玉ねぎ　¼個

1 clove garlic　にんにく　1かけかけ

1 stalk parsley　パセリ　1茎

1 stalk basil　バジル　1茎

3 Tbsp. olive oil　オリーブ油　大さじ3

A

　½ egg　卵　½個

　2 Tbsp. grated cheese　粉チーズ　大さじ2

　cup bread crumbs　パン粉　カップ

　pinch each, salt and pepper　塩、こしょう　少量

B

　2 Tbsp. butter　バター　大さじ2

　2 Tbsp. demiglace sauce　デミグラソース（缶詰）　大さじ2

　1 tsp. lemon juice　レモン汁　小さじ1

　dash water　水　少量

---

1. Remove the head, transparent backbone and sac of innards from the squid (page 126). Peel off the skin and rinse squid thoroughly. Chop legs into half-inch (1–cm.) lengths.

   イカは軟骨と内臓を抜き、皮をむいてよく水洗いしておく（126頁参照）。足は1cmくらいのぶつ切りにする。

2. Mince the onion, garlic, parsley and basil.

   玉ねぎ、にんにく、パセリ、バジルはみじん切りにしておく。

3. Combine the chopped legs, ② and Ⓐ to make the stuffing. Mix well. Place this mixture inside the body of the squid, secure with a toothpick.

   ぶつ切りにした足と②、Ⓐ をよくまぜ、イカに詰める。口はつまようじでとめる。

4. Heat 3 Tbsp. olive oil in a frying pan. Add the squid and stir-fry about 20 minutes.

フライパンに大さじ3のオリーブ油を熱し、転がしながら20分イカを焼く。

5. Add Ⓑ to the frying pan. Mix all ingredients and bring to a simmer.

Ⓑの材料をフライパンに入れてまぜ、煮立たせる。

6. Arrange squid on a plate and pour ⑤ over.

イカを盛りつけて、⑤ を振りかける。

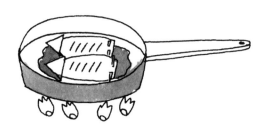

CLAM *OKARA*
あさりのおから

Serves 4　4人分　30 min.　30分　　　191 kcal

7 oz. *okara* (tofu lees)　おから　200g

4 dried *shiitake* mushrooms　干ししいたけ　4枚

½ carrot　にんじん　½本

2 deep-fried tofu pouches (*abura-age*)　油揚げ　2枚

1 can clams　あさり水煮缶詰　1缶　90g

Ⓐ

| **4 tsp. *dashi* broth**　だし　小さじ4

| **5 tsp. soy sauce**　醤油　小さじ5

| **4 Tbsp. sugar**　砂糖　大さじ4

Ⓑ

| **1 Tbsp. reserved water used to reconstitute the *shiitake* mushrooms**　干ししいたけのもどし汁　大さじ1

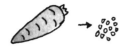

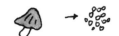

1. Pour boiled water over the *abura-age*, to reduce its oil content. Reconstitute the dried *shiitake* mushrooms by soaking them 30 minutes in 1 cup water (reserve 1 Tbsp. of the water).

   油揚げに熱湯をかけ油ぬきする。干ししいたけは、カップ1の水に30分浸けて戻す。

2. Mince the carrot, *abura-age* and *shiitake* mushrooms.

   にんじんと油揚げとしいたけを、みじん切りにする。

3. Heat the oil in a medium-sized frying pan. Fry ② and the clams, with their liquid, on low. Combine seasonings Ⓐ and add half to the frying pan.

   フライパンを熱し、②とあさりを缶の汁ごと入れる。弱火でいため、調味料Ⓐの半分の量を加える。

4. Add tofu lees and Ⓑ, cook on low. Add the other half of Ⓐ and continue to heat.

   おからとⒷを加えて弱火でいため、調味料Ⓐの残りを加える。

Desserts

デザート

CASTELLA

カステラ

10 servings　10人分　90 min.　90分　　　　　　　　282 kcal

8 eggs　卵　8個

2 cups cake flour (*hakurikiko*)　薄力粉　カップ2（200g）

2¾ cups sugar　砂糖　カップ2¾（300g）

3 Tbsp. milk　牛乳　大さじ3

4 Tbsp. honey　はちみつ　大さじ4

① Cut into square 7 or 8 newspapers

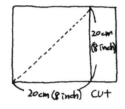

② Cut line —
Hold line……

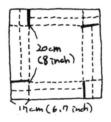

③ Make a box with 7 or 8 sheets and put z aluminum foil (50 cm. 19.7 inch) in it

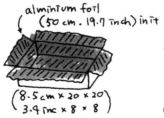

• 新聞紙 7.8枚重ね
全面に広げ正方形に切る.
図のように箱（8.5 x 20 x 20）
を作りアルミハクをしく.

1. Add the honey to the milk, and mix. In a small saucepan, heat over a low flame. Just before mixture comes to a boil, turn off the heat.

   小鍋に牛乳にはちみつをまぜ、弱火にかける。沸騰する寸前で火を止める。

2. Break the eggs into a small mixing bowl and add the sugar. Beat about 10 minutes with a hand-held electric mixer, till stiff. Add ① and beat a few more minutes.

   ボールに卵を割り入れ、砂糖を加える。ハンドミキサーで約10分、かたくなるまで泡立て、① を加え、さらに数分続ける。

3. Add sifted cake flour gradually and beat 2 to 3 minutes on medium. Pour into a mold made from sheets of newspaper.

   ふるった薄力粉を少しずつ加え、ミキサーを中速にして2～3分間泡立てたら、新聞紙で作った型に入れる。

4. Bake 8 to 10 minutes on the upper rack of an oven heated to 350°F (180°C).

   180℃に熱しておいたオーブンの上段で8～10分間焼く。

5. Move mold down to the lower rack. Lower the oven temperature to 325°F (160°C) and bake 1 more hour.

   ④ をオーブンの下段に移し、160℃で60分間焼く。

6. Take castella out of the oven and tear open the aluminum foil right away. Cover the castella, while it's still warm, with plastic wrap.

   すぐにアルミホイルをはがし、熱いうちにラップで包む。

EASY APPLE CAKE
簡単りんごケーキ

Serves 8　8人分　60 min.　60分　　　　　　　　　495 kcal

3 eggs　卵　3個

$2\frac{1}{4}$ cup sugar　砂糖　カップ$2\frac{1}{4}$（250g）

1 cup vegetable oil　サラダ油　カップ1

2 apples　りんご　2個

$2\frac{2}{3}$ cups cake flour (*hakurikiko*)　薄力粉　カップ$2\frac{2}{3}$（270g）

1 Tbsp. baking powder　ベーキングパウダー　大さじ1（10g）

dash vanilla　バニラエッセンス　少量

9–in. square baking pan　20 cm x 20 cmの型

---

1. Peel and core the apples. Cut into half-inch dice.
   りんごの皮をむき、芯を除き1cm角のさいの目に切る。

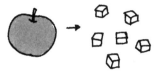

2. Beat the eggs in a small bowl. Add vegetable oil and vanilla, mix.
   小さめのボールで卵を割り溶き、サラダ油とバニラエッセンスを加えてまぜる。

3. In a separate bowl, combine sugar, cake flour and baking powder. Mix well and add to ②.
   別のボールで、砂糖、薄力粉、ベーキングパウダーをよくまぜ②に加える。

mix all the ingredients

4. Fold the diced apples into ③.
   ① のりんごを ③ に加える。

5. Pour ④ into an oiled baking pan.
   ④ をサラダ油をぬった天板か耐熱皿に流し込む。

6. Bake 40 minutes in an oven preheated to 350°F (180°C).
   あらかじめ180℃に温めておいたオーブンで40分焼く。

Bake at 180° for 40 minutes.

STEAMED CHESTNUT CAKE
栗入り蒸しケーキ

5 servings 5人分 60 min. 60分 458 kcal

½ cup butter　バター　カップ½（100g）

1 cup sugar　砂糖　カップ1（100g）

3 egg yolks　卵黄　3個

2 egg whites　卵白　2個

5 Tbsp. milk　牛乳　大さじ5（85cc）

7 oz. sweet chestnuts, bottled (*kuri no kanro-ni*)　栗の甘露煮　200g

2 cups bread crumbs　パン粉　カップ2（100g）

dash vanilla　バニラエッセンス　少量

small rectangular cake tin　25cmのパウンドケーキ型

1. Lightly butter the sides of the pan and lay a sheet of wax paper along the bottom.

   ケーキ型の内側にバターを塗って、底にクッキングシートを敷く。

2. Soften butter to room temperature. Cut up the chestnuts finely.

   バターを室温にもどしておき、栗は細かくきざんでおく。

3. Knead the butter in a small mixing bowl, till creamy.

   ボールにバターを入れ、クリーム状になるまで練る。

4. Add sugar a little at a time and mix well until creamy.

   少しずつ砂糖を入れ、やわらかくなるまでまぜる。

5. Add egg yolks, vanilla and milk gradually, mixing well with each addition.

   卵黄とバニラエッセンスと牛乳を少しずつ加え、よくまぜる。

6. Add chestnuts and bread crumbs, mix briefly.

   栗とパン粉を加え、さっとまぜる。

7. Place the bowl of egg whites inside another bowl, of ice water. Beat the egg whites until they stiffen.

   卵白を入れたボールの底が別のボールに入れた氷水にあたるようにして、角が立つまで泡立てる。

206

8. Fold ⑥ into ⑦. Mix with just a few strokes and pour into the pan.

   ⑥ を ⑦ に加え、さっくりとまぜ、それをケーキ型に入れる。

9. Butter one side of a sheet of aluminum foil and cover the top of the tin with it (buttered side down).

   アルミホイルの内側にバターを塗り、ケーキ型にかぶせる。

10. Place the cake in a preheated steamer and steam on medium 30 to 40 minutes.

    湯気の立っている蒸し器に入れ、中火で30分から40分蒸す。

CANDIED KUMQUATS

キンカンの甘露煮

Serves 4 4人分 40 min. 40分 316 kcal

1 lb. kumquats (*kinkan*) キンカン 500g

2 cups *shōchū* (Japanese distilled liquor) 焼酎 カップ2

2¼ cups sugar 砂糖 カップ2¼（250g）

1. Rinse the kumquats and blot them dry with paper towels. Poke holes in them here and there with a fork.

   キンカンを流水で洗いペーパータオルなどで水気をふき、フォークで穴をあける。

2. Combine all ingredients in a saucepan (if available, enameled or glass is best).

   すべての材料を鍋に入れる。鍋は、できればホーローかガラス製のものがよい。

3. Cover ② with a drop-lid (page 229) made of Japanese paper and simmer 30 minutes.

   ②に和紙で落とし蓋（229頁参照）をし、30分間煮る。

4. Let kumquats cool for a few minutes. Store refrigerated in a glass jar or other container.

   煮えたものを冷やしてびんなどに入れ、冷蔵庫で保存する。

❤ **By the way:** This dish keeps very well in the refrigerator. It's full of vitamin C and is good for keeping skin clear and preventing colds.

冷蔵庫に入れておけば保存が効く。ビタミンCが多いので、美容とかぜの予防などにもよい。

DAIKON HONEY GELATIN

大根のはちみつゼリー

Serves 4　4人分　15 min.　15分　　　　　　　　　　　　81 kcal

1⅔ oz. *daikon* radish　大根　50g

4 Tbsp. honey　はちみつ　大さじ4

1 Tbsp. gelatin　粉ゼラチン　大さじ1

4 Tbsp. white wine　白ワイン　大さじ4

mint leaves　ミントの葉

1. Soak the gelatin in white wine. Then heat the mixture in a ladle held carefully into a pot of water heating on the stove. When gelatin dissolves, remove from heat, combine with the honey and mix well.

   白ワインの中に粉ゼラチンを入れふやかしておく。それを器ごと、湯を入れた鍋につけ（湯せんにする）溶かす。溶けたらはちみつをまぜる。

2. Peel and grate the *daikon* radish, reserving both solids and liquids.

   皮をむいた大根をおろす。

3. Fold ② into ① and stir through gently, till mixture is smooth and creamy.

   ①と②を合わせ、なめらかになるまで泡立てないようにまぜる。

4. Spoon into 4 glasses and refrigerate to set. Just before serving, garnish with mint leaves.

   それを4つのグラスに分け、冷蔵庫で冷やす。仕上げにミントの葉を飾る。

POTATO DOUGHNUTS
ポテトドーナッツ

Serves 8 8人分 40 min. 40分 **511 kcal**

2 cups hot mashed potatoes (from flakes) マッシュポテト（市販のフレーク状のもの） カップ**2**

1 cup sugar 砂糖 カップ**1**

1 egg 卵 **1**個

1 cup heated milk 温めた牛乳 カップ**1**

½ cup butter バター **100g**

¼ tsp. salt 塩 小さじ**¼**

½ tsp. ground nutmeg ナツメグ 小さじ**½**

1 tsp. baking powder ベーキングパウダー 小さじ**1**

3½ cups cake flour (*hakurikiko*) 薄力粉 カップ**3½**

vegetable oil for deep frying 揚げ油（サラダ油）

1. Combine sugar, softened butter, milk and eggs in a large bowl and mix. Fold in the mashed potatoes.

   砂糖、室温でやわらかくしたバター、牛乳、卵を大きなボールに入れてまぜる。それにマッシュポテトを加えてさらによくまぜる。

2. In a small bowl, sift the baking powder, nutmeg, salt and cake flour together and add to ①, to make the batter. (Batter will be quite soft.)

   ① に、ベーキングパウダー、ナツメグ、塩、薄力粉を合わせてふるったものを入れまぜ、やわらかめの生地を作る。

3. Form ② into whatever shapes you like.

   ② を好みの形に作る。

4. Deep fry ③ in oil heated to 350°F (170–180°C) till golden brown, about 2 minutes.

   ③ を170～180℃に熱しておいた油できつね色になるまで、約2分揚げる。

5. Drain on paper towels. Serve piping hot.

   ペーパータオルにとり油を切ったら、温かいうちに食べる。

SWEET POTATO CHESTNUT BALLS
栗かのこ

Serves 4　4人分　80 min.　80分　　　　　　　　232 kcal

---

10 oz. sweet potatoes (*satsumaimo*)　さつまいも　大1本
（**300g**）

¾ cup sugar　砂糖　カップ¾（80g）

½ tsp. salt　塩　小さじ½

10 sweet chestnuts, bottled (*kuri no kanro-ni*)　栗の甘露煮
10粒（ビン詰）

---

1. Peel sweet potatoes. Cut them into slices half an inch thick.
   Soak them in a bowl of cold water for 30 minutes.

   さつまいもの皮をむき、1cm厚さくらいに輪切りし、30分間水
   にさらす。

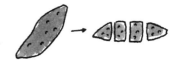

2. Place sliced sweet potatoes in saucepan and add water to
   cover. Bring to a simmer and cook until potatoes soften.
   Drain.

   さつまいもを鍋に入れ、かぶるくらいの水を加え、やわらかく
   なるまで煮た後、湯を捨てる。

3. While potatoes are hot, add 2 Tbsp. sugar and mash. Then
   push the potato mixture through a sieve. Add the remaining
   sugar and the salt.

   ② が熱いうちに大さじ2の砂糖を加えて、潰し、裏ごしをした
   後、残りの砂糖と分量の塩を加えて木べらかスプーンでまぜる。

4. Mix with a spatula or a wooden spoon until firm. When mixture cools, form it into 4 balls.

   固くなるまでよく練りあげ ③ が冷えたら、4つに分けてボール
   の形に丸める。

5. Cut chestnuts in half lengthwise. Press 5 halves into each
   sweet potato ball.

   栗を縦に半分に切る。さつまいもボールに切った栗を5個ずつ
   押しつけて飾りつける。

❤ **By the way:** This dessert goes nicely with green tea.

これはお茶にピッタリのデザート。

CHEESECAKE
チーズケーキ

Serves 4　4人分　30 min.　30分　　　　　　　　　　　445 kcal

1 cup cream cheese　クリームチーズ　カップ**1**

½ cup unsalted butter　無塩バター　カップ½

½ cup powdered sugar　パウダーシュガー　カップ½

1 egg　卵　1個

1 Tbsp. lemon juice　レモン汁　大さじ1

2 Tbsp. milk　ミルク　大さじ2

⅓ cup cake flour (*hakurikiko*)　薄力粉　カップ⅓（30g）

1 tsp. baking powder　ベーキングパウダー　小さじ1

4 tsp. cocoa powder　ココアパウダー　小さじ4

9–in. round baking pan　直径20cmのケーキ型

1. Oil pan's bottom and sides. Soften butter and cream cheese.
   バターを薄く型の側面と底に塗る。バターとクリームチーズは使いやすいように室温でやわらかくしておく。

2. In a blender, mix butter, cream cheese and powdered sugar.
   ミキサーでバター、クリームチーズ、パウダーシュガーをまぜる。

3. Beat the egg and add it to ② in 2 steps, mixing 10–20 seconds each time. Then add lemon juice and milk, mix again.
   レモン汁、牛乳を加えてさらにまぜる。

4. Sift cake flour and baking powder together. Add to ③, mix.
   薄力粉とベーキングパウダーは合わせてふるっておき、ミキサーに加え10秒まぜる。

5. Pour ⅔ of ④ into a bowl. Add cocoa to the other ⅓, mix.
   ④ から⅔をボールに取り、残りのココアをまぜる。

6. Pour mixture with no cocoa into pan first, and pour cocoa mixture over, diagonally, for a marbleing effect. Bake about 20 minutes at 400°F (200°C).
   ⑤ の⅔の生地を型に入れ、その上にココア生地を斜め模様に流し、200℃に温めておいたオーブンで約20分焼く。

ZWIEBACK CHEESECAKE
ビスケット台のチーズケーキ

Serves 4　4人分　60 min.　60分　　　　　　　500 kcal

10 slices zwieback　ビスケット　10枚（甘さの少ないもの、マリービスケットなど）

3 Tbsp. butter　バター　大さじ3

$1\frac{1}{4}$ cups cream cheese　クリームチーズ　カップ$1\frac{1}{4}$

$\frac{1}{2}$ cup sour cream　サワークリーム　カップ$\frac{1}{2}$

$\frac{1}{2}$ cup sugar　砂糖　カップ$\frac{1}{2}$

1 Tbsp. lemon juice　レモン汁　大さじ1

1 egg　卵　1個

9-in. round baking pan　直径20cmのケーキ型

1. Soften the butter and cream cheese to room temperature.

   バターとクリームチーズは室温に戻しておく。

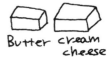

Butter cream cheese

2. Place zwieback in a clear plastic bag and close with a twist-tie. Pound gently on the bag till zwieback are crushed.

   ビニール袋の中にビスケットを入れて上からたたき、細かく砕く。

3. In a small mixing bowl, combine ② with the butter from ①. To make the crust, lay this mixture into the baking pan and spread it out and press it down evenly with your fingers.

   ② と ① のバターをボールに入れてまぜ合わせ、型の底に指で押さえるようにして平らにひく。

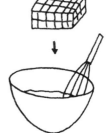

4. In another small bowl, beat the cream cheese well with a wooden spoon.

   クリームチーズを別のボールに入れ、木べらで練る。

5. Add sour cream, sugar, lemon juice and egg to ④, mix till smooth.

   ④ にサワークリーム、砂糖、レモン汁、卵を加えて、なめらかになるまでまぜ合わせる。

Add. lemon juice
sugar
Sour cream

6. Pour ⑤ over the crust prepared in ③.

   ③ の型に ⑤ を流し込む。

7. Bake 20–25 minutes in an oven heated to 350°F (170–180°C).

   170〜180℃に温めたオーブンで20〜25分間焼く。

CHOCOLATE BREAD PUDDING
パンチョコプリン

Serves 8　8人分　40 min.　40分　　　　　　　　　　416 kcal

8 slices bread　パン　8枚

dash vegetable oil　サラダ油　少量

3 eggs　卵　3個

3 cups milk　牛乳　カップ3

⅓ cup sugar　砂糖　カップ⅓

½ tsp. vanilla extract　バニラエッセンス　小さじ½

1½ cups semisweet chocolate chips　セミスイートチョコレートチップ　カップ1½

9–in. round baking pan　直径20cmのケーキ型

180° (350° F)

1. Lightly oil the bottom of the baking pan.

   型にサラダ油をぬっておく。

2. Cut the bread into ¾-in. (1.5-cm.) cubes. Lay the cubes into the bottom of ①.

   食パンを1.5cm角くらいに切り、① に入れる。

3. Combine the milk, sugar and eggs in a mixing bowl. Mix well and pour over ②.

   牛乳、砂糖、卵をボールに入れ、よくまぜたものを ② の上からかける。

4. Scatter chocolate chips over ③.

   チョコレートチップを ③ にちらす。

5. Bake in an over preheated to 350°F (170–180°C) about 35 minutes, till pudding is firm but still moist on the inside and top is a golden brown. Serve warm.

   170～180℃くらいに熱したオーブンで、プリンの表面に軽くこげ目がつき、中がしっとり仕上がるまで30分ほど焼く。

RAISIN BREAD PUDDING
レーズンブレッドプディング

Serves 4　4人分　20 min.　20分　　　　　　　　　283 kcal

4 slices raisin bread　レーズン食パン　4枚

2 eggs　卵　2個

2 cups heated milk　温めた牛乳　カップ2

½ cup sugar　砂糖　カップ½

dash vanilla　バニラエッセンス　少量

pinch cinnamon　シナモン　少量

2 tsp. butter　バター　小さじ2

9–in. square baking pan　20cm x 20cmのケーキ型

1. Toast the slices of bread and cut each into 4 triangles.
   食パンを焼いて4つの三角形に切る。

2. In a small bowl, combine and mix the heated milk and the eggs, sugar, vanilla and cinnamon.
   ボールに卵、砂糖、温めた牛乳、バニラエッセンス、シナモンを入れてまぜる。

3. Lightly butter 4 ovenproof dishes. Place 4 triangles of bread on each dish and pour the mixture over.
   耐熱容器4皿にバターを薄く塗り、パンを入れ、② を注ぐ。

4. Bake in a toaster oven for 10 to 20 minutes (or in a convection oven at 350°F/180°C about 10 minutes), till top is golden.
   オーブントースターで約10〜20分焼く。オーブンなら180℃で、10分くらい軽くこげ目がつくまで。

DESSERT RICE BALLS (*OHAGI*)

三色おはぎ（あんこ・きなこ・ごま）

Serves 6   6人分   60 min.   60分   467 kcal

---

2 cups glutinous rice (*mochi-gome*)   もち米   カップ2 （320g）

2½ cups water   水   カップ2½ （500cc）

A

| **Adzuki mixture**   あんの材料

| **1⅓ cups adzuki (*azuki*) beans**   あずき   カップ1⅓ （200g）

| **4 cups water**   水   カップ4

| **1 cup sugar**   砂糖   カップ1

| **½ tsp. salt**   塩   小さじ½

B

| **Soybean flour coating**   きな粉衣の材料

| **½ cup soybean flour (*kinako*)**   きな粉   カップ½

| **¼ cup sugar**   砂糖   カップ¼

| **½ tsp. salt**   塩   小さじ½

C

| **Sesame seed coating**   ごま衣の材料

| **4 Tbsp. black, roasted sesame seeds**   炒り黒ごま   大さじ4

| **2 Tbsp. sugar**   砂糖   大さじ2

---

1. Soak the adzuki beans overnight in a pot filled with a fairly large amount of water. Then heat the pot for 5 minutes on high and discard the water. Fill the pot with new water, in a 1–1 ratio with beans, and heat until beans are soft enough to be crushed between your fingers. Discard water again and use a wooden spoon to crush beans while adding the sugar and cooking on medium. Add salt. Keep stirring till most of the liquid boils down.

   たっぷりの水に浸けて一晩おいたあずきを新たに多めの水に浸し、強火で5分煮立て、ゆで汁を捨てる。その豆に分量の水を加え、指であずきがつぶれるくらいにやわらかくなるまで煮る。その後、残った煮汁を捨て、木ベラでつぶしながら砂糖を入れ中火で煮る。その中に塩を入れ、まぜながら水分をとばし、「あん」をつくる。

2. Rinse and soak the glutinous rice. Drain and cook it as you would any rice (page 220). When rice is done, crush about half the grains, leaving half intact.

もち米は洗って水に浸しておく。水を切り、分量の水を加え、普通のご飯と同様に炊きあげる（220頁参照）。炊きあがったもち米を粒が残る程度に潰す。

3. Shape rice into 18 balls, each about the size of an egg. Push a grape-sized ball of the adzuki mixture from Step ① into 6 of the balls, and smooth the rice around it.

潰したもち米で8個の楕円形のだんごをつくる。そのうちの6つには、① の "あん" を直径2cmくらいに丸めたものを入れる。

4. Coat the palm of your hand with the rest of the adzuki mixture from ① and roll 6 of the balls not containing adzuki, coating them in it. Then make the soybean flour coating Ⓑ and roll the other 6 balls in it.

残りのだんごのうち6つは、あんを手のひらに広げて包み、あとの6つは Ⓑ をまぜてつくったきな粉をまぶす。

5. Make sesame seed mixture Ⓒ and roll the balls from Step ③ in it, to coat them.

あん入りの6つのだんごに Ⓒ をまぜてつくったごまをまぶす。

6. Set all 18 balls out in an attractive way on a plate.

器に三色のおはぎを盛りつける。

Note: Be careful not to add the sugar too early. Let beans soften first, since they won't soften any further once sugar is added.

あずきがやわらくならないうちに砂糖を入れると、それ以上やわらくならないので注意。

RICE CREAM
ご飯のアイス

6 servings　6人分　300 min.　300分　　　　　　　246 kcal

1$\frac{2}{3}$ cups steamed rice　ご飯　180g

1$\frac{1}{2}$ cups milk　牛乳　カップ1$\frac{1}{2}$

2$\frac{1}{3}$ Tbsp. sugar　グラニュー糖　大さじ2$\frac{1}{3}$

1 cup fresh cream　生クリーム　カップ1

dash vanilla　バニラエッセンス　少量

1 Tbsp. orange curaçao　オレンジキュラソー　大さじ1

small metal bowl or pan　小ぶりの金属性ボールか鍋

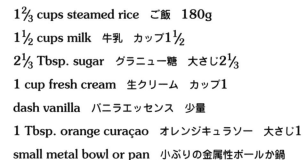

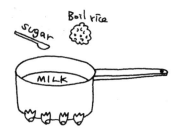

1. Place the rice and milk in a deep, sturdy saucepan and heat on high. Add the sugar and bring to a simmer. Reduce heat and simmer 15 to 20 minutes, stirring continuously to keep it from burning. Remove pan from heat and let it cool.

   ご飯と牛乳を厚手の深い鍋で強火にかけ、煮立ったらグラニュー糖を加え、弱火にして15〜20分、こげないよう木ベラなどでかきまぜながら煮て、冷ます。

2. When ① has cooled, combine it with the fresh cream in a food blender, mix till smooth.

   ① が冷めたら、生クリームを加え、ミキサーにかける。

3. Fold in the vanilla and orange curaçao. Pour the mixture into the cake tin.

   米のつぶつぶがなくなるまでまざったら、バニラエッセンスとオレンジキュラソーを入れて、型に流す。

4. Place in the freezer about 2 hours.

   ③ を冷凍庫に2時間入れる。

5. Mix with a spoon and then pat down smooth again. Return it to freezer for about 1 more hour.

   スプーンで均一になるようにかきまぜ、さらに1時間凍らす。

6. Repeat step ⑤. Rice cream is ready when it's velvety smooth.

   もう一度 ⑤ を繰り返す。なめらかになったら出来上がり。

Appendices
付録

HOW TO COOK RICE

米の炊き方

4 servings　4人分　　　　　　　　　　　　　　　　285 kcal

2 cups rice　米　カップ2（320g）	
2¼ cups water　水　カップ2¼	

Rinsing and draining

Place rice in a large bowl or pan. Add enough water to cover easily. Rinse rice by hand with a gentle kneading motion. Quickly discard water when it becomes cloudy, and add new. Repeat process 5 or 6 times till water is clear. Drain well in a colander.

とぎ方

米を大きなボールに入れ、水を十分に注ぐ。最初は、ゆっくりと米をかき回すようにして、浮いたごみを手早く流し、新しい水にとりかえて、5、6回米を握るようにとぎ、水をとりかえ2、3回同じ要領でとぐ。水が濁らなくなったらざるなどにあけよく水を切る。

Soaking

Pour 2¼ cups water over, and soak for 30 minutes. (Soaking makes rice sticky, so if you like drier rice, skip this step.)

水は、米の分量より若干多めのカップ2¼。炊きあがった米にねばりを出したいときは炊く前に30分ぐらい米を水に浸けておくとよい。

Cooking

1. Use a saucepan with a lid that fits tightly (or a rice cooker; see below). Cover and cook on high heat.

Since rice expands more than 2 to 3 times during cooking, be sure to use a deep pot with a heavy lid. Rice will boil over and will not become deliciously fluffy unless the pot is fairly deep and the lid is heavy.

炊き方

できるだけ重い蓋のついた深めの鍋を用意する。

米は、炊きあがるともとの量の2倍から3倍の量になるので、浅い鍋や、軽い蓋だと炊いている間に吹きこぼれることがあり、おいしく炊けなくなる。鍋に蓋をし強火で炊く。

Repeat 5 or 6 times

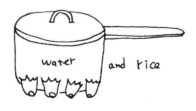

water and rice

2. When water comes to a boil, reduce heat to medium and cook 5–6 minutes.

沸騰したら中火にして5、6分炊く。

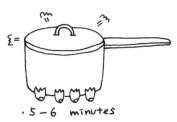

3. Reduce heat to low and cook 10–13 minutes.

さらに弱火にし、10分から13分くらい炊く。

4. Raise heat to high for 10 seconds, to cook off any remaining moisture. Take pot from heat and let pot stand 5–10 minutes on top of a dampened dishtowel, to steam. Just before serving, stir rice up gently from the bottom of the pot in a circular motion with a *shamoji* (wooden spatula). If you are not planning to use rice immediately, cover with a clean dishtowel and replace lid.

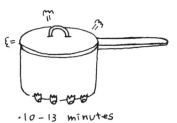

·10 – 13 minutes

最後に10秒強火にして蒸気をとばしたら鍋をおろし、5分から10分ぬれぶきんの上にのせ蒸らす。蒸らしたらしゃもじでまぜ、空気に触れさせふっくらと仕上げる。すぐに食べない場合は、鍋と蓋の間にきれいなふきんをはさんで蓋をしておく。これで余分な水分がふきんに吸収され、ご飯は水っぽくならない。

· 10 seconds

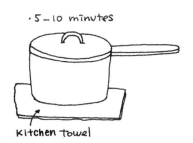

·5–10 minutes

Kitchen towel

Leftover rice can be frozen in individual portions and heated in a microwave as needed. Rice keeps nicely in the freezer for about two weeks.

ご飯が残った場合は、1人分の量ずつ冷凍して保存。食べるときに電子レンジにかける。こうしておけば、2週間は保存可能。

Nowadays most people in Japan use rice cookers. With a rice cooker, all you need to do is put in the proper amounts of washed rice and water, and press a button. The rest is automatic. In addition, the machine keeps rice warm for hours, which means that you can prepare it in advance.

ご飯を炊く場合、日本ではもっぱら自動炊飯器が使われる。とぎ終わった米と適切な分量の水さえ入れれば、あとはボタンを押すだけですべて自動的にふっくらとご飯が炊け、何時間も保温してくれる。これだと前もってご飯を炊いておけるので便利。

HOW TO MAKE *DASHI* BROTH

だしの取り方

There are 2 kinds of *dashi* made from kelp and bonito, known as primary and secondary *dashi*. Primary *dashi* is used in clear soups requiring a delicate flavor. Fuller-bodied secondary *dashi* is used as a base for simmering vegetables and as a broth for *soba* noodles. Many miso soup recipes call for kelp *dashi*, in which case either primary or secondary *dashi* can be used.

A third common type of *dashi* broth is made from dried sardines; some noodles or miso soup recipes specifically call for it.

Dashi also comes in an instant form, which is convenient even if not as delicious or nutritious. Instant *dashi* can substitute for any of the three *dashi* broths given here.

こんぶとかつお節だし・煮干しだし

こんぶとかつお節（削り節）でとるだしは、一番だしと二番だしがある。一番だしは、吸い物、味噌汁、蒸し物などに、二番だしは煮物やそばのつゆ、味噌汁などに使われる。煮干しだしは、味噌汁やうどんのつゆに使う。このほか、風味や栄養では劣るものの、インスタントのだしは、味噌汁、蒸し物、煮物、そば、うどんなどいろいろなものに使えるので便利。

KELP *DASHI*　こんぶだし

Primary *Dashi*

一番だし

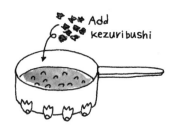

> 4 cups water　水　カップ4
>
> 6–inch length konbu kelp　出しこんぶ　40g (15cm)
>
> 3 cups dried bonito (kezuribushi) flakes　削り節　カップ3 (30g)

1. Rinse the kelp just a little by swiping at it with a damp cloth a few times. Don't wash off all the white powder, since that's what gives it flavor.

出しこんぶの表面を堅く絞ったぬれぶきんで数回ふき、表面のよごれを取る。こんぶ表面の白い粉はこんぶのうま味の素なので洗い落とさないように。

2. Combine 4 cups water and the kelp in a saucepan. If possible, let kelp soak 30 minutes before making broth. Then heat uncovered and, just before the water boils, remove kelp and set it aside. Lower flame, add the dried bonito, simmer once more. When broth boils, remove pot from heat right away and let sit for a few minutes.

鍋に水4カップとこんぶを入れる。できれば煮立てる前30分間くらい鍋の水に浸けておくとよい。鍋は蓋をせずに煮立たせ、沸騰する少し前にこんぶを取り出し、火を弱めてから削り節を入れ煮立たせる。沸騰したら火から鍋をおろし、そのまま数分おいておく。

3. Strain stock through a kitchen cloth or paper towel and set bonito aside. Yields about 4 cups of stock.

ふきんなどでだし汁をこす。削り節はとっておく。これで4カップ分のだしになり、料理に使える。

Secondary *Dashi*

二番だし

> **4 cups water** 水　カップ4
>
> **kelp and bonito reserved from the recipe above** 出しこんぶと削り節（一番だしで使用したもの）
>
> **1 cup new (unused) bonito flakes** 削り節（新たに加える分）カップ1（10g）

1. Place the kelp and bonito used once in the above recipe into a new pot of water, and heat until it begins to boil. Turn heat down to low, simmer 15–20 minutes.

一番だしで使ったこんぶと削り節を新たな水に入れ煮立たせる。煮立ったら火を弱め、15〜20分、好みの濃さで時間を加減しながら火にかける。

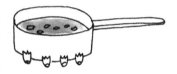

2. Add new bonito and immediately remove pot from heat. Let flakes fall to the bottom (30 seconds to 1 minute), skim foam from the surface. Strain.

新しい削り節を加え、すぐに鍋を火からおろし、30秒くらいおいて削り節が鍋底に沈むのを待つ。表面のアクをすくい取り、ふきんなどでこす。

3. Discard the solids. Yields 2–3 cups of stock.

こんぶと削り節は捨てる。これで2〜3カップの二番だしになる。

Dashi keeps in the refrigerator for about 3 days, and in the freezer for a week or two. (Pour it into an ice cube tray for easier freezer storage.)

だしは冷蔵庫で3日間くらいもち、冷凍庫では1〜2週間、さらにアイスキューブにしてフリーザーに入れておけばずっと保存がしやすくなる。

Sardine *Dashi*

煮干しのだし

This sardine *dashi* broth is a variation that can be used in place of kelp *dashi* in various kinds of recipes, including miso soups and *udon* noodles.

味噌汁やうどんのつゆによく合う。

> **3 generous cups water** 水　カップ3強
>
> **20 small dried sardines** 煮干し（頭とわたを除いてでき上がり重量の2〜2.5%）　20尾

1. Select thoroughly dried sardines. Remove the heads. Snap fish open and remove the black innards.

よく乾燥した煮干しをえらび、頭と内臓（黒いわた）を取り除く。

223

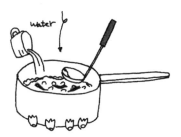

2. Place sardines in 3 generous cups water in a small saucepan and heat on medium. When liquid boils, reduce heat to low and simmer gently 4–5 minutes. Turn off heat. Skim fat and foam frequently.

カップ3強の水に13〜15gの煮干しを入れ中火にかけ、沸騰したら弱火にして静かに4〜5分煮て火を止める。煮ている間アクやアワはきれいに取り除く。

3. When sardines sink to the bottom of the pot, strain broth through a colander lined with a clean dishtowel. Yields 3 cups of stock.

煮干しが鍋底に沈んだら、ふきんを広げたボールに煮汁をあけてこす。これで、カップ3ほどのだしがとれる。

PREPARING FISH

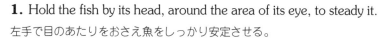

魚の下ごしらえ

Scaling Fish　うろこの引き方

1. Hold the fish by its head, around the area of its eye, to steady it.

左手で目のあたりをおさえ魚をしっかり安定させる。

2. With the blade of a kitchen knife, scrape the scales away in short strokes, from tail to head.

包丁の刃先を皮につけ、尾の方から頭に向かってうろこを逆立てるようにして削ぐ。

3. Turn the fish over and do the other side.

片方が終わったら同じように反対側もやる。

Cleaning Fish　わたの出し方

1. Insert the tip of the knife into the gill slit and cut the base of the gills free. Work the gill out.

指先でえらぶたを持ち上げ、包丁の刃先でえらのつけ根に切り込みを入れ、えらを引き出す。

2. Make a cut about 1 to 1½ in. (3 to 4 cm.) below the gill.

胸びれの下方に3、4センチの切り込みを入れる。

3. Insert the tip of the knife into the cut. Pull the entrails out through the cut.

その切り込みから刃先を入れ、わた（内臓）をていねいにかき出す。

4. Place some salt water in a shallow bowl. Place the fish in the water and use your fingers to rinse out its belly.

ボールに薄めの塩水を作り、魚を浸け、指で腹の中をきれいに洗う。

5. Wipe fish dry.

洗い終わったら水分をふき取る。

Filleting Fish　三枚おろし

1. Cut off the fish's head.

魚の頭を除く。

2. Slit open the belly and remove entrails. Rinse fish well.

腹にそって包丁を入れ内臓を除いて洗う。

3. Work the knife in next to the backbone and slide it along the length of the bone to free fillet on that side.

背と腹側から中骨にそって包丁を入れ、上側の身を切り離す。

4. Repeat for other side.

中骨のついている身も(3)の要領で骨から身を切り離す。

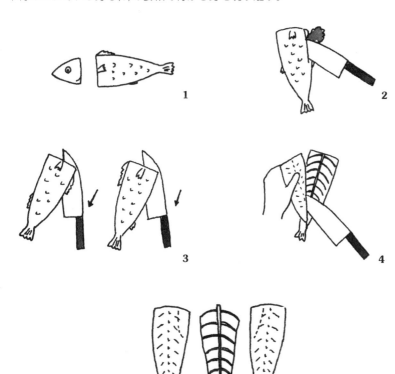

INSIDE A JAPANESE KITCHEN

台所用品

Bird's-eye view of a typical meal　日本の食卓

1	ご飯	rice	6	焼き魚	grilled fish
2	味噌汁	miso soup	7	茶碗蒸し	*chawanmushi*
3	箸	chopsticks	8	サラダ	salad
4	天ぷら	tempura	9	漬けもの	Japanese-style pickles
5	天つゆ	dipping sauce for tempura (*tentsuyu*)	10	醤油	soy sauce

万能包丁
all-purpose kitchen knife

出刃包丁
cleaver

菜切り包丁
vegetable knife

おろし金
graters

すり鉢とすりこ木
mortar and pestle

フライパン
cast-iron frying pan

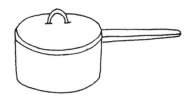

小鍋
saucepan

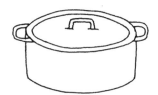

中鍋
soup pot

土鍋
earthenware pot

鉄製すきやき鍋
cast-iron *sukiyaki* pot

鉄鍋
cast-iron pot with wooden lid

ガス焼き網
range-top grill (*yakiami*)

ロースター
range-top roaster

金属製角蒸し器
Japanese-style square
metal steamer

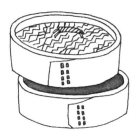

チョンロン（中国の蒸し器）
Chinese bamboo steamers

CUTTING METHODS

野菜などの切り方

斜め切り
cut on the diagonal
(*naname-giri*)

せん切り
julienne (*sen-giri*)

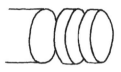

輪切り
cut into thick slices
(*wa-giri*)

みじん切り
mince (*mijin-giri*)

半月切り
cut down the middle lengthwise and then into half-moon slices (*hangetsu-giri*)

いちょう切り
cut down the middle lengthwise twice and then into quarter-slice (*ichō-giri*)

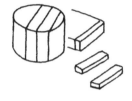

短冊(たんざく)切り
cut into thin rectangular blocks (*tanzaku-giri*)

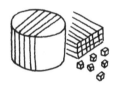

さいの目切り
dice (if half-inch or smaller); cube (if half-inch or bigger) (*sainome-giri*)

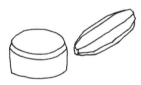

めんとり
peel and cut into plane surfaces (*mentori*)

ささがき
shave; cut into thin shavings (*sasagaki*)

ぶつ切り
chop roughly
(*butsu-giri*)

色紙(しきし)切り
cut into squares
(*shikishi-giri*)

小口(こぐち)切り
cut into thin slices
(*koguchi-giri*)

かつらむき
peel in a thin continuous sheet (*katsuramuki*)

乱(らん)切り
cut into rolling wedges (*ran-giri*)

くし形切り
cut into wedges (*kushigata-giri*)

MAKE YOUR OWN STEAMER

蒸し器

Japanese-style steamers are very different from the small, folding steamers used in the West. They are rather large and are made of several metal layers. At the bottom is a pot of water. Food is placed into a roomy middle section of one or more layers fitted over this; at the top is a lid.

Improvise your own steamer with a large soup pot or covered roaster. Remove both ends of a metal can and place the can inside the pot. Add water. Balance a heatproof metal or ceramic dish on top of the can and lay the foods to be steamed in the dish. (You may need 3 or 4 cans, depending on the amount of food.) Before placing the lid on, cover the top with a cloth, to absorb moisture that will collect there.

現在日本で一般に使われている金属製の角蒸し器は、欧米の小さな折りたたみ式蒸し器とは違ってサイズも大きく、一段あるいは二段に分かれる構造になっている。最下層で湯を沸騰させ、底板の穴を通して昇る湯気によって上段にある材料を蒸すしかけになっていて、この部分は空洞で蓋が乗る。

蒸し器がない場合には、空き缶を利用する方法がある。これは、大きめの鍋を用意し、空き缶の上下の蓋を取り去り、必要な数を鍋に据え、材料をのせた皿をその上に置く。最後に鍋に水を入れ、鍋の蓋と胴体の間にふきんをはさみ、水滴が落ちるのを防ぐようにする。

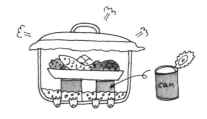

MAKE YOUR OWN DROP-LID

落とし蓋

A drop-lid is a lightweight wooden lid a little bit smaller than the pot. Place it right on top of food being simmered, to help deepen the flavor.

The drop-lid provides friction, forcing the flavor of ingredients to blend and to circulate well around the pot. Because it's made of wood, a drop-lid can rest directly on ingredients without harming the flavor. When you use one, though, be sure to rinse it with water first, to keep aromas from clinging to it.

If you don't have a drop-lid, improvise with the lid of a slightly smaller pot. Or take a piece of aluminum foil a little bigger than the pot, punch 2 or 3 holes in it and place it inside, tucking the edges over and around the ingredients.

落とし蓋は、煮物をするとき鍋のなかの材料に直接のせる木製の軽い蓋で、鍋の直径よりも小さくできている。落とし蓋をすると、煮汁はこの蓋にあたって上下よくまざり、鍋全体に味が回るようになる。木のふたは、材料に直接ふれても風味を損なうことはないが、使うときは必ず水にぬらしてから使う。乾いたままで使うと煮汁が浸透し、乾いてから煮汁のにおいがとれなくなる。落とし蓋がない場合は、鍋よりも小さい蓋を使うか、アルミホイールを鍋の直径よりも若干大きめにし、周辺を鍋の材料の周辺に差し込むようにする。

CUTS OF BEEF, PORK, CHICKEN

牛・豚・鶏の部位

On referring to meat in English

English makes very fine distinctions among parts of the animal and treatment of the meat.

However, one interesting difference between the two languages is that although we can refer in Japanese to "meat with the fat included," that same phrase is not used in English. Specific reference is made in English only to those steps which are taken to process meat in some way. So for instance, in English, rump with the fat included is simply "rump," although rump with fat removed is "rump, trimmed."

The word "lean" is used to refer to portions of the animal that contain very little fat from the start, such as top round or eye of the round.

Similarly, "chicken" would be assumed to contain the bones, unless some reference were made to removing the bones, such as "chicken, boned" or "chicken, boneless."

英語での「肉」の呼び方

英語には、肉の部位 や加工の仕方によって細かいくつもの呼び方がある。呼び方で特徴的なことは、肉が加工された場合、その加工の内容が表示されるという習慣があること。例えば、たんに "rump" といえば、「脂身のある」牛尻肉のことで、人工的に脂身が除かれたときは、"rump, trimmed" と表示される。もともと脂身が少ない「赤身」は、"lean" と呼ばれtop round（内もも肉）やeye of the round（しんたま）などが、それにあたる。同様に、鶏もも肉は骨のついた状態で売られることが一般的なので、骨を除いた場合のみ "boned" とか "boneless" と表示される。

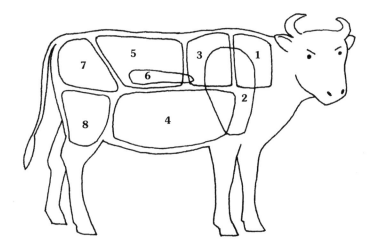

1	CHUCK	肩ロース
2	SHOULDER	肩
3	RIB	リブロース
4	FLANK	ばら
5	SIRLOIN	サーロイン
6	TENDERLOIN	ヒレ
7	RUMP	尻（ランプ）
8	ROUND	もも

1	BREAST	胸
2	INNER BREAST FILLET	ささ身
3	WING	手羽
4	THIGH	もも

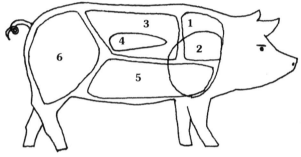

1	SHOULDER BUTT	肩ロース
2	PICNIC SHOULDER	肩
3	LOIN	ロース
4	TENDERLOIN	ヒレ
5	FLANK	ばら
6	HAM	もも

COOKING TERMS JAPANESE–ENGLISH
和英料理用語集

ア

アーモンド *(āmondo)* — almond

アーモンドスライス *(āmondosuraisu)* — almond slice

アイナメ *(ainame)* — greenling; rock trout

和える *(aeru)* — to dress; add dressing and mix [toss]

青のり *(aonori)* — aonori seaweed

赤貝 *(akagai)* — ark shell

あかかぶ *(akakabu)* — beet

アクをとる *(aku o toru)* — to improve [mellow] the flavor; remove the harshness; skim the fat

揚げる *(ageru)* — to deep fry

あさつき *(asatsuki)* — (Japanese) chive; allium

アサリ *(asari)* — short-necked clam

アジ *(aji)* — horse mackerel

味つけをする *(ajitsuke o suru)* — to season; flavor
　塩とこしょうで味つけをする *(shio to koshō de aji o tsukeru)* — to season a soup with salt and pepper

味の素 *(ajinomoto)* — monosodium glutamate [MSG]

あずき *(azuki)* — red adzuki bean

アスパラガス *(asuparagasu)* — asparagus

温める *(atatameru)* — to heat; warm

あなご *(anago)* — *anago* eel; conger eel

油 *(abura)* — oil
　—ぬきをする *(nuki o suru)* — to reduce the oil content
　—で揚げる *(de ageru)* — to deep fry in oil
　—を切る *(o kiru)* — to drain (of oil)
　—を熱する *(o nessuru)* — to heat oil
　—をひく *(o hiku)* — to oil (a frying pan, etc.)

あぶる *(aburu)* — to roast; broil; grill; toast

アマダイ *(amadai)* — red tilefish

アユ *(ayu)* — sweetfish

洗う *(arau)* — to rinse

泡立てる *(awadateru)* — to beat (eggs, etc.)

アワビ *(awabi)* — abalone

アンコウ *(ankō)* — angler; anglerfish

あんず *(anzu)* — apricot

イ

イカ *(ika)* — squid

イクラ *(ikura)* — salmon roe

石づき *(ishizuki)* — hard part at the bottom of a mushroom stem

伊勢エビ *(iseebi)* — Japanese spiny lobster

いためる *(itameru)* — to sauté
　きつね色になるまでいためる *(kitsune-iro ni naru made itameru)* — sauté till golden brown

いちじく *(ichijiku)* — fig

煎る *(iru)* — to roast; toast; cook in a (dry) frying pan till most of the liquid cooks off

イワシ *(iwashi)* — sardine

イワナ *(iwana)* — char

いんげん *(ingen)* — green bean

ウ

ウースターソース *(ūsutā sōsu)* — Worcestershire sauce

ウド *(udo)* — udo [a stout Japanese herb, the young shoots of which are used in salad]

うどん *(udon)* — (Japanese) *udon* noodle [a relatively thick white noodle made from flour, salt and water]

ウナギ *(unagi)* — (Japanese freshwater) eel

ウニ *(uni)* — sea urchin

梅 *(ume)* — (Japanese) plum

梅干し *(umeboshi)* — (Japanese) plum, pickled

裏ごしする *(uragoshi suru)* — to strain; sift

エ

枝豆 *(edamame)* — green soybean

えのきたけ *(enokitake)* — *enoki* mushroom

エビ *(ebi)* — shrimp

えんどう豆 *(endōmame)* — pea

オ

オーブントースター *(ōbun-tōsutā)* — toaster oven

オールスパイス *(ōrusupaisu)* — allspice

大さじ *(ōsaji)* — tablespoon; Tbsp.〔略〕

大皿 *(ōzara)* — platter; large plate

おから *(okara)* — tofu lees [crumbly white byproduct of tofu-making]

おく *(oku)* — to set aside; let sit

オクラ *(okura)* — okra

おじや *(ojiya)* — a simple *dashi*-based rice soup with egg

おたま *(otama)* — ladle

お茶漬け *(ochazuke)* — a simple green tea–based rice soup

おつまみ *(otsumami)* — snack; light food: finger food

落とし蓋 *(otoshibuta)* — drop-lid

おにぎり *(onigiri)* — rice ball

おやつ *(oyatsu)* — a snack; refreshments; (a child's) snack

オリーブ油 *(oribuyu)* — olive oil

おろす *(orosu)* — to grate

温度計 *(ondokei)* — thermometer

カ

解凍する *(kaitō suru)* — to thaw

貝割れ菜 *(kaiwarena)* — *daikon* radish shoot

カキ *(kaki)* — oyster

柿 *(kaki)* — (Japanese) persimmon

かき回す *(kakimawasu)* — to stir; mix well; stir up from the bottom

飾る *(kazaru)* — to decorate; garnish

カジキ *(kajiki)* — swordfish; marlin; spearfish

カシューナッツ *(kashuunattsu)* — cashew

数の子 *(kazunoko)* — herring roe

型 *(kata)* — mold

ケーキの型 *(kēki no kata)* — cake tin; baking pan

片栗粉 *(katakuriko)* — (dogtooth violet) starch

固まる *(katamaru)* — to harden; become hard [stiff]

固める *(katameru)* — to harden; make hard; freeze

カツオ *(katsuo)* — bonito

かつおぶし *(katsuobushi)* — dried bonito (flake)

かつらむきにする *(katsuramuki ni suru)* — to peel (daikon radish, etc.) in a thin continuous sheet

カニ *(kani)* — crab

かぶ *(kabu)* — turnip

かぼちゃ *(kabocha)* — (Japanese) squash; (Japanese) pumpkin [similar to acorn squash]

かまぼこ *(kamaboko)* — *kamaboko* [cake of pressed fish]

から揚げにする *(kara-age ni suru)* — to fry (without coating)

殻 *(kara)* — shell (of peanut, etc.); pod (of bean)

からし *(karashi)* — Japanese-style prepared mustard

からし菜 *(karashina)* — mustard green

カリフラワー *(karifurawā)* — cauliflower

カレー粉 *(karēko)* — curry powder

カレーソース *(karēsōsu)* — curry sauce

カレイ *(karei)* — flounder

皮 *(kawa)* — peel; skin

一をむく *(o muku)* — to remove the peel [skin]

(刃物・手で) — to peel (with a knife or by hand)

(刃物で) — to pare (with a knife)

乾かす *(kawakasu)* — to dry

かんてん *(kanten)* — agar (-agar); (Japanese) gelatin

かんぴょう *(kanpyō)* — gourd ribbon; dried gourd strip [shaved and dried bottle calabash pith]

がんもどき *(ganmodoki)* — fried tofu-and-vegetable patty

キ

きくらげ *(kikurage)* — tree cloud

きなこ *(kinako)* — soybean flour

キムチ *(kimuchi)* — kimchi

キャビア *(kyabia)* — caviar

キャベツ *(kyabetsu)* — cabbage

牛乳 *(gyūnyū)* — milk

きゅうり *(kyūri)* — cucumber

餃子 *(gyōza)* — Chinese-style dumpling

切る *(kiru)* — to cut

薄く切る *(usuku kiru)* — to slice thin

角切りにする *(kakugiri ni suru)* — to cut into cubes

細かく切る *(komakaku kiru)* — to chop finely; mince

さいの目に切る *(sainome ni kiru)* — to dice (½-in. or smaller)

せん切りにする *(sengiri ni suru)* — to julienne; cut into julienne slices

縦に切る *(tate ni kiru)* — to cut lengthwise

短冊切りにする *(tanzakugiri ni suru)* — to cut into thin rectangles

半月切りにする *(hangetsugiri ni suru)* — to cut into half-moon slices

半分に切る *(hanbun ni kiru)* — to cut in half

みじん切りにする *(mijingiri ni suru)* — to mince

横に切る *(yoko ni kiru)* — to cut crosswise

四つ切りにする *(yotsugiri ni suru)* — to quarter; cut into fourths

輪切りにする *(wagiri ni suru)* — to cut into thick slices

ぎんなん *(ginnan)* — ginkgo nut

ク

串 *(kushi)* — skewer

クジラ *(kujira)* — whale

砕く *(kudaku)* — to crush; pound; grind

グラニュー糖 *(guranyūtō)* — (granulated) sugar

くり *(kuri)* — chestnut

クリーム状にする *(cream jō ni suru)* — to cream; blend to the consistency of cream

グリーンピース *(gurinpīsu)* — (shelled) pea

くるみ *(kurumi)* — walnut

クローブ *(kurōbu)* — clove

くわい *(kuwai)* — water chestnut

加える *(kuwaeru)* — to add

ケ

計量する *(keiryō suru)* — to measure

計量カップ *(keiryō kappu)* — measuring cup

削り節 *(kezuribushi)* — dried bonito (flake)

コ

コーンスターチ *(kōnsutāchi)* — cornstarch

濃くする *(koku suru)* — to make strong [thick; rich]

固形スープ *(kokei sūpu)* — bouillon; soup stock

ココナッツ *(kokonattsu)* — coconut

小さじ *(kosaji)* — teaspoon; tsp. (略)

こしき *(koshiki)* — strainer; sieve

こしょう *(koshō)* — pepper

こしょうをふりかける *(koshō o furikakeru)* — to sprinkle with pepper

黒こしょう *(kuro-koshō)* — black pepper

白こしょう *(shiro-koshō)* — white pepper

こす *(kosu)* — to strain; pass through a sieve; sift

粉 *(kona)* — powder

粉チーズ *(kona chizu)* — grated cheese

こねる *(koneru)* — to knead; mix up (together)

ごぼう *(gobō)* — burdock root

胡麻 *(goma)* — sesame (seed)

白胡麻 *(shiro-goma)* — white sesame (seed)

黒胡麻 *(kuro-goma)* — black sesame (seed)

胡麻油 *(goma-abura)* — sesame oil

こまつな *(komatsuna)* — a variety of Chinese cabbage

小麦粉 *(komugiko)* — flour

ゴムベラ *(gomubera)* — rubber spatula

米酢 *(komesu)* — rice vinegar

衣 *(koromo)* — batter

コンソメ *(konsome)* — consomme; bouillon; soup stock

こんにゃく *(konnyaku)* — "devil's tongue jelly"

こんぶ *(konbu)* — kelp

サ

裂く *(saku)* — to tear

桜海老 *(sakuraebi)* — small shrimp

サケ *(sake)* — salmon

酒 *(sake)* — saké; Japanese rice wine

サザエ *(sazae)* — turban shell; turbo

233

ささみ *(sasami)*	chicken inner breast fillet	セロリ *(serori)*	celery
さつま芋 *(satsumaimo)*	sweet potato	ぜんまい *(zenmai)*	flowering fern
里芋 *(satoimo)*	taro; field yam		
砂糖 *(satō)*	sugar	**ソ**	
グラニュー糖 *(guranyūtō)*	(granulated) sugar	ソース *(sōsu)*	Worcestershire sauce
黒砂糖 *(kurozatō)*	brown sugar; muscovado sugar; unrefined sugar	そば *(soba)*	(Japanese) *soba* noodle [a thin, brownish gray buck-wheat noodle]
氷砂糖 *(kōrizatō)*	rock candy	そぼろ *(soboro)*	powdered fish
粉砂糖 *(konazatō)*	powdered sugar	そら豆 *(soramame)*	broad bean
サバ *(saba)*	mackerel		
サメ *(same)*	shark	**タ**	
さやえんどう *(sayaendou)*	snow pea; field pea	タイ *(tai)*	sea bream
サヨリ *(sayori)*	halfbeak	大根 *(daikon)*	*daikon* radish [giant white radish]
さらす *(sarasu)*	to soak in water to improve the flavor; [one method of blanching]	大豆 *(daizu)*	dried soybean
		炊き込みご飯 *(takikomi gohan)*	rice cooked together with other ingredients
サラダ菜 *(saradana)*	*saradana* [leafy salad green]	炊く *(taku)*	to steam; cook (rice)
サラダ油 *(saradayu)*	vegetable oil	たくわん *(takuan)*	*takuan* [pickled Japanese radish]
さんしょう *(sanshō)*	Japanese pepper tree; prickly ash	たけのこ *(takenoko)*	bamboo shoot
サンマ *(sanma)*	Pacific saury	タコ *(tako)*	octopus
		だし（汁）*(dashi-jiru)*	soup stock
シ		だしの素 *(dashi no moto)*	*dashi* broth in instant pow-dered form
しいたけ *(shiitake)*	*shiitake* mushroom		
塩 *(shio)*	salt	たたく *(tataku)*	to pound (meat, to tender-ize it)
軸 *(jiku)*	stem		
—を除く *(o nozoku)*	to remove the stem	タバスコ *(tabasuco)*	tabasco sauce
ししとうがらし *(shishitōgarashi)*	small green pepper	玉ネギ *(tamanegi)*	onion
シジミ *(shijimi)*	freshwater clam	タラ *(tara)*	cod
ししゃも *(shishamo)*	smelt	タラコ *(tarako)*	cod roe
しそ *(shiso)*	perilla leaf; Japanese mint	たらばガニ *(tarabagani)*	king crab
シタガレイ *(shitagarei)*	sole	タルタルソース *(tarutaru sōsu)*	tartar sauce
下ごしらえ *(shitagoshirae)*	prep cooking; preparations	たれ（特に酢が入ったもの）*(tare)*	gravy [particularly one containing vinegar]; sauce; broth
シナモン *(shinamon)*	cinnamon		
しぼる *(shiboru)*	to wring; squeeze		
じゃがいも *(jagaimo)*	(white) potato		
しゃもじ *(shamoji)*	(flat wooden) rice ladle	**チ**	
春菊 *(shungiku)*	(edible) spring chrysanthe-mum	ちくわ *(chikuwa)*	*chikuwa* [hollow, tube-shaped fish cake]
しょうが *(shōga)*	ginger (root)	ちくわぶ *(chikuwabu)*	*chikuwabu* [*fu* wheat gluten formed into the shape of a *chikuwa*]
紅しょうが *(benishōga)*	red pickled ginger		
焼酎 *(shōchū)*	Japanese distilled liquor		
醤油 *(shōyu)*	soy sauce	茶わん *(chawan)*	*chawan* rice bowl
薄口醤油 *(usukuchi shōyu)*	light soy sauce	朝鮮にんじん *(chosen ninjin)*	ginseng
濃口醤油 *(koikuchi shōyu)*	soy sauce	チリソース *(chiri sōsu)*	chili sauce
食紅 *(shokubeni)*	red food coloring	チリパウダー *(chiri paudā)*	chili powder
白魚 *(shirauo)*	whitebait	チリペッパー *(chiri peppā)*	red chili pepper
白子 *(shirako)*	(fish) milt	チンゲン菜 *(chingensai)*	bok choy [a variety of Chinese cabbage]
シラス干し *(shirasuboshi)*	dried young sardine		
白こしょう *(shiro-kosyō)*	white pepper		
		ツ	
ス		つける（水に）*(tsukeru)*	to dip; soak (in water, etc.)
酢 *(su)*	vinegar	漬ける *(tsukeru)*	to pickle; preserve; put up
炊飯器 *(suihanki)*	electric rice cooker	包む *(tsutsumu)*	to wrap (in); cover (with)
スズキ *(suzuki)*	sea bass	潰す（ジャガイモなどを）*(tsubusu)*	to mash (potatoes, etc.); crush
すだち *(sudachi)*	a small green citrus fruit used as a garnish		
		つめる *(tsumeru)*	to fill; package
すりこぎ *(surikogi)*	wooden pestle	缶につめる *(kan ni tsumeru)*	to can
する *(suru)*	to grind down; mash	びんにつめる *(bin ni tsumeru)*	to bottle
するめいか *(surumeika)*	dried squid		
		テ	
セ		電子レンジ *(denshi renji)*	microwave (oven)
セージ *(seiji)*	sage		
そーめん *(sōmen)*	(Japanese) *sōmen* noodle [a fine white noodle made of wheat]	**ト**	
		トースター *(tōsutā)*	toaster
ゼラチン *(zerachin)*	gelatin	とうがらし *(tōgarashi)*	red chili pepper
セリ *(seri)*	Japanese parsley		

豆腐 (tōfu)	tofu	
絹ごし豆腐 (kinugoshi-dōfu)	silken tofu	
もめん豆腐 (momen-dōfu)	firm tofu	
焼き豆腐 (yaki-dōfu)	lightly grilled tofu	
生揚げ (nama-age)	fried block of tofu	
油揚げ (abura-age)	deep-fried tofu pouch	
とうもろこし (tōmorokoshi)	corn	
溶かす (tokasu)	to dissolve, melt	
溶く（卵などを）(toku)	to beat (egg, etc.)	
とぐ（米などを）(togu)	to wash (rice)	
溶ける (tokeru)	to dissolve; melt	
ドジョウ (dojō)	loach [eel-like fish]	
トビウオ (tobiuo)	flying fish	
トマト (tomato)	tomato	
プチトマト (puchi-tomato)	cherry tomato	
トマトケチャップ (tomato kechappu)	ketchup; catsup	
トマトソース (tomato sōsu)	tomato sauce	
トマトピュレー (tomato pyurē)	tomato purée	
トマトペースト (tomato pēsuto)	tomato paste	
トラフグ (torafugu)	a variety of globefish	
トリ貝 (torigai)	cockle	
鶏肉 (toriniku)	chicken	
ドレッシング (doresshingu)	(salad) dressing	
どんぶり (donburi)	(large) *donburi* rice bowl	

ナ

長いも (nagaimo)	(Chinese) yam; cinnamon vine	
長ねぎ (naganegi)	(Japanese) leek	
なす (nasu)	eggplant	
なずな (nazuna)	shepherd's purse	
納豆 (nattō)	*nattō* [fermented soybeans]	
ナツメグ (natsumegu)	nutmeg	
鍋 (nabe)	pot: saucepan; skillet; frying pan	
圧力鍋 (atsuryoku nabe)	pressure cooker	
シチュー鍋 (shichū nabe)	stew pot	
煮込み用鍋 (nikomi-yō nabe)	sturdy soup pot [saucepan]; crock pot	
深鍋 (fuka nabe)	deep-sided pot	
鍋つかみ (nabetsukami)	potholder	
ナマズ (namazu)	catfish	
なめこ (nameko)	*nameko* mushroom	

ニ

握る (nigiru)	to squeeze; grip; press	
肉 (niku)	meat	
子牛の肉 (ko-ushi no niku)	veal	
鹿肉 (shika niku)	venison	
羊の肉 (hitsuji no niku)	mutton	
皮なし (kawa nashi)	skinned; skinless	
骨なし (hone hashi)	boned; boneless	
肉たたき (nikutataki)	mallet (for tenderizing meat)	
ニジマス (nijimasu)	rainbow trout	
ニシン (nishin)	herring	
煮干し (niboshi)	dried small sardine	
—だし (dashi)	sardine *dashi* broth	
にら (nira)	(Japanese) scallion	
煮る (niru)	to cook; heat	
弱火で煮る (yowabi de niru)	to simmer	
とろ火で煮る (torobi de niru)	to stew	
強火で煮る (tsuyobi de niru)	to boil on high (heat)	
煮込む (nikomu)	to simmer; stew	
煮詰める (nitsumeru)	to cook till boiled down	
にんじん (ninjin)	carrot	
にんにく (ninniku)	garlic	

ネ

ねかす (nekasu)	to let sit; leave	
熱する (nessuru)	to heat	

ノ

海苔 (nori)	*nori* seaweed	

ハ

バカ貝 (bakagai)	round clam	
白菜 (hakusai)	Chinese cabbage	
はさむ (hasamu)	to sandwich	
パンにハムをはさむ (pan ni hamu o hasamu)	to sandwich some ham between slices of bread	
バジル（バジリコ）(bajiru)	basil	
はす (hasu)	lotus (root)	
ハゼ (haze)	goby; mudskipper	
パセリ (paseri)	parsley	
バター (batā)	butter	
—を溶かす (~ o tokasu)	to melt butter	
—をぬる (~ o nuru)	to butter	
無塩バター (muen batā)	unsalted butter	
はちみつ (hachimitsu)	honey	
はっかの葉 (hakka no ha)	mint leaf	
発酵させる (hakkō saseru)	to ferment	
バニラエッセンス (banira essensu)	vanilla (extract)	
バニラビーンズ (banira binzu)	vanilla bean	
パプリカ (papurika)	paprika	
ハマグリ (hamaguri)	clam	
ハマチ (hamachi)	young yellowtail	
ハモ (hamo)	pike eel	
春雨 (harusame)	glass noodle	
パン粉 (panko)	bread crumb	

ヒ

火 (hi)	heat; flame	
弱火 (yowabi)	low; a low flame	
中火 (chūbi)	medium; a medium flame	
強火 (tsuyobi)	high; a high flame	
ピーナッツ (pinattsu)	peanut	
ピーマン (piman)	green pepper	
ひき肉 (hikiniku)	ground	
豚ももひき肉 (buta momo hikiniku)	ground fresh ham	
牛赤身ひき肉 (gyū akami hikiniku)	lean ground beef	
ピクルス (pikurusu)	(Western-style) pickle	
ひじき (hijiki)	a black variety of seaweed	
ピスタチオ (pisutachio)	pistachio nut	
浸す (hitasu)	to soak; steep	
ひっくり返す (hikkurikaesu)	to turn over; flip	
ひとつかみ (hito tsukami)	generous amount	
ひとつまみ (hito tsumami)	pinch; small handful	
—の塩 (no shio)	pinch of salt	
火にかける (hi ni kakeru)	to put on the stove; heat; cook	
冷やす (hiyasu)	to chill; refrigerate	
ヒラメ (hirame)	flounder	

フ

ふ (fu)	bread-like food made of wheat gluten	
ブーケルガルニ (būkerugaruni)	bouquet garni	
ふかす (fukasu)	to steam	
ふき (fuki)	coltsfoot	
フグ (fugu)	blowfish	
ふたをする (futa o suru)	to cover	
沸騰させる (futtō saseru)	to bring to a boil	

235

フナ (funa)		carp
ふやかす (fuyakasu)		to soak; steep
ブリ (buri)		yellowtail
ふりかける (furikakeru)		to sprinkle
ふるい (furui)		sieve; sifter
ふるいにかける (furui ni kakeru)		to sieve; sift; put through a sieve [sifter]
ブロッコリー (burokkori)		broccoli

ヘ

ベーキングパウダー (bēkingu paudā)		baking powder
ベーコン (bēkon)		bacon
紅花油 (benibanayu)		safflower oil
ペパーミント (pepāminto)		peppermint
へら (hera)		spatula

ホ

ホウボウ (hōbō)		gurnard
ほうれん草 (hōrensō)		spinach
干し柿 (hoshigaki)		dried persimmon
干し椎茸 (hoshishiitake)		dried *shiitake* mushroom
干しぶどう（レーズン） (hoshibudō)		dried grape
ホッケ (hokke)		atka mackerel
ボラ (bora)		mullet
ポン酢 (ponzu)		shaddock vinegar

マ

マーガリン (māgarin)		margarine
まいたけ (maitake)		*maitake* mushroom
前もって温める (maemotte atatameru)		to preheat
まく (maku)		to sprinkle
マグロ (maguro)		tuna
マス (masu)		sea trout
混ぜる (mazeru)		to mix
泡立つように混ぜる (awadatsu yō ni mazeru)		to beat until frothy
かき混ぜる (kakimazeru)		to beat
軽くかき混ぜる (karuku kakimazeru)		to mix gently
ざっくり混ぜる (zakkuri mazeru)		to fold in a few quick strokes
均一になるように混ぜる (kin'itsu ni naru yō ni mazeru)		to mix well until blended
手早く混ぜる (tebayaku mazeru)		to beat quickly, until frothy
マダイ (madai)		red sea bream
マダコ (madako)		common octopus
マッシュルーム (masshurūmu)		mushroom
松茸 (matsutake)		matsutake
松の実 (matsu no mi)		pine nut
まぶす (mabusu)		to dust (with flour, etc.)
小麦粉をイカにまぶす (komugiko o ika ni mabusu)		to dust squid with flour
マヨネーズ (mayonēzu)		mayonnaise
マリネにする (marina ni suru)		to marinate

ミ

みがきにしん (migakinishin)		dried filleted herring
ミキサー (mikisā)		blender
水 (mizu)		water
水切りをする (mizukiri o suru)		to drain (the water)
水でもどす (mizu de modosu)		to reconstitute by soaking in water
水につける (mizu ni tsukeru)		to soak in water; dip into water

味噌 (miso)		fermented soybean paste
赤味噌 (akamiso)		red miso
白味噌 (shiromiso)		white miso
甘味噌 (amamiso)		reduced-salt miso
満たす (mitasu)		to fill
鍋をスープで満たす (nabe o sūpu de mitasu)		to fill a pot with soup
みつば (mitsuba)		trefoil
みょうが (myōga)		a variety of ginger
みりん (mirin)		sweet saké (for cooking)
ミント (minto)		mint

ム

蒸し器 (mushiki)		steamer
蒸し煮にする (mushini ni suru)		to braise
蒸す (musu)		to steam

メ

紫キャベツ (murasaki-kyabetsu)		red cabbage
芽キャベツ (mekyabetsu)		brussels sprout
目刺し (mezashi)		dried sardine

モ

餅 (mochi)		cake of glutinous rice
もち米 (mochigome)		glutinous rice
もやし (moyashi)		bean sprout
盛る (moru)		to serve; heap (in a bowl)

ヤ

焼き海苔 (yakinori)		toasted *nori* seaweed
焼く (yaku)		to cook; bake; grill
味付けをして焼く (ajitsuke o shite yaku)		to flavor and grill [broil; barbecue]
あぶって焼く (abutte yaku)		to toast; roast; broil
網で焼く (ami de yaku)		to cook (on a range-top grill); grill
大きな肉を時間をかけて焼く (ōkina niku o jikan o kakete yaku)		to roast
オーブンで焼く (ōbun de yaku)		to bake
きつね色に焼く (kitsune-iro ni yaku)		to heat to a golden brown
直火で焼く (jikabi de yaku)		to broil
鉄板などに油をひいて焼く (teppan nado ni abura o hiite yaku)		to fry; sauté
照り焼にする (teriyaki ni suru)		to broil
天火で焼く (tenpi de yaku)		to bake
丸焼きにする (maruyaki ni suru)		to barbecue; roast whole
たれなどをつけながら焼く (tare nado o tsukenagara yaku)		to baste [apply sauce, etc., while cooking]
蒸し焼にする (mushiyaki ni suru)		to roast in a covered pan
薬味 (yakumi)		condiment; garnish
山いも (yamaimo)		yam
ヤリイカ (yariika)		a variety of squid

ユ

湯がく (yugaku)		to blanch, scald
ゆず (yuzu)		citron peel
ゆすぐ (yusugu)		to rinse
ゆでる (yuderu)		to boil, cook
ゆば (yuba)		soy milk skin [a byproduct of tofu making; the skin that collects at the top of a vat of soy milk]

ゆりね (yurine)		lily bulb

ラ

ラード (rādo)		lard
ライム (raimu)		lime
ライ麦 (raimugi)		rye flour
らっきょう (rakkyō)		shallot pickled in light vinegar

リ

りんご (ringo)		apple
りんご酢 (ringo-su)		apple vinegar

レ

レーズン (rēzun)		raisin
冷却する (reikyaku suru)		to cool
冷蔵する (reizō suru)		to refrigerate
冷凍する (reitō suru)		to freeze
レタス (retasu)		lettuce
レモン (lemon)		lemon
レモン汁 (lemonjiru)		lemon juice
レモンピール (remon piru)		lemon peel
れんこん (renkon)		lotus root

ロ

ローズマリー (rōzumari)		rosemary
ローリエ (rōrie)		bay leaf

ワ

ワイン酢 (wainzu)		wine vinegar
ワカサギ (wakasagi)		freshwater smelt
ワカメ (wakame)		*wakame* seaweed
わけぎ (wakegi)		Welsh onion
分ける (wakeru)		to divide
わさび (wasabi)		Japanese horseradish
わらび (warabi)		bracken
割る（卵を）(waru [tamago o])		to break (an egg)
四割りにする (yotsuwari ni suru)		to cut into fourths; quarter
八割りにする (yatsuwari ni suru)		to cut into eighths

BASIC COOKING TERMS ENGLISH–JAPANESE
英和料理基礎用語集

A

alcohol; liquor *sake*　　　　　　酒
apple *ringo*　　　　　　　　　　りんご

B

bake (bread, etc.)　　　　　　　　(パンなど)をオーブンで焼く
　(pan nado) o ōbun de yaku
baking powder *bēkingu paudā*　ベーキングパウダー
bean *mame*　　　　　　　　　　豆
beat (an egg) *(tamago) o toku*　(卵)を溶く
beef *gyūniku*　　　　　　　　　牛肉
beer *bīru*　　　　　　　　　　　ビール
blanch *... o yugaku*　　　　　…を湯がく
blueberry *burūberi*　　　　　　ブルーベリー
boil *... o yuderu*　　　　　　…をゆでる
　bring ~ to a boil　　　　　…を沸騰させる
　　... o futtō saseru
　boil ~ down *... o nitsumeru*　…を煮詰める
bone *hone*　　　　　　　　　　骨
　to bone *... no hone o nozoku*　…の骨を除く
bonito flakes (dried) *kezuribushi*　削り節
bouillon cube *kokei sūpu*　　固形スープ
broil (with direct heat)　　　　(直火で)…を焼く
　(jikabi de) ... o yaku
burdock root *gobō*　　　　　　ごぼう

C

cabbage *kyabetsu*　　　　　　キャベツ
cake *kēki*　　　　　　　　　　ケーキ
cake flour *hakurikiko*　　　　薄力粉
canned goods *kanzume*　　　　缶詰
carrot *ninjin*　　　　　　　　にんじん
celery *serori*　　　　　　　　セロリ
chicken *toriniku*　　　　　　鶏肉
chop *... o kiru*　　　　　　　…を切る
　cut ~ up roughly　　　　　…をぶつ切りにする
　　... o butsugiri ni suru
clam (short-necked) *asari*　　アサリ
combine *... o ~ ni mazeawaseru*　…を～にまぜ合わせる
　combine A with B　　　　　AをBに加える
　　A o B ni mazeawaseru
cool; chill *... o samasu*　　…を冷ます
cook *... o ryōri suru*　　　…を料理する
cookie; cooky *okashi*　　　　お菓子
cornstarch *kōnsutāchi*　　　コーンスターチ
cover *futa*　　　　　　　　　蓋
　to cover ~ *... ni futa o suru*　…に蓋をする
crab *kani*　　　　　　　　　　カニ
crisp *(tabemono nado o)*　　　(食べ物など)をパリパリにな
　paripari ni naru made yaku　　るまで焼く
cube *... o kakugiri ni suru,*　…を角切りにする、…をさい
　... o sainome ni kiru　　　　の目に切る
cucumber *kyūri*　　　　　　　きゅうり
cut *... o kiru*　　　　　　　　…を切る
　cut ~ in half　　　　　　　…を半分に切る
　　... o hanbun ni kiru

cut ~ into fourths; quarter　　…を四等分にする
　... o yontōbun ni suru
　cut ~ into eighths　　　　　…を八等分にする
　　... o hattōbun ni suru
cutting board *manaita*　　　まな板

D

deep fry *... o ageru*　　　　…を揚げる
dessert *dezāto*　　　　　　　デザート
dice *... o sainome ni kiru*　…をさいの目に切る
dish; plate; platter *sara*　　皿
dissolve *... o tokasu*　　　…を溶かす
　stir to help ~ dissolve　　…をかきまぜて溶かす
　　... o kakimazete tokasu
dress; spoon dressing over　　…を和える
　and toss *... o aeru*
dust with flour　　　　　　　　小麦粉をまぶす
　komugiko o mabusu

E

egg *tamago*　　　　　　　　　卵
　hard-boiled *yude-tamago*　ゆで卵
　soft-boiled *hanjuku (tamago)*　半熟(卵)
　scrambled *iri-tamago*　　いり卵
　sunny-side up *medama-yaki*　目玉焼き
eggplant *nasu*　　　　　　　なす

F

fillet (meat, fish, etc.)　　　　(肉など)を切り身にする、(魚)
　(niku nado) o kirimi ni suru,　を三枚におろす
　(sakana) o sanmai ni orosu
fish *sakana*　　　　　　　　　魚
flour *komugiko*　　　　　　　小麦粉
freeze *... o reitō suru*　　　…を冷凍する
fruit *kudamono*　　　　　　　くだもの
frying pan *furaipan*　　　　フライパン

G

garlic *ninniku*　　　　　　　にんにく
gelatin (powdered) *kona-zerachin*　粉ゼラチン
ginger root *shōga*　　　　　しょうが
grain *kokumotsu*　　　　　　穀物
green pepper *piman*　　　　　ピーマン

H

honey *hachimitsu*　　　　　　はちみつ
horseradish *wasabi*　　　　わさび

I

ingredients, cooking *zairyō*　(料理の)材料

K

kelp *konbu*　　　　　　　　　こんぶ
ketchup; catsup *tomato kechappu*　トマトケチャップ
knead *... o koneru*　　　　…をこねる
knife (kitchen) *hōchō*　　　包丁

L

leek, Japanese *naganegi* 長ねぎ

M

mash (potatoes, etc.) (じゃがいもなど)をつぶす
  (jagaimo nado) o tsubusu
meal; dinner; fare *shokuji* 食事
measure *hakaru* 計る
meat *niku* 肉
menu; bill of fare *menyū; kondate* メニュー、献立
microwave oven *denshi renji* 電子レンジ
milk *gyūnyū* 牛乳
mince …を刻む、みじん切りにする
  … o kizamu, mijingiri ni suru
miso; fermented soybean paste 味噌
  miso
mix A and B *A to B o mazeru* AとBをまぜる
mushroom *kinoko* きのこ(類)
  mushroom *masshurūmu* マッシュルーム
  shiitake s*hitake* しいたけ
  enoki *enoki* えのき
  matsutake *matsutake* 松茸
  maitake *maitake* まいたけ
  shimeji *shimeji* しめじ

O

oil *abura* 油
  sesame oil *goma-abura* ごま油
  vegetable oil *saradayu* サラダ油
onion *tamanegi* 玉ねぎ
orange (mandarin) *mikan* みかん

P

pan *nabe* 鍋
  frying pan *furai pan* フライパン
  saucepan *nabe* 鍋
pare; remove a peel [skin] with a (刃物で皮など)をむく
  knife, etc. *(hamono de kawa*
  nado) o muku
pea *endōmame* えんどう豆
peel; remove a peel [skin] with a (刃物または手で皮など)をむく
  knife or by hand *(hamono mata*
  wa te de kawa nado) o muku
pepper *koshō* こしょう
plum (Japanese) *sumomo* すもも
pork *butaniku* 豚肉
pot; soup pot *nabe* 鍋
potato *jagaimo* じゃがいも
preheat オーブンを前もって温める
  ōbun o maemotte atatameru
prep cooking *shitagoshirae* 下ごしらえ
pumpkin, Japanese *kabocha* かぼちゃ

R

red chili pepper *tōgarashi* 唐がらし
refrigerate *… o reizō suru* …を冷蔵する
refrigerator *reizōko* 冷蔵庫
rice
  uncooked *kome* 米
  cooked; steamed *gohan* ご飯
  brown *genmai* 玄米
  rice bowl (small) *chawan* 茶碗
  (large) *donburi* どんぶり
roast *… o abutte yaku* …をあぶって焼く

S

saké *nihonshu; sake* 日本酒、酒
salad *sarada* サラダ

salmon *sake, sāmon* サケ
salt *shio* 塩
sauté *… o itameru* …をいためる
seasoning; flavoring *chōmiryō* 調味料
seaweed *kaisō* 海草
shell *kara, saya* 殻、さや
  to shell ~; remove from the shell 殻から…を取り出す
    kara kara … o toridasu
  to remove from the pod; hull さやをとる
    saya o toru
shellfish *kai* 貝
side dish *okazu* おかず
simmer *(torobi de yukkuri to)* (とろ火でゆっくりと)…を煮る
  … o niru
skin *kawa* 皮
  to skin ~; remove the skin from …の皮を除く
    … no kawa o nozoku
soy sauce *shōyu* 醤油
spice *supaisu* スパイス
spinach *hōrensō* ほうれん草
sprinkle (sauce or dressing, etc.) (ソースやドレッシングなど)
  (sōsu ya doresshingu nado) をかける
  o kakeru
squash, Japanese *kabocha* かぼちゃ
squid *ika* イカ
staple food *shushoku* 主食
starch *katakuriko* 片栗粉
steam; cook (rice); steam (food (米)を炊く、…を蒸す
  in a steamer) *(kome) o taku,*
  … o musu
sugar *satō* 砂糖

T

tofu (bean curd) *tōfu* 豆腐
  firm *momen-dōfu* もめん豆腐
  "silken" *kinugoshi-dōfu* 絹ごし豆腐
toaster oven *ōbun-tōsutā* オーブントースター
tuna
  canned *tsuna* ツナ
  fresh *maguro* マグロ
trim (the fat) …の脂身を除く
  … no aburami o nozoku

V

vegetable *yasai* 野菜
vinegar *su* 酢

W

whitefish *shiromi-zakana* 白身魚
wine *wain* ワイン
Worcestershire sauce *usutā sōsu* ウスターソース

Index

240

さくいん

The Students of Bunkyo Women's College Who Helped Make STONE SOUP

STONE SOUPに協力してくた文京女子短期大学学生のみなさんです。

緋田 市恵 Ichie Aida	小林 ひとみ Hitomi Kobayashi	日野 麻美 Mami Hino
相原 貴子 Takako Aihara	小林 美奈古 Minako Kobayashi	平井 友紀 Yuki Hirai
青木 由香 Yuka Aoki	小日向 桜 Sakura Kohinata	平田 恵子 Keiko Hirata
青木 理恵子 Rieko Aoki	小安 美保 Miho Koyasu	深沢 道代 Michiyo Fukazawa
赤石 幸子 Sachiko Akaishi	近藤 麻由美 Mayumi Kondō	福田 純子 Junko Fukuda
浅野 照江 Terue Asano	斎藤 美香 Mika Saitō	藤井 佳弥子 Kayako Fujii
阿相 陽子 Yōko Asō	嵯峨 まゆみ Mayumi Saga	藤江 洋美 Hiromi Fujie
荒井 亜希子 Akiko Arai	逆井 恵美 Emi Sakai	冨士谷 明子 Akiko Fujitani
荒川 みどり Midori Arakawa	酒井 恵美子 Emiko Sakai	船木 宏美 Hiromi Funaki
飯野 久美子 Kumiko Iino	佐藤 絵理 Eri Sato	船越 千恵美 Chiemi Funakoshi
井口 美貴 Miki Iguchi	佐藤 しのぶ Shinobu Satō	古畑 万里子 Mariko Furuhata
池谷 知春 Chiharu Iketani	佐藤 千恵 Chie Satō	星野 幸子 Sachiko Hoshino
砂金 歩美 Ayumi Isago	佐藤 裕美子 Yumiko Satō	堀内 佳代 Kayo Horiuchi
石川 陽子 Yōko Ishikawa	佐野 あゆみ Ayumi Sano	堀内 美穂 Miho Horiuchi
石田 美緒子 Mioko Ishida	佐野 奈都子 Natsuko Sano	前川 治子 Haruko Maekawa
和泉 彩子 Ayako Izumi	椎貝 優子 Yūko Shiigai	前田 忍 Shinobu Maeda
磯道 智美 Tomomi Isomichi	澁田 麻里子 Mariko Shibuta	松井 静子 Shizuko Matsui
市川 亜矢子 Ayako Ichikawa	島崎 佳代子 Kayoko Shimazaki	松井 稚恵 Chie Matsui
市川 忍 Shinobu Ichikawa	清水 幸子 Sachiko Shimizu	松崎 亜紀子 Akiko Matsuzaki
伊藤 千絵 Chie Itō	清水 寛子 Hiroko Shimizu	松本 久美子 Kumiko Matsumoto
伊藤 優子 Yūko Itō	白井 智子 Tomoko Shirai	丸山 佳美 Yoshimi Maruyama
伊藤 由美 Yumi Itō	信田 真由美 Mayumi Shinda	水谷 由里子 Yuriko Mizutani
稲葉 しのぶ Shinobu Inaba	菅又 有希子 Yukiko Sugamata	三橋 尚恵 Hisae Mitsuhashi
猪又 智子 Tomoko Inomata	菅原 淳子 Junko Sugawara	緑川 美穂 Miho Midorikawa
今井 裕美 Hiromi Imai	杉山 真紀 Maki Sugiyama	三橋 奈保子 Naoko Mihashi
岩崎 直美 Naomi Iwasaki	杉山 ルミ Rumi Sugiyama	三平 由美子 Yumiko Mihira
岩瀬 わかな Wakana Iwase	鈴木 栄美 Emi Suzuki	宮内 洋子 Yōko Miyauchi
岩見 香織 Kaori Iwami	鈴木 香織 Kaori Suzuki	宮本 こずえ Kozue Miyamoto
植松 千晴 Chiharu Uematsu	鈴木 雅代 Masayo Suzuki	三好 恵美子 Emiko Miyoshi
宇治 礼子 Reiko Uji	鈴木 美保 Miho Suzuki	村石 朋子 Tomoko Muraishi
臼田 香織 Kaori Usuda	須田 佳代子 Kayoko Suda	村田 恵 Megumi Murata
梅津 珠見 Tamami Umetsu	関口 朋子 Tomoko Suzuki	室井 紀子 Noriko Muroi
浦部 八重子 Yaeko Urabe	関本 朋子 Tomomi Sekimoto	毛利 清美 Kiyomi Mōri
漆田 美穂子 Mihoko Urushida	関本 朋美 Tomomi Sekimoto	茂木 朋子 Tomoko Motegi
江原 里美 Satomi Ebara	瀬戸 律子 Ritsuko Seto	守本 桂子 Keiko Morimoto
遠藤 小百合 Sayuri Endō	瀬戸口 澄子 Sumiko Setoguchi	森本 隆理子 Ruriko Morimoto
大熊 優美 Yumi Ōkuma	反町 恵美子 Emiko Sorimachi	矢島 典子 Noriko Yajima
太田 雅美 Masami Ōta	大門 美香 Mika Daimon	矢吹 順子 Junko Yabuki
大竹 みゆき Miyuki Ōtake	高田 早苗 Sanae Takada	山内 美乃 Yoshino Yamauchi
大塚 三由起 Miyuki Ōtsuka	高野 典子 Noriko Takanoyama	山口 晃子 Akiko Yamaguchi
大野 あずさ Azusa Ōno	高橋 あゆみ Ayumi Takahashi	山口 麻美 Asami Yamaguchi
小笠原 理佳 Rika Ogasawara	高橋 美佳 Mika Takahashi	山崎 文子 Ayako Yamazaki
岡野 めぐみ Megumi Okano	高山 吉江 Yoshie Takayama	山本 佳苗 Kanae Yamamoto
小川 美貴子 Mikiko Ogawa	瀧田 貴子 Takako Takida	山本 早和子 Sawako Yamamoto
小椋 美奈子 Minako Ogura	竹井 美如 Mie Takei	山本 智恵美 Chiemi Yamamoto
小田 育子 Ikuko Oda	竹原 美緒 Mio Takehara	湯浅 弥生 Yayoi Yuasa
尾出 久美子 Kumiko Ode	田中 希世子 Kiyoko Tanaka	吉岡 由紀恵 Yukie Yoshioka
小野 明子 Akiko Ono	田中 真紀子 Makiko Tanaka	吉川 恵子 Keiko Yoshikawa
貝沼 美知代 Michiyo Kainuma	田中 雅美 Masami Tanaka	吉沢 朋子 Tomoko Yoshizawa
柏 恵理子 Eriko Kashiwa	谷口 智美 Tomomi Taniguchi	吉田 美都子 Mitsuko Yoshida
加藤 友美 Tomomi Katō	千葉 庸子 Yōko Chiba	四元 幸恵 Yukie Yotsumoto
加藤 典子 Noriko Katō	長 美智子 Michiko Chō	米田 あき Aki Yoneda
加藤 裕子 Hiroko Katō	土橋 美香 Mika Tsuchihashi	和井田 かよ子 Kayoko Waida
加藤 陽子 Yōko Katō	恒成 恵美子 Emiko Tunenari	渡部 規子 Noriko Watanabe
金子 真規 Maki Kaneko	角田 知子 Tomoko Tsunoda	渡部 靖子 Yasuko Watanabe
金田 裕子 Yūko Kaneda	照井 雅子 Masako Terui	渡辺 絵里 Eri Watanabe
加納 由香 Yuka Kanō	遠山 直子 Naoko Tōyama	渡辺 美紀 Miki Watanabe
亀井 理栄 Rie Kamei	利根川 亜希 Aki Tonegawa	
川合 由夏 Yuka Kawai	富田 香 Kaori Tomita	
川内 朋美 Tomomi Kawauchi	富張 由理 Yuri Tomihari	
川崎 淳子 Junko Kawasaki	砥綿 悦子 Etsuko Towata	
川島 由美子 Yumiko Kawashima	中川 佳江 Yoshie Nakagawa	
蒲原 あけみ Akemi Kanbara	中島 昭江 Akie Nakajima	
菊田 陽子 Yōko Kikuta	仲地 佐恵 Sae Nakachi	
菊池 愛 Ai Kikuchi	永松 久美子 Kumiko Nagamatsu	
北川 浩子 Hiroko Kitagawa	中村 千華 Chika Nakamura	
木津谷 圭子 Keiko Kitsuya	中村 涼子 Ryōko Nakamura	
木村 勝美 Katsumi Kimura	中山 明子 Akiko Nakayama	
木村 知子 Tomoko Kimura	西田 淳子 Junko Nishida	
日下 里絵 Rie Kusaka	西原 綾 Aya Nishihara	
草間 みゆき Miyuki Kusama	西山 和美 Kazumi Nishiyama	
工藤 綾子 Ayako Kudō	根岸 伸枝 Nobue Negishi	
窪田 有紀 Yuki Kubota	野崎 弥生 Yayoi Nozaki	
呉本 里美 Satomi Kuremoto	野村 晃子 Teruko Nomura	
黒木 聡美 Satomi Kuroki	野本 悦子 Etsuko Nomoto	
小泉 由美子 Yumiko Koizumi	萩巣 千恵子 Chieko Hagisu	
小坂 志穂 Siho Kosaka	長谷川 美紀 Miki Hasegawa	
興石 尚美 Naomi Koshiishi	秦野 紀子 Noriko Hatano	
小圓 夢代 Yumeyo Kozono	羽鳥 由佳 Yuka Hatori	
小垰 愛 Ai Kodao	原 順子 Junko Hara	
後藤 奈都子 Natsuko Gotō	張替 美由紀 Miyuki Harigae	

Notes on Cooking

とってもかんたんマイレシピ
STONE SOUP

1996年 3 月22日　第1刷発行
1999年10月 1 日　第3刷発行

編者　渡辺節子

装幀　ポイントライン

発行者　野間佐和子

発行所　講談社インターナショナル株式会社
〒112-8652　東京都文京区音羽1-17-14
電話 東京　03-3944-6493（編集部）
　　　　　　03-3944-6492（業務部・営業部）

印刷所　大日本印刷株式会社

製本所　株式会社国宝社

定価はカバーに表示してあります。

© Setsuko Watanabe 1996, Printed in Japan

ISBN4-7700-2061-9